MONTEREY
COUNTY GUIDE

A Community Resource by Patricia Hamilton

PARK PLACE PUBLICATIONS
PACIFIC GROVE, CALIFORNIA

The Tapestry of Eden

Here is a land of many faces
of many colors and hearts,
whose ancestors built adobes
and fished a burgeoning bay,
and prepared to go to war.
And those who come today
seek knowledge, or a glimpse,
a taste, of this singular paradise.
All of these people – and more –
woven lovingly together
in the fabric of the land,
a tapestry of pine-lined shores
and redwood forest primeval,
with snow-capped hills and open fields
that form an earthen bed
for acre upon acre of golden poppies,
sleeping only a breath away
from fresh-plowed furrows
and heaving vineyards
basking in the sun.
Surely this is Eden,
and we welcome all who come
to stand in the dazzling light
of our splendid garden home.

~ *Joelle Steele*
From A Tapestry of Eden

PARK PLACE PUBLICATIONS
PACIFIC GROVE, CA

www.montereycountyguide.com

SECOND EDITION
1st Printing
1st Edition 1999 published as
"Your Personal Guide
to Monterey County"

Copyright ©2000
Park Place Publications
1.Monterey Bay Region (Calif.)–
Tours. 2. Monterey Bay National
Marine Sanctuary Region (Calif.)
tours. 3. Pacific coast (Calif.)–
Tours. I. Title
917.9476

Printed in U.S.A.

For information regarding
advertising and bulk purchases,
please contact
Park Place Publications
P.O. Box 0£0
Pacific Grove, CA 93950
831-649-6640

ISBN 1-877809-44-6

ABOUT THE AUTHOR

A 4th generation Pagrovian, Patricia Hamilton is descended from the Rev. Sylvanus G. Gale, Methodist minister in the Pacific Grove Retreat, 1890-93. Her daughter, son-in-law, and grandson live in Sacramento, California.

After a career as a controller with an international restaurant corporation, Hamilton began writing and publishing interior landscape contractor books in 1982, which she continues to market internationally, with several books she publishes by other local authors.

In 1994, she enrolled in UC Santa Cruz, completed her degree in Philosophy at the University of Lancaster, England, then lived in Spain where she taught English in Elche, near Valencia. She wrote and published two books abroad: "Peace Consciousness in Northern Ireland and Findhorn, Scotland," a UCSC President's Fellowship, and "I Can't Be Bothered," about her mates in Lancaster. In 1997 she published "Tell Me More Ancestor Stories, Grandma!," by 9th generation local author, Diana J. Dennett.

"Many of my international friends wanted to visit me here on the famous Monterey Peninsula but had heard it was very expensive. To encourage them to come, I began to collect items of interest that were low cost or free; people here wanted the information too, and the rest, as they say, is history."

Welcome to Monterey County!

The best things in life *are* in Monterey County! And a lot of them are *free*! Enjoy the finest restaurants, shopping, and lodgings in the world. Experience the natural wonders of the Monterey Bay National Marine Sanctuary: tidepool, kayak, surf, dive, swim, or just wade in the water. Meander among the succulents and along the sandy beaches to take in the most beautiful sunsets in the world. Walk on Mother Earth in the Ventana Wilderness and along the cliffs of Big Sur, glimpse the Monarchs in their habitat, and sit among the wildflowers at Garland Park. Have a family night out at your library's storytime, experience the performing arts, tell your story at "Open Mic" night, and take an art walk among the galleries to heighten your sense of the beautiful and the divine. Visit the lighthouse and the museums, walk the Path of History, get a blast from the past at Cherry's Jubilee on Cannery Row, watch the sea lions jump and play off Pt. Joe on the 17-Mile Drive, and cheer marathon runners. Volunteer to be a docent at the State Parks, help the disabled enjoy an outing, meet with friends at the club, surf the Net. Take advantage of the many free offers: airplane rides, golf lessons, coffee, maps, tennis lessons, tours, wine-tasting, food samples, and much, much more; support those who are giving. They're all here in the *Monterey County Guide* – stress relievers, fitness enhancers, family values and quality of life times. As local artist and poet Joelle Steele so aptly puts it, *Surely this is Eden, and we welcome all who come to stand in the dazzling light of our splendid garden home.*

How to Use This Guide

To make it easy to spot what you're looking for, the following symbols and categories are used throughout the book:

■	ATTRACTIONS
●	SHOPS, ART GALLERIES, LIBRARIES, BOOKSTORES
▲	PARKS AND RECREATION
◆	ENTERTAINMENT
➤	ADDITIONAL OFFERS & VOLUNTEER FUN

A simple caveat before you begin: hours and admission policies are subject to change without notice. Please call ahead and be flexible. If you find that an attraction has changed its date or hours, drop us a postcard with the details so we can delete or change the entry in future editions. The Calendar of Events gives dates for the year 2000; call them for subsequent years' date, or check on-line at www.montereycountyguide.com.

We've added many new places and events to this second edition and would like to add new things of all kinds as they come up. You can help by letting us know what they are. We also give free listings to all merchants, clubs, organizations, and individuals who offer free things for any reason; such as a thank-you for patronage, to entice others to try a service or product, to give back to the community, to educate and inform, to help others, etc. Most free offerings are underlined so they're easy to spot!

Acknowledgments

I wish to thank my friends and family who encouraged me and supported me throughout the many months I spent doing research and putting this book together: Kathy Slarrow, Shirley Blank, Leonard Epstein, Robert Hamilton, Jane Hammond, Elizabeth Holliday, Diana J. Dennett, Joelle Steele, Yvette Carroll, Anne and Robert Packard, Sally Higgins and Melanie McCoy. We are all connected in community and we support each other.

Much appreciation goes to the many kindhearted people in the community who responded to my requests for information, facts, and pictures: All of the Monterey County Chambers of Commerce and Business Associations, the Visitor's Centers, Armanasco Public Relations, the librarians, the art galleries and bookstores, Mike O'Brien at Camera World, Dave Schaechtele at the California State Parks Department, and the many merchants, clubs, and others who sent in their free listings in response to the press releases. There are too many to mention individually, but I remember you all and thank you.

Photograph Credits

Cover: Sea otter at Moss Landing, Captain Yohn Gideon, Elkhorn Slough Safari; Pacific Grove, Moe Ammar; Carmel Valley, Karen Neely; LONE CYPRESS TREE & GOLF COURSE – Pebble Beach Company, used by permission; South County courtesy of Monterey County Vintners & Growers; all other photos by the author.
Author and Chu-Chu the Cat: Kathy Slarrow
Carmel: Artists on beach, Fr. Serra Sarcophagus, beach with surfers, street scene with chairs, Carmel Plaza - Randy Wilder
Street scene with leaves - Dane Thompson Filmcraft
Golden Bough - Marv White
Marina: Foundrymen - Chris Gage, Firemen Sculpture - artist Betty Saletta, photo Chris Gage, Artichoke fields, close-up - Sharon Green, Marina Boardwalk - Sharon Fong, Elkhorn Slough Safari - Melanie Gideon
Monterey: Robert Louis Stevenson, California State Historic Parks, DPR
Pacific Grove: Caledonia Park, American Tin Cannery, City Hall, Golf, Lovers Point, Recreation Trail and Hopkins Marine Station - Don Gruber
Back Cover & Pebble Beach: PEBBLE BEACH, the LONE CYPRESS TREE, their respective images are trademarks, service marks, and trade dress of Pebble Beach Company, used by permission
Salinas: Creekbridge Community Park - Duane Meneely Photography, National Steinbeck Center - Stuart Schwartz, Airplanes - Sharon Lanine.
Most all other photos were taken by the author, however, a few photos were supplied without the photographer being identified. We regret this oversight and are very happy to give credit when it is known.

Steps Through Monterey County

Welcome to Monterey County, one of the ecological wonders of the world. We're delighted to have you with us and we'd love to have you back.

Make the most of your stay. Check with your lodging facility for educational materials about the geography, customs, and cultures of Monterey. When you are here make friends with the locals, they are anxious to tell a story or just give directions.

Help us set an example for all. Through our actions toward preserving and protecting the Monterey Bay National Marine Sanctuary, the coastline, the parks, and all our local beauty, we can pass on an important lesson to current and future generations.

Leave only footprints. Take the time to enjoy walking, biking, sightseeing, picnicking, tide pooling, and boating. But as you do, please help us maintain the natural balance of this paradise by refraining from feeding the wildlife, disturbing any living or natural objects, and leaving places you visit as you found them.

Please respect the privacy of others. Inquire before photographing.

Lessen the impact. Walkways, pathways, and boardwalks were built for you. Environmental and forestry staff members work hard to foster growth on dunes, in forests and parks.

Environmental program at work. When possible we sincerely appreciate your help with energy and water conservation, as well as participation in recycling programs.

Getting from here to there. We encourage visitors and residents alike to use environmentally sound methods of transportation. Many walking and biking trails are available, and please ask about Monterey's transit system.

Driving through Monterey County. The beauty can be distracting, so please keep your attention level up and remember to park in designated parking areas. Please turn off your engine if stopped for more than one minute.

Look for establishments that support "Steps through Monterey County." The environmental caravan is gaining steam and you can help.

After you leave, please share your experiences with others. Monterey County is a very special place. We want everyone to come and enjoy what we know as paradise. We're happy to share it with you!

Monterey County Hospitality Association
140 W. Franklin, Monterey, CA 93940
Telephone: 831-649-6544

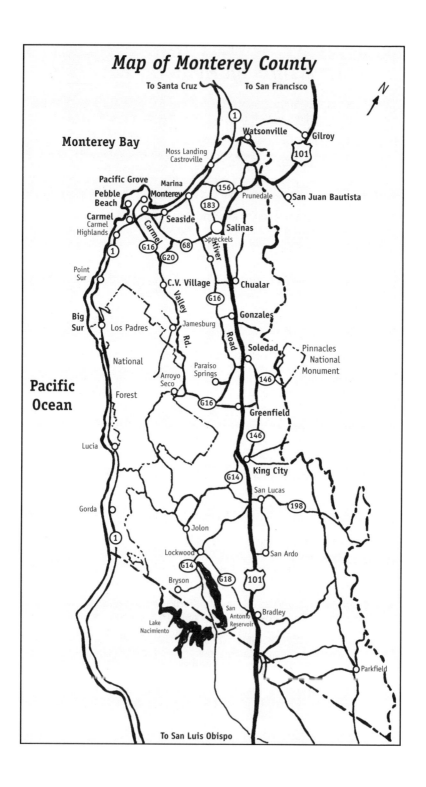

Map of Monterey County

To Santa Cruz

To San Francisco

N

Monterey Bay

①

Watsonville

Gilroy

101

Moss Landing
Castroville

Pacific Grove

Marina

156

Prunedale

San Juan Bautista

Pebble Beach

Monterey

183

Carmel

Seaside

Salinas

Carmel Highlands

68

Spreckels

Carmel

G16

G20

1

Point Sur

C.V. Village

Chualar

G16

Big Sur

Los Padres

Valley

Jamesburg

Gonzales

Rd.

Road

Soledad

Pinnacles
National
Monument

National

Paraiso Springs

Arroyo Seco

146

Pacific Ocean

Forest

G16

Greenfield

146

Lucia

King City

G14

Gorda

San Lucas

198

Jolon

Lockwood

San Ardo

G14

1

Bryson

G18

101

San Antonio Reservoir

Bradley

Lake Nacimiento

Parkfield

To San Luis Obispo

Table of Contents

Monterey with Kids

Wildlife Viewing, Petting

Agriculture

Art & Culture

Historical, Museums

Sports, Playgrounds, Recreation Centers

The Unique and The Unusual

Helpful Information

Area Code for Monterey County is 831

Police, Fire, Animal Rescue/Shelter, Hospitals

Emergency Calls Only   911
Non-Emergency Calls:
- Carmel Police, 624-6403. Fire, 624-1718.
- Carmel Highlands Fire, 624-2374.
- Mid-Carmel Valley Fire, 624-5907.
- Carmel Valley Fire, 659-2021.
- Cypress District Carmel/Rio Rd. Fire, 624-4511.
- Del Rey Oaks Police, 375-8525. Fire, 646-3900.
- Gonzales Police, 675-5010. Fire, 675-5000.
- Greenfield Police, 674-5118.
- King City Police, 385-4848. Fire, 385-3430.
- Marina Police, 384-7575. Fire, 384-7575.
- Monterey Police, 646-3830. Fire, 646-3900.
- Monterey County Sheriff, 755-3950.
- Pacific Grove Police, 648-3149. Fire, 648-3110.
- Salinas Police, 758-7236. Fire, 758-7261.
- Sand City Police, 394-6811. Fire, 646-3900.
- San Lucas Police, 627-2018.
- Seaside Police, 394-6811. Fire, 899-6262.
- Soledad Police, 678-1332. Fire, 755-5111.
- SPCA Animal Rescue, 373-2631 ext.0, 646-5534.
- Monterey County Animal Shelter, Salinas: 758-7285, Peninsula: 384-1396.
- Community Hospital of Monterey Peninsula, Holman Highway, 624-5311.
- Natividad Medical Center, 1441 Constitution Blvd., Salinas, 755-6268.

Officer Shen invites young people into the Monterey Police Station, 351 Madison Street, to collect the police sports cards, each with a personal message. Shen's: "As long as you do your best, you will always be a winner!"

Transportation Information

Monterey-Salinas Transit bus. Monterey 899-2555, Salinas 424-7695. Companions ride free during Clean Air Month (May). Free rides to Laguna-Seca races-call 424-7695. www.mst.org.com.

Waterfront Area Visitor's Express, between Memorial Day and Labor Day weekends, from 9am-6:30pm.$1 ticket good 9am to 6:30pm 899-2555.

Monterey Peninsula Airport: Alaska Airlines, 800/252-7522; Air Canada, 800/776-3000; America West Airlines, 800/235-9292; American Eagle, 800/433-7300; Northwest Airlines-KLM, 800/225-2525; United Airlines, 800/241-6522; US Airways Express, 800/428-4322. www.montereyairport.com.

Monterey-Salinas Airporter Airbus: To and from San Fran and San Jose airports. 14 scheduled departures daily. Call for reservation, 883-2871.

Amtrak Coast Starlight, 800-USA-RAIL. www.amtrak.com.

Monterey County Bicycle Map, to receive a free map, call 755-8961.

Yellow Taxi: Monterey, 646-1234. Carmel, 624-5180. Salinas, 443-1234.

Visitor Information Centers

- Big Sur Chamber of Commerce, 667-2100.
- Cannery Row Foundation, on the bay side of 640 Wave, on the Recreation Trail, in the green antique railroad car.
- Carmel Business Association, 624-2522.
- Carmel Tourist Information Center, 624-1711.
- Carmel Valley Chamber of Commerce, 659-4000.
- Castroville Chamber of Commerce, 633-6545.
- Gonzales Chamber of Commerce, 675-9019.
- Greenfield Chamber of Commerce, 674-3222.
- Hispanic Chamber of Commerce, 757-1251.
- King City Chamber of Commerce, 203 Broadway, 385-3814.
- Marina Chamber of Commerce, 384-9155.
- Monterey Chamber of Commerce of the Monterey Peninsula, 649-1770.
- Monterey County Travel & Tourism Alliance, 626-1424.
- Monterey Peninsula Visitors and Convention Bureau, 649-1770.
- Moss Landing Chamber of Commerce, 633-4501.
- Pacific Grove Chamber of Commerce, 373-3304.
- Pájaro Valley Chamber of Commerce, 724-3900.
- Prunedale Chamber of Commerce, 663-0965.
- Salinas Valley Chamber of Commerce, 424-7611.
- Seaside/Sand City Chamber of Commerce, 394-6501.
- Soledad-Mission Chamber of Commerce, 678-2278.

Local Radio Stations

KAZU 90.3FM	KBOQ 95.5FM	KMBY 104.3FM	KRML 1410AM
KUSP 88.9FM	KWAV 97FM	KPIG 107.5 FM	KDON 102.5FM
MAGIC 63AM	KBTU 101.7FM	KRQC 92.7FM	KISS 103.9FM
KNRY 1240 AM	KTOM 100.7FM	KXDC 101.7FM	KOCN 105.1FM
KSCO-AM 1080	KLOK 99.5/99.9, KHDC 90.9:Local Spanish radio stations.		

Local Television Stations/Special Programs

"Eye on This Morning," KION-TV CBS46, local news and entertainment program, weekdays 6-9am. www.kiontv.com.

"Access Monterey Peninsula," community access television beginning Feb. 2000. If you have a show idea, call 333-1267. www.ampmedia.org.

"Central Coast Magazine," AT&T Channel 2, Mon-Sat, 9:30am; Mon-Fri, 2:30, 5:30; Mon-Sun 9:30pm; presents local art, activities, history, people and places. 899-7100.

"Classic Arts Showcase" videos to tempt you to visit the arts. "Life in the Arts," interactive classroom. 59 KMST, Monterey County Educational TV.

Monterey County Office of Education–755-6424, Arts–883-1331.Instructional Television always has something of interest: MonPen & Salinas: Channel 26; No County-34; Fort Ord-5; Greenfield & King City-38; Gonzales & Soledad-8; Bradley, San Ardo & San Lucas-55. For more information, call 755-6424.

8 KSBW (NBC)	11 KNTV (ABC)	35 KCBA (FOX)	15 KCU (SPANISH)
9 KQED (PBS)	54 KTEH (PBS)	36 KICU (IND)	67 KSMS (SPANISH)
25 KCAH (UHF)			

Tour Operators

- A-1 Chartered Limo Service, 899-2707.
- Adventure Tours, 375-2409.
- AgVenture Tours, 643-9463.
- Bay Bikes, 646-9090.
- Cannery Row Walking Tours, 373-5727.
- Carmel Valley Trail Rides, 625-9500.
- Carol Robles' Monterey County Tours, 751-3666.
- Destination Monterey Carmel, 373-0508.
- Elkhorn Slough Safari Nature Tours, 633-5555.
- Gael's Monterey Peninsula Tours, 373-2813.
- Monterey Bay Nature Tours, 375-3226.
- Monterey Bay Scenic Tours, 372-MBST. Multi-lingual tours.
- Native Guides, 625-8664.
- Otter-Mobile™ Tours and Charters, 649-4523, fax 333-0832. Audio tour of 17-Mile Drive available; Steinbeck tour out soon. <u>Owner offers free tours to allied trades. Free hotel pick-up.</u>
- Prime Connections, 800-954-8687.
- Reuben W C Limo & Tour Service, 393-2243.
- Steinbeck Country Tours, 659-0333/625-5107.
- USA Hosts, 649-5115.
- Your Maitre d' Limousines, 624-1717.

Map of the Monterey Peninsula

Lover's Point

Monterey Bay Aquarium

Coast Guard Wharf

Cannery Row

Fisherman's Wharf

Fisherman's Wharf #2

Ocean View Blvd.

Pacific Grove Municipal Golf Course

Asilomar Ave.

Sunset Drive

Lighthouse Ave.

Ocean View Blvd.

17th

American Tin Cannery Central Ave.

Wave

Dennis the Menace Park

Pine

17 Mile Drive

Siney

Lighthouse Ave.

Historic Downtown

Lighthouse Ave.

Foam

Hawthorne

Dale

Scott

Turnel

Pearl

Pacific Grove

David Ave.

Prescott

Forest Ave.

McClellan

Lyndman

Franklin

Jefferson

Madison

Monterey

Calle Principal

Van Buren

Washington

Alvarado

Pearl

Webster

Pearl

Camino El Estero

Lake El Estero

Freemont St.

68

Spanish Bay Golf Course

Seventeen Mile Gate

Sunset Drive

Forest Lake

Samuel F. B. Morse Gate

Veterans Memorial Park

Harris

Polk

Abrego

Madison

Pacific Street

Cass St.

El Dorado

Iris Carmon Rd.

Seventeen Mile Drive

Monterey Peninsula Country Club

Del Monte Forest

68

Soledad

Munras Ave.

Del Monte Shopping Center

Spyglass Golf Course

Poppy Hills Golf Course

Pebble Beach

Peter Hay Golf Course

Seventeen Mile Drive Gate

Seventeen Mile Drive Gate

Cypress Point Golf Course

Pebble Beach Golf Courses

The Lodge

1

Carmel Beach

Carmel

Carpenter

5th

6th

Ocean

7th

8th

Carmel Valley Road (G-16)

San Antonio

Camino Real

Scenic Drive

Lincoln

Dolores

San Carlos

Mission

Junipero

Carmel Rancho Blvd.

Rancho Cañada Golf Club East & West

Quail Lodge

Schulte Rd.

Carmel Mission

The Barnyard Rio Rd.

1

Crossroads Shopping Center

Point Lobos

Carmel Highlands

To Big Sur (26 Miles)

Calendar of Events

Updates at www.montereycountyguide.com

You will have a lot of fun when you join the festivities in Monterey County and will find all the details on the page referenced. Most events usually occur on the same day or weekend of the same month each year. Year 2000 shown. Dates and times subject to change, so it's best to call ahead.

ONGOING

			Page
Weekly	FARMERS MARKETS	Monterey	109
Weekly	FARMERS MARKETS	Salinas	201
Weekly (summer)	FARMERS MARKET	Carmel	62
Monthly	FLEA MARKET	Monterey	109

JANUARY

January	DINE OUT FOR DAFFODILS	Monterey	117
January-March	WHALE WATCHING	Big Sur	21
January 1	RIO GRILL'S RESOLUTION RUN	Carmel	47
January 11	MUSIC SOCIETY PERFORMANCE	Carmel	47
January 15-31	WHALEFEST 2000	Monterey	117
January 17	MARTIN LUTHER KING JR. PARADE	Seaside	236
January 17	A VILLAGE AFFAIR	Carmel Vy	70
January 20-23	MONTEREY SWINGFEST	Monterey	117
January 23-24	MONTEREY SYMPHONY	Carmel	47
January 25	MONTEREY SYMPHONY	Salinas	205

FEBRUARY

Jan 31-Feb 6	AT&T NATIONAL PRO-AM	Pebble Bch	194
February all month	BLACK HISTORY MONTH	Seaside	236
February 6	A TASTE OF PACIFIC GROVE	Pacific Grove	172
February 7	MUSIC SOCIETY PERFORMANCE	Carmel	47
February 12	A DAY OF ROMANCE IN OLD MONTEREY	Monterey	117
February 12	AN EVENING AT THE BUCKEYE	Carmel Vy	70
February 12-13	A WHALE OF AN ART SHOW	Monterey	117
February 13	TOGETHER WITH LOVE	Pacific Grove	172
February 16	MARDI GRAS	Cannery Row	153
February 20-21	MONTEREY SYMPHONY	Carmel	47
February 22	MONTEREY SYMPHONY	Salinas	205
February 23-27	MASTERS OF FOOD & WINE	Carmel	47, 223
February 24-April 2	GUYS & DOLLS	Carmel	47

JULY

Page

July 8	SLOAT'S LANDING	Monterey	121
July 8	WORLD SUPERBIKE RACE NITE	Cannery Row	153
July 9-Aug 13	BLUES AND ART IN THE PARK	Seaside	237
July 10	"GREAT BALLS OF FIRE"	Carmel Vy	71
July 13-16	COWBOY CRAZY DAYS	Seaside	237
July 15-16	DOG SHOWS AND OBEDIENCE TRIALS	Carmel	49
July 15-16	DEL MONTE KENNEL CLUB SHOW	Carmel Vy	71
July 15-18	CALIFORNIA RODEO	Salinas	207
July 15-Aug 6	CARMEL BACH FESTIVAL	Carmel	49
July 17-21	CA STATE AMATEUR GOLF	Pebble Bch	194
July 22-23	CRAFTS FAIRE	Monterey	122
July 25-29	FEAST OF LANTERNS	Pacific Grove	173
July 25-30, Aug 1-6	EQUESTRIAN CLASSICS	Pebble Bch	194
July 28-30	NATIONAL HORSE SHOW	Monterey	122
July 30	ANTIQUE STREET FAIRE	MossLanding	86

AUGUST

August	GREAT TOMATO CONTEST AND PARTY	Monterey	122
August	TURKISH ARTS & CULTURE FESTIVAL	Monterey	122
August	AIRPORT OPEN HOUSE	Salinas	207
August	CHILDREN'S MASQUERADE	Salinas	207
August	MONTEREY BAY RIB COOKOFF	Seaside	237
August	FALL FUN FEST	Seaside	237
August	STEELHEAD RESCUE	Carmel Vy	71
August	YOUTH PAGEANT & TALENT SHOW	Marina	80
Aug-Nov	WINE HARVESTING	Wineries	223
August 3-6	STEINBECK FESTIVAL XIX	Salinas	207
August 4-6	CARMEL VALLEY FIESTA	Carmel Vy	71
August 5	WALK FOR THE GOLD	Seaside	237
August 11-Oct 15	SHAKE-SPEARE FESTIVAL	Carmel	49
August 12	WINEMAKER'S CELEBRATION	Carmel Vy	71
August 12-13	CELEBRATION SIDEWALK SALE	Monterey	122
August 12-13	WINEMAKERS' CELEBRATION	Wineries	223
August 12-13, 26-27	Y'ART SALE	Big Sur	21
August 14-18	NCGA AMATEUR GOLF	Pebble Bch	194
August 15-20	MONTEREY COUNTY FAIR	Monterey	122
August 16-20	BLACKHAWK CLASSIC CARS	Pebble Bch	194
August 17-19	BROOKS USA AUCTION	Carmel Vy	71
August 18	CONCOURSO ITALIANO	Carmel Vy	71

OCTOBER

			Page
November 23	THANKSGIVING DINNER	Castroville	91
November 24	CHRISTMAS TREE LIGHTING	Cannery Row	154
November 24	9th ANNUAL BUY NOTHING DAY	National	
November 25	THANKSGIVING DINNER	Monterey	126
November 25	THANKSGIVING DINNERS	Salinas	209
November 27	TREE LIGHTING	Pacific Grove	175

DECEMBER

December	ARTISTS' MINIATURES	Monterey	126
December	LAS POSADAS	Salinas	209
December	DOLLS' TEA PARTY	Seaside	238
December	CHRISTMAS TREE LIGHTING	Marina	80
December	MRWMD RECYCLED ART FESTIVAL	Marina	80
December 1	TREE LIGHTING CEREMONY	Monterey	126
December 1	CARMEL LIGHTS UP THE SEASON	Carmel	51
December 2	CHRISTMAS PARADE	Soledad	217
December 2	CHRISTMAS TREE LIGHTING	Carmel Vy	73
December 2-3	CHRISTMAS FESTIVAL	Carmel	51
December 3	HOLIDAY ARTS & CRAFTS FESTIVAL	Monterey	126
December 5	CHRISTMAS AT THE INNS	Pacific Grove	175
December 6-11	STREETS OF BETHLEHAM	Salinas	209
December 7, 9	CHRISTMAS IN THE ADOBES	Monterey	126
December 8	LA POSADA	Monterey	126
December 8-10	COWBOY POETRY & MUSIC	Monterey	126
December 8-31	SPECIAL CHRISTMAS FESTIVITIES	Monterey	126
December 9	SANTA'S ARRIVAL	Monterey	127
December 9	SNOW IN THE PARK	Pacific Grove	175
December 9	HAPPY HOLIDAY PARADE	Seaside	238
December 9	SANTA FLY-IN	Carmel Vy	73
December 10	"BRIGHTEN THE HARBOR"	Monterey	127
December 15-31	CANDY CANE LANE	Pacific Grove	175
December 16-17	LIVING NATIVITY	Pacific Grove	175
December 21-31	HOLIDAY PLAYLAND & POSADA	Seaside	238
December 25	CHRISTMAS COMMUNITY DINNER	Monterey	127
December 25	CHRISTMAS DINNER	Seaside	238
December 25	POTLUCK CHRISTMAS DINNER	Marina	80
December 26	KWANZAA CELEBRATION	Salinas	209
December 31	FIRST NIGHT® MONTEREY	Monterey	127
Dec-Jan	THE CALIFORNIA CHALLENGE	Monterey	127

Volunteer To Have Fun

Junior Friends of the Pacific Grove Library and librarian Lisa Maddalena

Many volunteer opportunities appear throughout the text of this book as free ways to attend festivals and events, to meet other people and help out around the community, and to help others enjoy all the wonderful things to see and do. If you are a volunteer, I salute you. If you haven't yet tried this form of 'entertainment,' I heartily recommend it. You will profit in ways you never imagined.

Jefferson Awards Program

Jacqueline Kennedy Onassis and the Honorable Robert Taft Jr. established the Jefferson Awards in 1972 as a way to recognize volunteerism in our local communities. The goal is to honor local volunteers who have made exceptional contributions in their communities. Nomination forms are available at your local Chamber of Commerce or Volunteer Center. Call Julie Ann Lozano at 758-8888 ext. 236 for more information.

Volunteer Center of Monterey County

The Volunteer Center is a CLEARING HOUSE for volunteers and organizations that match the needs of each. Annually, The Volunteer Center volunteers provide over $1,700,000 in service hours to the community. Fee to the individual or the organization: NONE.
- Management assistance to strengthen or expand programs.
- Computer group collects, refurbishes, & distributes computers.
- Language services to agencies and their clients.
- The Human Race raises hundreds of thousands of dollars.
Be a part of it all! Become a member, buy a T-shirt, volunteer your time to make Monterey County the best it can be!

301 Lighthouse Avenue, Suite 203, Monterey, CA 93940
jmaines@mbay.net http://www.yesillhelp.org
Phone: 831-655-9234   1-800-776-9176

Monterey Bay National Marine Sanctuary

Established in 1992, the Monterey Bay National Marine Sanctuary (MBNMS) is the largest of twelve Marine Sanctuaries nationwide, encompassing over 5,300 square miles of water, and stretching along the Central California Coast from Marin County near San Francisco to Cambria in San Obispo County. Their mission is to manage marine areas of national significance, to protect their ecological and cultural integrity for the benefit of current and future generations. Bay Net volunteers are part of this process.

➤ **Interpretive Center for the Sanctuary.** Free admission, Mon-Fri, 9am-5pm. Special events and programs. 299 Foam Street at D Street. Call for information, 647-4201. www.mbnmsf.org.

➤ **Great American Fish Count,** held during the first two weeks in July, is sponsored by the MBNMS Program, REEF Environmental Education Foundation and the American Oceans Campaign. Free. Karen, 647-4253.

➤ **Ocean Project,** 50 institutions working together for the oceans: www.theoceanproject.org.

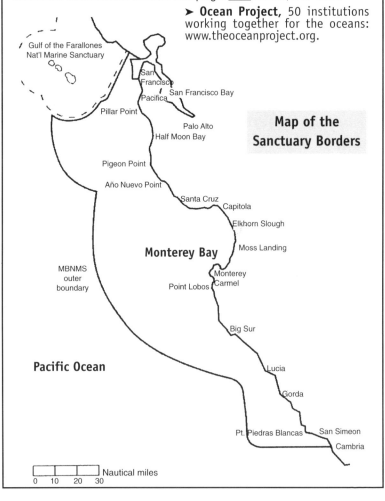

Map of the Sanctuary Borders

BAY NET

Those people in the blue jackets, with the telescopes trained on sea otters and other interesting bay sights, are volunteering to serve two hours a week after their Bay Net Shoreline Docent Training. They are trained to answer questions about the Marine Sanctuary and other tourist needs. _Take a free peek!_

Bay Net is the first of its kind in the nation to train docents to educate the public about a national marine sanctuary. It was established in 1995 on the Monterey Peninsula and now also serves in Santa Cruz. For more information or to volunteer, please call Milos Radakovich at 643-2638, or e-mail: milos@mbay.net. Visit them on the web at: www.mbay.net/~baynet.

WHALES ON WHEELS & SAVE THE WHALES

Purpose: To educate children and adults about marine mammals, their environment, and their preservation. Bring hands-on marine mammal artifacts to classroom for a fee, or you can help save the whales by _Adopting A Whale_ and supporting the WOW program. Only $15 per kit which includes:

- 8x10 color photo of orca in the wild
- Orca box to color, cut out & assemble
- Adopting A Whale certificate
- Newsletter with orca information

For more information, call Maris at 831-899-9957 or send your name and address with $15 to Whales on Wheels, 1192 Waring, Seaside, CA 93955.

Linking Thoughts
with Daniel Koffman

Whether considering all the events and activities of Monterey County Community Organizations while reading *Community Links*, or, all the great possibilities available to you in *Your Personal Guide (YPG)*, a single consideration emerges. So many choices, so little time!

This is a problem–a good problem–but a problem nonetheless!

The straight answer is, there are no wrong choices! So, how do you choose? There's great merit in doing a slow scan of all the information. *YPG's* format offers a Table of Contents which gets your review off to a speedy start. Look for the words and phrases that "speak to you:" music, hiking, food, lecture, park, great for children–whatever generally interests you.

In both *Links* and *YPG*, in most cases, phone numbers are listed for more information. Make a call. A great investment of a dime before you spend the time. You'll get a keen sense of the event, activity or attraction from the call. If you get a real person on the line (it does happen), your questions will get answered and you'll be more comfortable before you arrive. You'll have a better time.

Any choice will enrich you personally in some way. Go with a friend and your relationship will have a new sharing. Go with your spouse or significant other and your bond will deepen. Go with your child and you'll recreate the wonder of curiosity and new experience you had as a kid, remember? Your child will see and appreciate this in you. Go with the whole family and enjoy the magic of discovery. Fight the urge to be the expert, and instead, listen to the conversation and the new sharing. It'll be music to your ears! You'll be creating new memories.

This is the essence of family values: shared experiences, fresh memories, children seeing adults in new situations and watching their reactions. That's how we learn.

I envisioned *Community Links* years ago as a way to do something equally for all community organizations. The common problem for all community organizations is that there can never be enough publicity for events and activities. *Links* provides print, daily radio, TV, and internet publicity for all participating organizations, at no cost whatsoever. Fact is, in this way, I did not have to make a choice to work with one or another group; I chose them all.

Community Links and *YPG* offer the palette of possibilities to you and your family. Play, learn, enjoy, participate, help, support, contribute, sing, dance, eat, listen–do something!

Youth Organizations

OmBuddies – Mission is to match preschool to teenage children with seniors in nursing homes and board & care residences (assisted living), building bridges across the generations, one visit at a time. Through weekly visits, kids and elders develop lifelong friendships while having fun participating in recreational and educational activities. 2200 Garden Road, Monterey. 831-333-1300, fax 831-333-1323. E-mail: ombug@aol.com. Web: www.montereynet.com/ombudsman.html.

Monterey County 4-H – The purpose of 4-H is to help youth develop into responsible, self-directed, productive citizens of the world, and to improve the well-being of youth and society through the use of research-based, learn-by-doing education experiences. Ages 9-18. 1432 Abbott Street, Salinas. 831-759-7360, fax 831-758-3018. E-mail: cemonterey@ucdavis.edu.

Community Partnership for Youth – Mission is to provide enriched afterschool and intersession opportunities from elementary through high school. The organization offers alternatives to violence, builds resiliency and provides students structure through joint school/parent/community partnerships. CPY forms relationships with the children and is committed to their continued well being. Research has shown that children who establish relationships with adult volunteers or mentors are more successful in school and socially than those who do not. P.O. Box 42, Monterey. 831-394-4279, fax 831-394-4279. E-mail: respect@cpy.org.

Community Links Monterey County©

"Getting The Word Out About Monterey County's Community Organizations Via Print, Radio, Television, Telecommunications & the Internet"

Daniel Koffman's comprehensive vehicle for local organizations:

- On The Radio - KAZU 90.3FM, KBTU 101.7FM, KPIG 107.5FM, CD93.5FM, KBOQ 95.5FM, KMBY 104.3FM
- On Television - KION-TV CBS 46 (6am-9am), AT&T Cable daily.
- On the Internet - www.communitylinks.net
- Telecommunications - Toll-Free Hotline 1-888-21-LINKS.
- Pick up Community Links© at the libraries, bookstores, Bagel Bakeries, Borders Books, Meals on Wheels, Visitor Information Center, Bay Bookstore and others. Call for a complete list of distribution points, call 1-888-21-LINKS.

Community of Caring™

Community of Caring Monterey Peninsula is a nonprofit organization dedicated to improving the quality of life for youth and families in our communities. This collaboration sponsors community-based programs and services targeted toward achieving progress on priority issues identified by the TELLUS project and community discussion.

The goals of *Community of Caring Monterey Peninsula* are:

- Promote a healthy set of community norms and values
- Foster a better connection between the community and the education system
- Embrace and promote our rich diversity
- Reduce substance abuse
- Enhance personal safety
- Expand parent education and support mechanisms
- Create additional activities available for youth
- Reduce the incidence of HIV and teen pregnancy

Community of Caring Monterey Peninsula is a coalition of the three Peninsula public school districts, institutions of higher education, the seven Peninsula cities, public and nonprofit agencies, businesses, youth, and the community at large dedicated to teaching and supporting youth and families in everyday life.

We believe in five core values that can empower people to be responsible, caring members of a community:

1. *Caring* for one another
2. *Respect* for one another
3. *Trust* in one another
4. *Responsibility* for one another
5. *Family* loyalty to one another

Get involved by:

- Being part of the community-wide effort
- Making yourself, your business, school or organization a part of Community of Caring Monterey Peninsula
- Practicing the core values
- Getting others involved

To participate in the Community of Caring Monterey Peninsula, call 831-646-3760, or write to P.O. Box 1031, Monterey, CA 93942.

City of Monterey Volunteer Program

The City of Monterey is a special city with a rich and varied history of Native Americans, Spanish and Mexican territories, and as the birthplace of California. You can immerse yourself in a kaleidoscope of historical facts and places. Our beautiful Monterey Bay Marine Sanctuary beckons visitors from all over the world seeking a close up view of sea otters, whales and other aquatic residents or to walk the Path of History and our numerous parks and wonderful recreation trails. Not just visitors, but all of us enjoy this beautiful City and environment.

Be part of this special City! You can volunteer in a variety of programs and services. The City of Monterey is committed to provide opportunities to local citizens for learning about City government through volunteering within various departments and helping with special events.

Current Volunteer Opportunities

Colton Hall Museum: hosts, hostesses

City of Monterey Library: Bookstacks Assistants, Homework Pals Program, Outreach Volunteers, California Collection Volunteers

Public Works: Adopt-A-Park, Beach or Street, Gardening, Information Walkers' Club, Storm Drain Stenciling/Monitoring, Special Events Recycling Team

Fire Department: Neighborhood Emergency Response Team (NERT)

Recreation & Community Services: Preschool Volunteers, After School Activities Volunteer, Recreation Center Receptionist, Special Events, Playground Volunteers

We also encourage "on-call" volunteers

How it works

- Call for complete program information
- Complete an Interest Form
- Meet with the Volunteer Coordinator, Complete Orientation
- Interview with Supervisor
- Start your Assignment!

For a complete information packet with current volunteer opportunities, call 646-3719.

Big Sur

The Phoenix Shop

Coast Galleries

Willow Creek Beach

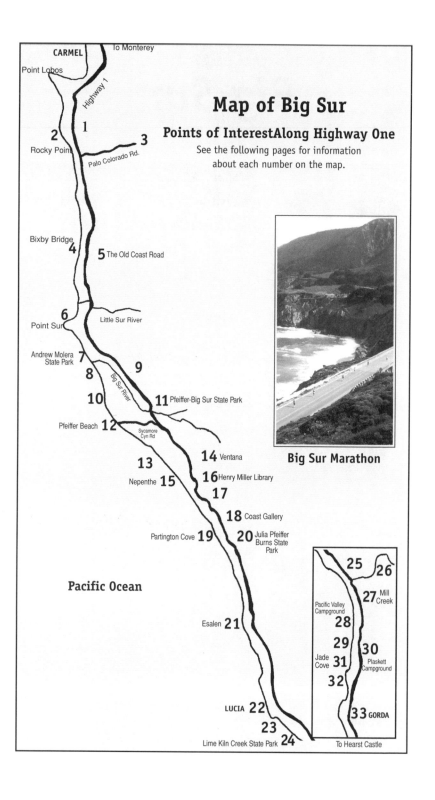

CARMEL

To Monterey

Point Lobos

Highway 1

2   1

Rocky Point   3

Palo Colorado Rd.

Map of Big Sur

Points of InterestAlong Highway One

See the following pages for information
about each number on the map.

Bixby Bridge

4   5 The Old Coast Road

6

Point Sur   Little Sur River

Andrew Molera
State Park   7

8   9

Big Sur River

10   11 Pfeiffer-Big Sur State Park

Pfeiffer Beach 12

Sycamore
Cyn Rd

14 Ventana

13   16 Henry Miller Library

Nepenthe 15

17

18 Coast Gallery

Partington Cove 19   20 Julia Pfeiffer
Burns State
Park

Big Sur Marathon

Pacific Ocean

Esalen 21

25   26

27 Mill
Creek

Pacific Valley
Campground

28

29   30

Jade
Cove 31   Plaskett
Campground

32

LUCIA 22

23   33 GORDA

24

Lime Kiln Creek State Park   To Hearst Castle

Big Sur

Area Code for Monterey County is 831

Helpful Information

● **Visitor Information Center**, Mon-Wed-Fri, 9:30am-1pm, at the Big Sur Station, 667-2100. www.bigsurcalifornia.org.

● **Virtual Tour**. "Drive" Hwy 1 at www.webtraveler.com/locales/bigsur.

▲ **U.S. Forest Service**. Park reservations call Parknet at 1-800-444-PARK. $4-$6/car day use, 8am-sunset. Camping, summer: River site $23, other $20. Nov-Mar, all sites $16. Free ranger shows around a campfire 8pm nightly (except Fri) June-Aug. When you stay, adjacent parks are free the next day. Call for yearly date of free admission: 649-2836, 385-5434.

▲ **California State Parks** and **Monterey County Parks**. Information: 888-588-CAMP, or 755-4899, 667-2315, http://cal-parks.ca.gov. May open some parks free to the public during May, State Parks Month; call 800-777-0369.

Calendar of Events

Year 2000 dates shown. Updates at www.montereycountyguide.com.
Please call in advance to verify as information is subject to change.

January/March   **WHALE WATCHING**   **FREE**
Watch the great gray whales on their annual migration down the California coast-line. Vista points: Pt. Lobos, Soberanes Pt., Pt. Sur. Pregnant females lead from the Bering Sea to calving lagoons off Mexico's Baja Peninsula.

April 30   **BIG SUR INTERNATIONAL MARATHON Spectators FREE**
15th annual. The Big Sur International Marathon is a spectacular road race set along one of the most breathtaking courses in the world. Race begins at 7am, awards at noon. Benefit for local charities, volunteers always needed. Free training clinics held in Nov. and Dec. Call the Marathon Office, 9-5 Mon-Fri, at 625-6226, fax 625-2119. www.bsim.org.

May 5-7   **BIG SUR JAZZ FEST**   **$$**
At Pfeiffer-Big Sur State Park. For more info, call 667-1530.

May 20-21   **EXPERIMENTAL MUSIC FEST**   **$$**
Henry Miller Library. Experimental musicians from all over the country. Sat-Sun. $7-$10. Library has many events—call for calendar, 667-2574. E-mail: bsxmfest@excite.com. www.henrymiller.org.

June-Sept   **GARDEN FAIRE**   **FREE**
Music, crafts, art, beadwork, herbal works, vintage clothing. Every Saturday, 1 to 6pm, at Loma Vista Cafe Gardens at Big Sur Shell Station. 667-2818.

August 12-13, 26-27   **3RD ANNUAL Y'ART SALE**   **FREE**
Live music, poetry readings, and drumming, 11am-7p-m. Take Highway 1 to Palo Colorado, go 2 miles, look for the dome house. Sofanya, 626-2876.

October 28   **BIG SUR RIVER RUN**   **$$**
Pfeiffer Big Sur State Park 10K run, 5K walk benefits local nonprofits. Register 7am, run/walk 10am. Pre-register 624-4112. www.bigsurriverrun.org.

1 Garrapata State Park, 7 miles south of Carmel, and just past Malpaso Creek. <u>Free</u>. Park off the highway on either side, approach from the north is shown. 2,879 acres of hiking trails, sandy beaches, rocky shores, dense redwood forests. Trail heads along the beach are indicated on numbered gates, or sign posts,

at turnouts. Enter gate 13, 15 or 16 to reach Soberanes Point and magnificent views. Rock climbing at south end on the beach. Watch for dangerous surf. Dogs must be on a leash or under direct voice control. Dawn to dusk.

2 Rocky Point, now the site of Rocky Point Restaurant, with an expansive southern view of the coastline. Open for breakfast, lunch and dinner. 831-624-2933.

3 Los Padres National Forest, 3 million acres of wilderness covering the Santa Lucia Mountains from Salinas down to the Pacific Ocean along the Big Sur coast. Hundreds of streams flow into the Little and Big Sur Rivers or directly into the ocean. There are hot springs at Tassajara and Esalen. Mountain lions and wild pigs may be seen; streams support fresh trout and steelhead. Rare spottings of the southern bald eagle and American Peregrine falcon. A popular hike begins at the U.S. Forest Service, Bottcher's Gap, public campground at the eastern end of Palo Colorado Road. Picnics, bring water; restrooms, wildflowers. Other trails lead into the Ventana Wilderness from the Big Sur Station and the Pacific Valley Station. Maps and permits can also be obtained at these stations.

4 Bixby Creek Bridge was the largest single span concrete arch bridge in the world when it was built in 1932. It is 550' long and 260' high. There are more than 20 original concrete bridges along Highway 1 in Big Sur. Many have pull outs nearby where you can get a closer look.

5 The Old Coast Road turns inland from Bixby Creek Bridge on Highway 1, crosses Bixby Creek, climbs Serra Grade, crosses Little Sur River, and rejoins Highway 1 at Andrew Molera State Park. Impassable in wet weather. Views, wildflowers, slow-going but worth it. 4-wheel drive recommended.

6 Point Sur State Historic Park, 19 miles south of Carmel. Adults $5. A century-old lighthouse, dramatically perched on a seaside plateau, with spectacular views, whale watching and guided three-hour tours that explore the light station and surrounding buildings. Participants should be prepared for a one-mile hike that climbs 300 feet and a 65-step staircase.

Tours of the light station and grounds: Saturday 10am and 2pm, Sunday 10am year-round; additional summer tours Wednesday 10am and 2pm. Space is limited; show up early. A free video of the lighthouse can be viewed at Big Sur Station, 8 miles south. Volunteer to be a docent. 625-4419, 624-7195.

7 Andrew Molera State Park. 4800 acres of meadows and woodlands. Big Sur Cultural and Natural History Center at the Ranch House. Circa 1930 kitchen, exhibits on birds of Big Sur, ranching and other cultural and natural history displays. 11am-3pm, Mon-Fri. 667-2521. The Big Sur River winds through the park. Hiking trails, horseback riding, secluded beach, bicycle trails, camping, grasslands, redwood forests, birds, and wildlife. An easy hike is the Bobcat Trail and River Trail Loop, 3 miles. Take the headlands trail from the north end of the parking lot, through the Trail Camp, past historic Cooper Cabin, Big Sur's oldest structure, to the picturesque and popular beach.

Park along Highway 1 and walk in for free. Day use fee, $4 per car. Trail map available at Ranger check-in. 667-2315. **Molera Horseback Tours**, at the park, fees vary, 625-5486. Site of **Ventana Wilderness Sanctuary**.

8 Big Sur River Inn. Music in the summer, Sundays 1-5pm. No cover, full bar, full menu. 625-5255, 800/548-3610.
- **Heartbeat Gift Gallery**, next to the Big Sur River Inn. Jewelry, crafts, gifts, unique drums and musical instruments. 667-2557.
- **General Store** has provisions and more. 7:30am-7pm. 667-2700.
- **Big Sur Village Pub**; **Big Sur Towing**, 667-2181.

9 Ripplewood Resort, accommodations, grocery and gas, Sun-Thurs, 8am-8pm, Fri-Sat, 8am-9pm, 667-2242. **Big Sur Library**, Mon-Wed-Fri. 12-6. 667-2537.

10 Fernwood, small settlement with a motel, gas, bar, grill, grocery, gift shop, and 65-site private campground with showers. 667-2422.

11 Pfeiffer-Big Sur State Park, 26 miles south of Carmel, turn left off the highway into the park entrance. Fee. 821 acres, nature Center. Call for

Ventana Wilderness Sanctuary

Mission: To perpetuate the animal and plant species native to the central California coast through wildlife and habitat restoration, education and research programs. Founded in 1977 by local residents. At the Research and Education Center at Andrew Molera State Park, you can <u>participate free in hands-on bird banding and the release of condors back into the wild</u>. Follow the road to the left of the park entrance one mile. Bird banding takes place every day except during inclement weather. For more condor, membership, or volunteer information, please contact The Ventana Wilderness Sanctuary, Box 99, Monterey, CA 93940. 831-624-1202.

Condor in flight

Creamery Meadow, within the park, is a 90 acre site for field study of birds and wildlife. Follow instructional signs.

information about guided nature walks, campfires, and programs for children. Trails include: Pfeiffer Falls and Valley View Trail, 1.3 miles, a one-hour stroll through redwood groves to the 60-foot falls. The 3-mile Oak Grove Trail is an easy hike. Adjacent to the softball field is the "Pioneer Tree," one of Big Sur's largest redwoods, whose top has been severed by lighting. Redwoods may live for 2000 years and grow to 350' tall. 667-2270. Junior Rangers Program, ages 7-12, 667-2315. All year camping, showers, laundry, no hook-ups. Reservations a must in summer. **Big Sur Lodge** is at the river crossing. Cottages, heated pool, grocery store, gift shop, restaurant. 7am-11pm. www.bigsurlodge.com. 800-424-4787, fax 831-667-3110. **Big Sur Campgrounds and Cabins**, 90 sites, showers, playground, river, 667-2322. **Riverside Campgrounds and Cabins**, 50 sites, rooms, cabins, showers, laundry, motorhomes, 667-2414. **Sykes Hot Springs** is a 10 mile hike in to natural hot springs where you can soak in rustic tubs. Will reopen in Spring 00; pick up a trail map at Big Sur Center.

12 Pfeiffer Beach, at the foot of Sycamore Canyon Road, the only paved, ungated road west of Highway 1 between the Big Sur post office and Pfeiffer-Big Sur State Park. Fee. Make a very sharp turn onto the narrow and winding road and follow for 2 miles. Not recommended for RVs or trailers as there are overhanging trees. Large parking area, short, well-marked path to the beach, restrooms. White sands dominated by dramatic large rocks that change colors with the light, and with waves crashing through.

13 Big Sur Center, gifts, gas, video rental, cafe, grocery store.

◆ **Loma Vista Cafe Garden** has music Saturdays, 2-5pm, during the summer. No cover. 667-2818.

◆ **Garden Gallery** has 50 local artists and cactus gallery. Stop in!

14 Store and Gallery at Ventana. Local artists, jewelry, pottery, gifts and more. 9am-10pm daily. 667-2787. On the west side of Highway 1 is the **Post Ranch Inn**, shop for fine gifts; call for dinner reservations at the elegant **Sierra Mar** restaurant, 667-2200. **Ventana Campground**, primitive camping, no vehicles over 20', campsites, showers, extra fee for dogs. Privately owned, 624-4812 or 667-2331. **Ventana Inn & Spa**, luxurious accommodations, 667-2332, 800-628-6500.

15 The Phoenix Shop at Nepenthe. Impressive wooden phoenix sculpture in the garden is pictured at right. Gifts, books, jewelry, toys, and clothing. Restaurant, bar, fabulous views, al fresco dining. 10:30am-7pm summer, 10:30am-6pm winter. 667-2347.

• **Hawthorne Gallery**, 48485 Highway 1, across from Nepenthe. Contemporary painting, indoor/outdoor sculpture, blown glass, ceramics. Representing five Hawthornes, Albert Paley, and selected guests. 667-3200. "Ekheahan" sculpture on view at Post Ranch Inn.

16 Henry Miller Library with rare books and artwork of Henry Miller, the great American writer and artist who lived in Big Sur from 1944-1962. Just south of the quiet village of Big Sur, about 30 miles south of Carmel. Tues-Sun, 11am-5pm, Thurs-Sun during winter. Literary, music, and art events, exhibits, workshops and more! Call for free calendar of events. Picnicking encouraged. www.henrymiller.org, hmlib@henrymiller.org, 667-2574.

17 Deetjen's Big Sur Inn, bed and breakfast inn, serves non-guests breakfast and dinner by reservation. A rustic Norwegian-style inn built in the 1930s. Big Sur traditional hospitality at its finest. 667-2377.

18 Coast Gallery Of Big Sur, 3 miles south of Nepenthe. Historic showplace for local artists and craftsmen. Henry Miller watercolors. Gallery, gift shop, cafe, candle studio, and boutique. One of the world's largest collections of American crafts. 9-5 daily. 667-2301. www.coastgalleries.com.

19 Partington Cove is a secluded beach at the end of an old dirt road, once a shipping point for tanbark oak by early pioneers. No fee. A picturesque hike takes you from the point where Highway 1 curves across Partington Canyon. Enter at the gate for a steep walk down, past an interesting sign about the undersea forest, branch to the left across a narrow wooden bridge and through a tunnel and onto the beach. Branch to the right leads to Partington Cove with dangerous surf on the rocks. Another trail, on the east side of Highway 1, leads upstream into Partington Canyon, through a beautiful redwood canyon and to the remains of an old tanbark cabin, eventually reaching the Tin House with beautiful coastal views. 4-5 miles. Rumor has it the house was build as a guest house for Franklin D. Roosevelt by Lathrop Brown who lived on the coast further south. John Partington logged tanoaks in the 1880s for tannic acid used to cure leather before the invention of synthetics in the 1930s.

20 **Julia Pfeiffer Burns State Park**, 3500 acres. Fee. Large underwater park with canyons and caves for experienced divers. Ten-minute hike on a cliffside trail leads to an 80-foot waterfall into the Pacific Ocean, giant redwoods, ocean views. A popular, six-mile trail leads hikers on a tour through the park. Two primitive hike-in campsites are available. Trail brochures available, restrooms, pay phone, no dogs. 667-2315.

21 **Esalen**, 45 miles south of Monterey. A center to encourage work in the humanities and sciences with public seminars, work-study, conferences, research. Nightly hot springs: 1-3:30am, $10, reservations, 667-3047. To request a catalog: 667-3000. www.esalen.org.

22 **Lucia,** overnight accommodations in a comfortable atmosphere. Fine restaurant featuring al fresco dining overlooking the South Coast. Provisions also available. 667-2391.

23 **Immaculate Heart Hermitage, New Camaldoli**, the self-sufficient community of Camaldolese Monks, offers retreats to men and women. Gift shop sells their famous Hermitage fruitcake, religious artifacts, and books. For retreats: Guestmaster, Immaculate Heart Hermitage, New Camaldoli, Big Sur, CA 93920, 831-667-2456, 800-826-3740. www.contemplation.com

24 **Lime Kiln Creek State Park**, offers hikes to historic kilns and coastal access with campsites for a fee. 43 tent and trailer sites, 15' trailer max. and 21' motorhome max, showers, grovery, 667-2403 or 667-2315.

25 **Kirk Creek and Campground**, has fee campsites on an open bluff above the ocean. Follow Kirk Creek trail on the east side for ocean views. 33 trailer and tent sites-16' trailer max. Bike and hiker sites. 385-5434.

26 **Nacimiento-Fergusson Road** off Highway 1 is very steep (to 4000'), windy and narrow as it cuts through the Ventana Wilderness. Ocean views, wildflowers, redwoods, oaks. At the summit is the **Los Padres National Forest Ranger's Station** with information, maps, water, and camping permits. Past Ft. Hunter Liggett Military Base at Jolon, Mission San Antonio de Padua (see Dutton Hotel ruins and the Hacienda designed as a hunting lodge for W.R. Hearst by Julia Morgan in 1935).

27 **Mill Creek** picnic area and a small beach. Free.

28 **Pacific Valley Center** was to reopen with a big millennium party, December 31, 1999. Call owner Harry Harris at 805/927-8655 for details. His plans for the Center include a restaurant, bar, gift shop, mini-market, campground, and 6 luxury units next year. **The Big Sur Jade Co. and Museum** will reopen with new jewelry at the same location, with free admission.

Willow Creek beach access at right.

29 **Sand Dollar Beach**, 1 mile south of U.S. Forest Service station in Pacific Valley and 14 miles north of San Luis Obispo County line, across from **Plaskett Creek Campground**. Free. Widest expanse of sand and mildest weather on the coast.

30 **Plaskett Campground**, a beautiful spot on the east side with big trees and ocean views, fire pits. Fee. 44 tent and trailer-16'max. Bike and hiker sites. 667-2315.

31 **Jade Cove**, 2 miles south of Sand Dollar Beach, is famous for its jade reserves and popular with beachcombers and rockhounds. Free.

32 **Willow Creek picnic area**, pictured below, is a good place to look for jade pieces among the rocks on the beach. Free. *Remember: Never turn your back to the surf on any Big Sur beach, to avoid being swept away.*

33 **Gorda**, the southernmost town in Monterey County on the Big Sur Coast, 66 miles from Carmel, with gas, cabins, grocery store, espresso, info. October Oktoberfest. Lodging: 805-927-4600. See llamas grazing behind a fence on an adjacent lot. **Treebones Campground**, private, at Los Burros Road, to open early 2000.

➤ **Hearst Castle** at San Simeon is 26 miles south of Gorda. Call for tour reservations, 800-444-4445.

Big Sur Arts Initiative

The Big Sur Arts Initiative was formed in 1998 by local parents and artists to provide arts, music and science enrichment programming in the community. During the first year, BSAI has worked with First Night of Monterey, Dance Kids, Inc., local actors, artists and musicians and a host of volunteers to put on workshops, classes and special events for all the children of Big Sur. Their mission is to enrich lives in the Big Sur community through the arts.

Hidden Gardens, A Big Sur Garden Tour

A summer fundraiser for the BSAI: The free opening of **The Children's Garden** at the Captain Cooper School includes The Garden Market with perennials, supplies and sculpture; presentation; demonstrations, and entertainment by and for the children.

Plus **The Garden Tour** ($30) of several Big Sur gardens, June 24, 2000. In 1999, the gardens visited included the Esalen Institute, Post Ranch Inn, Sierra Mar at the Post Ranch Inn, and Loma Vista.

To learn more about the Big Sur Arts Initiative, or to volunteer to help at these and other events, call 831-667-1530. www.bigsurarts.org.

The Big Sur Land Trust

Since 1978, The Big Sur Land Trust has been dedicated to the preservation of natural resources and open space in Big Sur and the Monterey Peninsula. The 1,100 acre Mitteldorf Preserve is home to  Monterey County's largest redwood tree, spring and fall activities and hikes. The Lodge, pictured here, may also be rented for that perfect occasion. Call 831-625-5523. www.bigsurlandtrust.org.

Spring Hikes

Join us for a hike among the wildflowers and the redwoods. Hikes are free for members and $10 for guests. Open to the public. Call for details and to reserve your space.

FREE Environmental Day Camp

Throughout July, children ages 8-16 can learn first hand about nature at the Mitteldorf Redwood Preserve and the Pt. Lobos Ranch. Camp lasts $3^1/_2$ days and includes a sleepover and tons of fun! Call for applications for day camp, and their poetry and art contests.

Art and Poetry Contests

"Walk on the Wild Side" 1999 childrens' art contest winner: Whale by Marc McMillan, Carmel, 8 yrs old. 1st place, 5-8 yr olds.

Carmel-by-the-Sea

The Otsey Totsey Doll House sketch by Grant Wallace

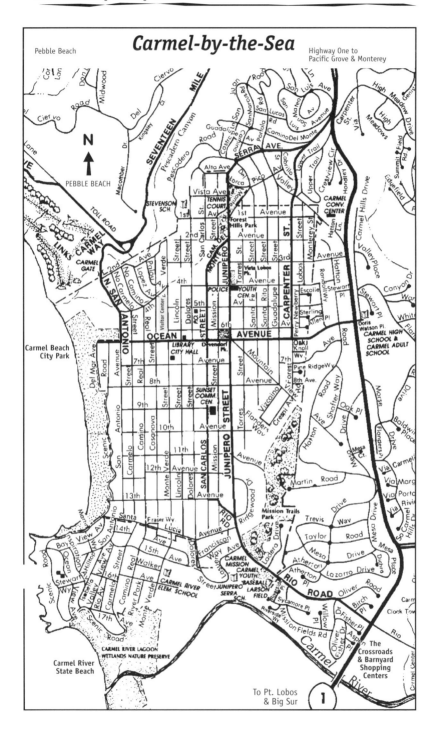

Downtown Walking Tours
Charming Shops & Courtyards

Start on Monte Verde, half a block south of Ocean Avenue, in front of City Hall. Although Clint Eastwood is no longer Mayor, he is still active in local politics. You might see our current mayor, Ken White, arriving at the office. As you face City Hall, you will see a pathway passing next to one of Carmel's Inns. Go up this path, and you will be in the Court of the Golden Bough.

A small stationery shop with its warm cottage atmosphere and stone fireplace will be on your right as you enter the court. Walk through, under an arcade, and up the stone-flagged path onto Ocean Avenue. Turn right, and up half a block to Lincoln Street.

Turn right again and on the west, or right side, halfway along the block is the La Rambla building, a Spanish style building with wrought iron balconies, built in 1929. Through the center of this building is an arcade leading to a garden shop with fountains and sculptures.

Returning on to Lincoln, turn left to Ocean and turn east, or right, up Ocean, halfway along the block and on the right-hand side, is a tiny arched entrance way to Der Ling Lane. A shop runs along one side of this quaint lane. Paved in Carmel stone, with an arched roof of creepers and flowers, this attractive little lane leads to another garden area, a peaceful and quiet spot, and a gallery in the back.

Return to Ocean, continue up to Dolores. Stop in the Carmel Drug Store for souvenirs. (They also offer delivery and free blood pressure testing.) Open 8am-10pm daily. Turn right, or south on Dolores, and halfway along the block on the west side, is Piccadilly Park. Benches, placed outside at the entrance and inside in shady spots, are ideal places to sit for a snack or rest break.

Back on Dolores, cross the street toward a quaint little English tea room, Tuck Box Restaurant in the Hansel & Gretel design, and on that side of the street, still walking south, you will come to El Paseo Building, almost on the corner. Walk into this little courtyard with its brick flagstone, and see the two Spanish figures that were sculptured by Jo Mora in 1928. Real estate offices and shops here often have fireplaces; the light from the flickering fires adds a further attraction. Walk out of this courtyard, by the other exit, onto 7th Street and turn left, or east, towards San Carlos.

Downtown Carmel

Visitor's Center Monte Verde btwn 5th & 6th
831-624-2522
www.carmel-by-the-sea.com

Cross San Carlos continuing on 7th and just past the old-fashioned grocery store, on the left you will see steps leading up into the Court of the Fountains. Walk into the courtyard. Pass the pool and fountain, pass two attractive gazebos, and turn right, out of the court and onto Mission Street.

Cross Mission Street, turn up (left) toward Ocean, and right, down the steps into the Carmel Plaza. Fifty-seven stores and restaurants, two hours free parking with validations at covered parking garage at Mission and 7th. There are benches and comfortable resting places among flowers, trees and a fountain. Restrooms are on the 3rd level at the top of the escalator.

When you leave the Carmel Plaza, coming back onto Mission Street, turn up to the right toward Ocean Avenue. You can cross Ocean and enter Devendorf Park to stroll or rest. In the northwest corner of the park is a statue of Fr. Junipero Serra and memorials dedicated to Carmel residents who served in W.W.II. There are public restrooms located in the far corner of the park.

You can continue exploring the Courtyards of Carmel crossing through the park to 6th Avenue. At the corner of 6th & Mission, turn to the north, or right, and walk up the west side of Mission to the Jordan Center which contains an art gallery, coffee house/restaurant, and shops.

The next pathway is the May Court, a little further to the north you'll come to the Mission Patio which is occupied by a variety of artisans – a furniture maker, jeweler, designer, sculptor, and even a Christmas shop. In the back of the Mission Patio on the left, you will see steps leading to The Mall, the next courtyard on your tour. The Mall connects Mission Street to San Carlos and is filled with art galleries, shops, jewelers and a small pub. Stroll through The Mall to San Carlos. Immediately across San Carlos are two pathways that will lead you through to Dolores Street.

Cross to the corner of San Carlos & 6th, you'll see "Cottage Row," a corner of Carmel cottage-like shops. Go north up San Carlos on the west side and you will see a small sign indicating passage to Dolores Street. If you choose to take this route you will be lead through one of Carmel's hidden treasures, the Secret Garden. If you continue north on San Carlos, you will pass the office of the Carmel Business Association/Carmel Visitors Information Center. This would be a good time to stop in for more information on inns, dining, points of interest, etc.

Just past the Visitor Information Center is a pathway leading to the old Hog's Breath Restaurant (closed in 1999) and the second passageway to Dolores Street. Walk down the path, through the patio (notice the mural of Carmel Valley by local artist, G.H. Rothe) and down the pathway to Dolores Street. Carmel's post office is located on the corner of Dolores & 5th – Carmel does not have street addresses, everyone goes to the post office to receive mail....it is a wonderful place to greet locals!

On the northwest corners of 5th & Dolores are benches where you can rest or enjoy a snack. Walk south on Dolores on the west side to Su Vecino Court/San Remo Cortiles. This is yet another courtyard filled with artisans, restaurants, and shops that will lead you through to the next street, Lincoln.

On the northwest corner of Lincoln & 6th, you will find **The First Murphy House**, built at the turn of the century. Park offers a lovely deck with a spectacular view of Carmel Bay; public restrooms. Home to Carmel Heritage Society which has annual tours of historic homes & inns, video library and self-guided historical tours. Free admission, Wed-Sun, 1-4pm. 624-4447. www.carmelheritage.org

Crossing 6th to the south, you will see the Pine Inn courtyard. The Pine Inn is Carmel's oldest hotel, and the brick-paved, flower-filled courtyard is charming. Walk through the courtyard and exit on Ocean Avenue. To the west, or the right, is Monte Verde. By crossing to the south, you will find yourself at the beginning of your tour. *Text courtesy Carmel Business Assn.*

Free Cheese, Candy, and more...

➤ Between walks, stop at **The Cheese Shop** in the Carmel Plaza and taste your way through the world of cheeses. Sample before you buy!

➤ **Stefan Mann Luggage,** Dolores, between 5th & 6th, will give you a free packing demonstration tailored to your needs. 9am-7pm. 625-2998.

➤ **Carmel Candy**, in the Carmel Plaza, will give you a free taste of their homemade fudge. Open 10am-6pm daily, 625-3559.

➤ **Carmel Walks**, Sat 10am & 2pm, Tues-Fri, 10am. $15 per person. 2 hour guided walk through Carmel courtyards. Meet in the outdoor courtyard of The Pine Inn on Lincoln St. at Ocean Ave. Reservations: 642-2700.

➤ **Historic walking tour** with Kay Prine, first Saturdays. Meet at the Murphy House, Lincoln & 6th. $7. Call 624-4447 for times.

➤ **Happy Dog Tours**, 647-1921.

Interesting Architecture Walks

Most are private homes, please do not disturb.

Frank Lloyd Wright House

Overlooking the ocean, on west side of Scenic Road, east of Martin Way.

Robert Stanton Buildings

Robert Stanton was a prominent architect and civic leader who designed Monterey Peninsula College, the Monterey County Courthouse in Salinas and numerous buildings with an Old World quality in Carmel.

Fisher Cottage	1926	West side Carmel btwn 11th & 12th
Young Cottage	1926	Southwest corner Carmelo & 11th
Church of the Wayfarer	1923-40	Northwest corner Lincoln & 7th
Normandy Inn	1927-50	Southwest corner Casanova & Ocean
N.B. Flower Shop	1942	Southwest corner Ocean & Monte Verde

Hugh Comstock Houses

Hugh Comstock started building 'doll houses' in 1924 for his wife, Mayotta Brown's, 'otsey-totsey' dolls. He used only native and natural materials, and fashioned each house with his own hands, although he was not trained as an architect or builder. You will enjoy a walking tour to view these lovely and unique houses, listed here in the order in which they were built.

HOUSE	DATE	LOCATION
Hansel & Gretel	1924-25	East side Torres btwn 5th & 6th
Ober Cottage	1925	Northeast corner Torres & 6th
Snow White's	1926	West side of Lincoln btwn 12th & 13th
Comstock Studio	1926-40	Northwest corner Santa Fe & 6th
The Woods	1927	Northeast corner Ocean & Torres
Our House	1928	West side Santa Fe btwn 5th & 6th
"Maples"	1928	West side Santa Rita btwn 6th & Ocean
Yellow Bird	1928	South side 6th btwn Santa Fe & Santa Rita
Comstock Cottage	1928	North side Ocean btwn Santa Fe & Santa Rita
The Doll's House	1928	Northwest corner Santa Rita & Ocean
Birthday House	1928	Southwest corner 6th & Santa Rita
Twin on Palou	1929	West side N. Casanova & East side Palou
Curtain Calls	1929	West side Junipero btwn 2nd & 3rd
Jordan House	1929	Southwest corner Vista & Mission
Angel	1929	West side San Antonio btwn 10th & 11th
Los Arboles	1934	East side Santa Fe btwn 8th & 9th
Welsh Cottage	1937	South side 8th btwn Santa Fe & Mt. View
Post Adobe	1937	South side 8th btwn Santa Fe & Mt. View
Slaughter House	1941	Northeast end of 6th near Perry Newberry
Windhorst	1942	West side Santa Fe btwn 2nd & 3rd
Village Inn	1954	Northwest corner Ocean & Junipero

A Self-Guided Walking Tour of the Heritage Trees of Carmel-by-the-Sea

Provided by the Friends of Carmel Forest

Choosing the Heritage Trees

Carmel-by-the-Sea from its beginning has been known as "a village in a forest." As part of the celebration of the 80th anniversary of Carmel's incorporation (1917), the public was invited to nominate candidates for Heritage Tree designation. Final selection was made by the Celebration Committee: Robert Condry, Dr. Roy L. Thomas, Steve Brooks, Gary Kelly, and Howard Skidmore.

The Heritage Trees are a Legacy

Lift up your eyes! In every part of Carmel you will see the lofty crowns of magnificent trees. The trees are a legacy to us from the past. Men and women in years gone by planted and nurtured many of the big trees we see today. Now it is for us not only to enjoy this heritage, but to preserve and protect it. The trees of choice for many, today seen all over town, were the native Monterey Pine and Coast Live Oak. The pine is native only to the Monterey Peninsula and to four small areas along the Pacific Coast. The Monterey Cypress is also seen and is native to Cypress Pt. and Point Lobos. Also seen today are immense Coast Redwoods and the Blue Gum Eucalyptus, said to have been imported from Australia to California in 1856.

Blue Gum Eucalyptus the Largest Tree

Standing by itself on the northwest corner at Ocean and San Antonio Avenues is the largest tree in the village, a Blue Gum Eucalyptus, at 22 feet 8 inches around the trunk. How did this immense tree, presumably predating any real-estate development in Carmel, come to be planted where it is? Possibly it marked a boundary around the grounds of the original rancho. A house said to have been built in 1846, making it the oldest in the village, is located in a windbreak grove of eucalyptuses a few hundred yards to the north. One theory is that the Spanish padres brought the Australian eucalyptus to California even before 1856. A possible support for this idea is the size of the two trees of the species just a few steps from the 1771 Carmel Mission. One tree is 34 feet in girth, the other 26 feet. They are by the so-called bunk house at the historic Mission Ranch, just outside the boundaries of Carmel-by-the-Sea.
(Text by Howard Skidmore)

Locating the Heritage Trees

In tree locations, the abbreviations "we," "es," etc., refer to "west side of street," "east side of street," etc.; 3 so. of 4th" refers to 3rd house south of 4th Ave." Tree measurements are in feet and inches of circumference, taken $4^1/_2$ feet above natural ground level. For multi-trunked trees, such as Coast Live Oaks, when a figure is given it is for the compounded circumference (not the total circumference) for all trunks. "Sea-shaped" refers to the seaside effects of wind, fog, and salt air. *(A complete list of heritage trees and a map is available at City Hall, Monte Verde between Ocean and 7th, and the Park Branch, Mission at 6th.)*

Ocean Avenue between Junipero and Monte Verde:

● "The Patriarch," sw corner of Devendorf Park, a Coast Live Oak, 12+ft, may be the largest oak in the village.

● Center Island at San Carlos, ws, Monterey Pine, 9ft.

● Center Island between Lincoln and Monte Verde, "The Contortionist," Toyon, sea-shaped.

North of Ocean, West of San Carlos:

● Lincoln, es, between 5th & 6th, Blue Gum Eucalyptus, 14+ft, largest of species downtown.

● Lincoln and 2nd, sw corner in street, Monterey Pine, 15+ft, largest pine on city property.

● Monte Verde and 4th, 30 Blue gum Eucalyptuses along so. side 4th to San Antonio. Trees line what was early road leading to rancho on west side of San Antonio.

North of Ocean, East of San Carlos:

● San Carlos and 5th ne corner, in lodge courtyard, Coast Redwood 16+ft. Largest tree in downtown.

South of Ocean, West of San Carlos:

● San Carlos and Santa Lucia, nw corner, in courtyard, Monterey Pine, 17ft, largest pine in Carmel, said to be largest in county. Private property.

● Monte Verde es so. of Ocean, City Hall, in front, Coast Redwood, 11+ft.

● Camino Real and 8th se corner, Monterey Pine 13+ft, to left of entrance to historic La Playa Hotel (built in 1904 and restored in 1984).

● San Antonio between 10th and 12th, "The Arcade," large Monterey Cypresses meet overhead. Planted in early 1900s.

● Scenic & Ocean, 2 w on Ocean, ns, "Contortionist II," Acacia, sea-shaped.

Friends of Carmel Forest

To become a member, write to P.O. Box 344, Carmel, CA 93921

Other Places of Interest

■ **Robinson Jeffers' Tor House and Hawk Tower**, 26304 Ocean View Ave. near Stewart Way.  The former home of poet Robinson Jeffers, whose poetry was inspired by the rugged Big Sur coast. The 1918 Tor House contains original furnishings and Jeffers' memorabilia. Drive by Hawk Tower (1920) on Stewart Way. Jeffers gathered the stones from nearby Carmel Beach and the outside retaining wall contains rock from the Temple of Peking, lava from Hawaii, and a piece of the Great Wall of China. He built Hawk Tower as a symbol of his love for his wife, Una. Tours of the gardens, house, and Tower, Fri-Sat, every hour, on the hour, 10am-3pm. Only 6 people can be accommodated on each tour, so reservations must be made ahead. $7 adults, $4 college, $2 high school, no children under 12. Robinson Jeffers Festival, in October, affords a <u>free walk</u> with poets. 624-1813.www.torhouse.org.

■ **The Basilica of Mission San Carlos Borromeo del Rio Carmelo** (Carmel Mission Basilica), 3080 Rio Road and Lausen Drive (831) 624-1271, 624-3600. <u>Grounds and Mission are free</u>.  Originally founded by Father Junipero Serra, June 3, 1770, in Monterey (now the Royal Presidio Chapel), the church was moved to this site in 1771. The present stone church was dedicated in 1797. Father Junipero Serra is buried in the Basilica. A donation of $2 for adults and $1 for children 5 and older is requested to visit the museum to continue the restoration which is privately funded. The Mission is considered the most authentically restored Franciscan mission. Open Mon-Sat, 9:30am-4:15pm, Sunday, 10:30am-4:15pm. Open until 7:15pm, June through August. This is a fabulous place to connect with the history of the Monterey Peninsula, and a sight not to be missed. The rooms are filled with utensils, clothing, tools, baskets, church vestments and more. The courtyard and gardens have several benches for resting and meditating, old statues, and a collection of specimen plants, native shrubs, and flowers.

Masses: Sat 5:30pm; Sun 7, 8, 9:30, 11, 12:30 and 5:30pm; weekdays: 7am, 12noon and 5:30pm (in Blessed Sacrament Chapel); Eve of Holy Days, 5:30pm; Holy Days: 7, 9:30, 11am, 12:30 and 5:30pm. Mission: St. Francis of the Redwoods Mass, Sunday, 10:30am.

Gift Shop is open 9:30am-4:30pm. 624-3600.

Mission San Carlos Borromeo del Rio Carmelo
Joelle Steele, 11x17 watercolor, 1996.

Art Gallery Walk

Carmel is known for its artists and galleries. There's the whimsy of Will Bullas, the poignancy of Rodrique's Blue Dog, sculpture by MacDonald, New Renaissance Masters, and everything in-between. You can spend an entire lifetime soaking up the art treasures found here. Be prepared to add to your own art collection. More galleries open every month. If you have time, visit the **Carl Cherry Center for the Arts,** founded by local artist Jeanne D'Orge, at 4th Ave. and Guadalupe St. 624-7491; and the **Sculpture House & Gardens Gallery** on Hwy One in the Carmel Highlands, 624-2476.

Mission Street

- **Dyansen Gallery**, in the Carmel Plaza. Contemporary art, graphics, and sculpture. Sun-Thur 10-6, Fri-Sat 10-9. 625-6903.

- **It's Cactus**, between Ocean and 7th. Imported handmade folk art of all things rare and unusual. 626-4213.

- **Edward Montgomery**, between Ocean & 7th. Contemporary paintings, prints, and sculpture. Daily 10-6, Sun 12-5. 622-9292, 800-323-4221.

- **Cottage Gallery**, near 6th. Traditional art: landscape, seascape, still life. Daily 10-5. 624-7888.

- **Alexander of Florence**, between 5th & 6th. Original contemporary Italian art. Open daily. 620-0732.

San Carlos Street

- **Jones & Terwilliger**, btwn 5th & 6th. 30 artists; oils & sculpture. Daily 10-6. Fri-Sat 10-10. East Gallery: 626-9100. West Gallery: 626-7300.

- **European Galleries**, between 5th & 6th. Contemporary originals. Daily 10-6, Fri-Sat 10-10. 624-2010.

- **Andrew T. Jackson Studio**, at 6th. 626-8354.

- **Mudzimu Gallery**, San Carlos Mall btwn 5th & 6th. Contemporary African stone sculpture. Daily 11-6, closed Tues. 626-2946.

- **Silver Light Gallery**, at Ocean. Photography. Daily 10-5. 624-4589.

- **Will Bullas Fun Art**, between Ocean & 7th. Humorous, appealing work. 11am-3pm daily. 625-4112.

- **Elke & Delaila**, at 6th. Daily 11-6. 624-8024.

- **Trotter Galleries**, at 7th. Early California. 625-3246.

- **Winters Fine Art Galleries**, Doud Arcade and Plaza San Carlos. Wide selection. Daily 10-5, closed Sun. 626-5452, 626-5535.

- **Richard MacDonald**, near 6th. Figurative sculpture by MacDonald. Daily 10-6, Fri-Sat 10-9. 624-8200.

- **New Renaissance Masters**, between 5th & 6th. Limited editions of Masters. Sun-Thur 10-6, Fri-Sat 10-10. 622-5255.

- **Simic New Renaissance**, between 5th & 6th. Original Impressionism and Realism. Mon-Wed 10-6, Thur-Sat 10-10, Sun 10-8. 624-7522.
- **Center for Photographic Art**, Sunset Cultural Center, San Carlos and 8th. Fine art photographs and exhibitions. Tues-Sun, 1-5pm. 625-5181.
- **Sunset Center**, San Carlos and 8th. Monthly art demonstrations, monthly showcase artists. Call for details, 372-2841.

Dolores Street

- **Joie De Vivre Gallery**, between 5th & 6th. Contemporary Masters from Italy, Spain, France, China, and the United States. Sun-Thurs 10-6, Fri-Sat 9-9. 620-0156.
- **Richard Thomas Galleries**, between 5th & 6th. Contemporary masters and traditional. 625-5636.
- **Gallerie Amsterdam**, between 5th & 6th. European paintings. Sun-Wed 10-6, Fri-Sat 10-10.
- **Golf Art & Imports**, between 5th & 6th. Golf-themed art, collectibles, and antiquities of all kinds. Mon-Sat 10-5, Sun 11-5. 625-4488.
- **Pitzer's of Carmel**, on 6th. Original paintings, sculpture, prints, and porcelain. Mon-Sat 10-6, Sun 10-5. 625-2288, 800/843-6467.
- **Photography West Gallery**, S.E. corner of Ocean. Classical and contemporary photography. Fri-Mon 10-6. 625-1587.
- **Bleich Gallery West**, south of Ocean. George J. Bleich, a renowned plein-air painter. Daily 10:30-5:30. 624-9447, 372-2717.
- **China Art Center**, between 7th & Ocean. Impressive collection of museum-quality paintings from the Sung and Ming Dynasties to modern times, silk, screens, furniture, jewelry. Mon-Sat 10-6. 624-5868.
- **Gallery 21**, between Ocean & 7th. Collection of Eyvind Earle, a former Disney animation artist. Daily from 10am. 626-2700.
- **Zimmerman Gallery**, between Ocean & 7th. Marc Zimmerman combines classical Renaissance with contemporary. Daily 10:30-5. 622-9100.
- **David Lee Galleries**, at 7th.
- **New Masters Gallery**, between Ocean & 7th. Contemporary paintings and sculpture. 625-1511.
- **Gallery 1000**, between Ocean & 7th. Original oils and watercolors. Daily 10-6. 624-9094.
- **Carmel Art Association Galleries**, between 5th & 6th. Oldest gallery (1928) with over 120 artists. There are some interesting sculptures in the front garden. Daily 10am-5pm. 624-6176.

- **Highlands Sculpture Gallery**, between 5th & 6th. Innovative gallery of sculpture, monotypes, paintings. 624-0535.
- **Galerie Plein Aire**, btwn 5th & 6th. 625-5686. www.galeriepleinaire.com
- **47 Gallery Sur, Inc.**, at 6th. Nature photography. Daily 10-6. 626-2615.
- **Josephus Daniels Gallery**, 6th, Su Vecino Ct., upstairs. Prints and photographs. Tue-Sat 1-5, Sun 1-4. www.danielsgallery.com. 625-3316.
- **Savage Contemporary Fine Art**, between 5th & 6th. Contemporary figurative and abstract. Daily 10-6. 626-0800, 888/626-0808.
- **James J. Rieser Fine Art**, between 5th & 6th. Early California paintings and local artists. Daily 11-5. 620-0530.
- **S.R. Brennen Galleries**. Corner of 5th. Eclectic collection. 10-6 daily. 625-2233.
- **William A. Karges Fine Art**, at 5th. Early California impressionists. Daily 10-5. 625-4266.
- **Atelier Carmel**, at 5th. Classic fine art. Daily 10-6. 625-3168.

Sixth Avenue

- **Classic Art Gallery**, at San Carlos. Traditional fine art. Daily 10-6, Fri-Sat 10-9. 625-0464.
- **Regal Art Galleries**, between San Carlos & Dolores. Original paintings and sculptures. Sun-Thurs 10-6, Fri-Sat 10-10. 624-8155.
- **Howard Portnoy Gallerie**, between Dolores & San Carlos. French impressionists; figurative bronze sculpture. Daily 1-5. 624-1155.
- **The Decoy**, between Dolores and Lincoln. Wildlife, waterfowl, and sporting dog themes. 625-1881.
- **Martin LaBorde Gallery**, between Lincoln & Dolores. LaBorde's paintings, serigraphs, and drawings. 10-6 daily. 620-1150.
- **Weston Gallery**, between Dolores & Lincoln. Photography of the 19th and 20th centuries. Wed-Mon 10:30-5:30, closed Tues. 624-4453.
- **D.E. Craghead/Fine Art Gallery**, between Dolores & Lincoln. Diverse paintings and sculpture. Daily 10-5:30. 624-5054.
- **Phillips Gallery of Fine Art**, between Dolores & Lincoln. Original paintings, stone sculptures. Sat-Thurs 10-6, Fri 10-8.
- **Gallery Americana**, corner of Lincoln. Contemporary paintings and sculpture. Mon-Sat 10-5:30, Sun 10-5. 624-5071.
- **Lynn Lupetti Gallery**, between Dolores & Lincoln. Luminous paintings by Lupetti, other fine artists. Daily 10-5. 624-0622.
- **Rodrigue Studio**, between Lincoln & Dolores. "Blue Dog" series. Daily 10-6. 626-4444.

- **Loran Speck Art Gallery**, near Dolores. Speck retrospective on Dutch and Italian painters of the Renaissance. Daily 10:30-5pm. 624-3707.
- **Lilliana Braico Gallery**, near Dolores. Mediterranean scenes, abstracts, portraits, and florals. Fri-Tues 11-5, Wed-Thurs by appt.
- **Winfield Gallery**, 6th Ave. Contemporary fine art and crafts. 624-3369.
- **Garcia Gallery**, between Dolores & San Carlos, upstairs. Danny Garcia impressionism, realism, and abstraction. Daily 10-5. 624-8338.
- **Zantman Art Galleries, Inc.**, at Mission. Paintings and sculpture of living American, European and Asian artists. Daily 10-5. 624-8314.

Lincoln Street

- **Avalon Gallery**, between Ocean & 7th in Morgan Court. Contemporary handmade works on paper, fine woodworking, and nudes. Wed-Mon 11-5 and by appt. 622-0830.
- **G.H. Rothe Gallery I & II**, between Ocean & 7th in Morgan Court. Original mezzotints, oils, pastels, mixed media, pencil, and watercolors. Daily 10-6. 624-9377.

Seventh Avenue

- **Nancy Dodds Gallery**, between San Carlos & Dolores. Contemporary works on paper: watercolors, etchings, oil, lithographs and monotypes. Mon-Sat 10:30-5:30, Sun 12-5. 624-0346.
- **Chapman Gallery**, between San Carlos & Mission. Works by past and present masters, including Hank Ketcham, S.C. Yuan, and Gail Reeves.

Tue-Sat 11-5. 626-1766. The Chapman Gallery dog, Hardy, is a BIG attraction; stop in with the kids to say hello. The Gallery will also give a free art print, similar to the one shown above, to anyone who mentions this book.

- **Unitarian Universalist Church of the Monterey Peninsula**, 490 Aguajito Road, shows local artists and sponsors many free events. Call for more information and a calendar, 624-7404.

Public Libraries & Bookstores

• **Harrison Memorial Public Library**, Ocean Ave. and Lincoln, 624-4629. Reference: 624-7323. Hours: Mon-Wed, 10am-8pm, Thurs-Fri, 10am-6pm, Sat-Sun, 1-5pm. 7 internet stations. Outreach Program: For people unable to come to the library. Delivery of books and books-on-tape, loan equipment which helps physically challenged people use library materials, braille and talking books. 624-7323. Audiovisual collection of local history includes tapes which can be viewed from 1-5pm, Tues-Fri.: "Big Sur, The Way It Was," "Don't Pave Main Street," "Ford Ord, A Place in History," "Longtimers" Part I and II," "Remembering Carmel" Part I, II and III. Become a Friend and help at the annual tea and book sale. www.hm-lib.org.

• **Library Park Branch**, 6th Ave. and Mission St. 624-1366. Tue, 10am-8pm, Wed-Fri, 10am-6pm, Sat, 1pm-5pm. Local History Dept with hundreds of books on California and Carmel, biography and art. Local authors and artists, historical photographs, and Carmel newspapers on microfilm. 624-1615. The Youth Services Dept has library materials for infants through young adults and books about parenting. Programs: Tues, 10:30am, preschool, 7pm, families; Wed, 10:30am, preschool; Fri, 10:30am, babies and toddlers, 11:15am, toddlers and preschool. Youth services: 624-4664.

• **Kingdom Come Books and Gifts**. Christian Bookstore. Protestant, Catholic, Jewish books, gifts, music, jewelry, greeting cards, Hermitage fruitcakes. Mon-Sat 10am-5:30pm. 26386 Carmel Rancho Lane. 624-1290.

• **Pilgrims' Way Bookstore**. Metaphysical books and music, astrology reports, incense, gifts. Lectures & book signings. Mon-Sat 10am-6pm, Sun 11am-5pm. Dolores & 6th Ave. www.pilgrimsway.com. 624-4955.

• **Sierra Club–Ventana Chapter**. Nature books and trail guides. Ocean between Dolores & San Carlos, upstairs. 624-8032.

• **Books, Inc.** Carmel Plaza. Weekly book club. Call Kate or Katie for dates and times, 625-1440.

• **Thunderbird Bookshop and Cafe**. Book signings and weekly lectures. Local art on the walls, cozy cafe with fireplace, solarium patio. They read and select the best books available and present them on tables: "Really Great Reading" and "May Recommends." Visit website for a listing of free events, including book clubs. 360 The Barnyard. 10-9 daily. 624-1803. www.thunderbirdbooks.com.

Poets & Writers Invited

➤ **Poetry on the Beach**, in the Bohemian tradition, at sunset on last Saturdays with Tad Wojnicki at Carmel Beach, foot of 13th Avenue. Bring a potluck dish, flashlight, poem/story, or a fire log. 770-0107.

➤ **Creative With Words** publications for poets/writers. Submit entries to *The Eclectics*, writers age 20 and up, and *We Are Writers, Too!*, age 19 and under. Write or fax for details and entry forms: PO Box 223226, Carmel 93922. Fax 655-8627.

Calendar of Events

Year 2000 dates shown. Updates at www.montereycountyguide.com.
Please call in advance to verify as information is subject to change.

JANUARY

January 1   **RIO GRILL'S RESOLUTION RUN**   Spectators FREE
New Year's Day 10K race to benefit the Suicide Prevention Center. 6.8 mile foot race over roads, trails and scenic beaches. 3 mile Family Fun Run is ideal for all ages and capabilities. From The Crossroads, through Carmel, and ending at the Carmel Mission. Participants: $21 adults, $16 ages 12 and younger. Registration includes a long sleeve T-shirt, brunch, and entry for prize drawings. Crossroads Shopping Center, Highway 1 at Rio Road. Info 644-2427; to volunteer 375-6966.

January 11   **CARMEL MUSIC SOCIETY PERFORMANCE** $$
Sunset Center Theater, pianist Jean-Yves Thibaudet. Tickets 625-9938.

January 23-24   **MONTEREY SYMPHONY** $$
Sunset Center Theater, Roberto Minczuk, conductor. Ginastera, Barber, Copland. Tickets 624-8511.

FEBRUARY

February 7   **CARMEL MUSIC SOCIETY PERFORMANCE** $$
Sunset Center Theater, The Moscow Chamber Orchestra. Tickets 625-9938.

February 20-21   **MONTEREY SYMPHONY** $$
Sunset Center Theater, Vladimir Spivakov, conductor and violinist. Mozart and Tchaikovsky. Tickets 624-8511.

February 23-27   **MASTERS OF FOOD & WINE** $$
14th Annual at the Highlands Inn, various times. Exceptional gastronomic event with internationally famous chefs and winemakers. Lunches, dinners, winery tours, wine tastings. 624-3801. www.Hyatt.com.

February 24-April 2   **GUYS & DOLLS** $$
Golden BoughTheatre, Monte Verde btwn 8th & 9th. Pacific Repertory Theatre. 622-0100. www. pacrep.org.

MARCH

March   **ANNUAL KITE FESTIVAL**   Spectators FREE
Date is kept secret to avoid crowds–see local papers. Kites must be homemade except for the kids-only commercial category. Noon registration, judging begins at 12:30. Carmel Beach at the end of 13th Avenue. For more information about categories, prizes and rules, contact Carmel Community Activities, 626-1255.

March 7-April 15   **PICASSO AT THE LAPIN AGILE** $$
By Steve Martin, at the Circle Theatre, Casanova btwn 8th & 9th. 622-0100. www. pacrep.org.

March 19-20   **MONTEREY SYMPHONY** $$
Sunset Center Theater, Alexander Anissimov, conductor. John O'Conor, piano. Glinka, Shostakovich and Brahms. Tickets 624-8511.

March 25   **CARMEL MUSIC SOCIETY COMPETITION**   FREE
Sunset Center Theater, 24th annual vocal competition, free and open to the public. To participate call 659-8274.

APRIL

April-Sept **GARDEN TOURS** **FREE**
Guided tours of The Barnyard gardens every Sunday at noon. Led by horticulturist Margo Grych. Meet at The Thunderbird Bookstore. 624-8886.

April 12 **CARMEL MUSIC SOCIETY PERFORMANCE** **FREE**
Sunset Center Theater, Felix Fan, cellist and winner of the 1999 23rd annual Instrument Competition will perform at 8pm. 625-9938.

April 16-17 **MONTEREY SYMPHONY** **$$**
Sunset Center Theater, Jean Louis Steuerman, conductor and pianist. Haydn, Mozart and Beethoven. Tickets 624-8511.

April 29 **5TH ANNUAL HOME & GARDEN AFFAIR** **$$**
Garden tour and festival with gardening demonstrations, music, entertainment, and refreshments. 1-4pm. The Barnyard Shopping Village, Highway 1. 624-8886.

April 30 **BIG SUR INTERNATIONAL MARATHON Spectators FREE**
15th Annual. Includes the 26.2 mile footrace, the marathon Relay Teams, the 21 mile non-competitive Power Walk, 5K footrace, and the 10.6 mile noncompetitive walk – all to raise money for charities. Eclectic musicians play along the course. Volunteers always needed. Free training clinics held in November thru April. Sign up to run/walk on-line: www.bsim.org or call 625-6226, fax 625-2119.

MAY

May **CARMEL ART FESTIVAL** **FREE**
Local art, youth art, sculpture-in-the-park exhibit, and demonstrations. Various locations. Includes 7th Annual Plein Air Event at Galerie Plein Aire. 624-2522.

May/Aug **FOREST FILM FESTIVAL** **$$**
Outdoor Forest Theater, Santa Rita & Mtn View. Films at 8:30pm. $5. 626-1681.

May 6-7 **ORCHID MAYFAIRE** **FREE**
Spectacular orchid show presented by the Carmel Orchid Society. Crossroads Shopping Center, Rio Road and Highway 1. Contact Sheila Bowman, 622-0292.

May 6-7 **28TH ANNUAL CHAMBER MUSIC CONCERTS** **FREE**
Saturday at 1pm, an afternoon of performances by chamber ensembles from the nation's top university music departments and conservatories, judged by a panel of renowned chamber musicians. Sunday at 3pm, competition Finalists Concert. Sunset Center. Chamber Music Monterey Bay. 625-2212, fax 625-3055.

May 7 **ROBINSON JEFFERS GARDEN PARTY** **$$**
Annual celebration of literature at the Tor House, 26304 Ocean Ave. at Carmel Point. Sunday, 2-5pm.

May 12 **BAGPIPE PARADE** **FREE**
Kick-off to Scottish Games and Celtic Festival. Meet the bagpipers in Devendorf Park at 4:30pm, watch the parade down Ocean Avenue at 5pm. 484-2834.

May 21-22 **MONTEREY SYMPHONY** **$$**
Sunset Center Theater, Federico Cortese, conductor, Symphony Chorus. Bellini, Cherubini and Saint-Saëns. Tickets 624-8511.

May 26-July 2 **A FLEA IN HER EAR** **$$**
By Georges Feydeau. Golden BoughTheatre, Monte Verde btwn 8th & 9th. Pacific Repertory Theatre. 622-0100. www. pacrep.org.

JUNE

June/July   **FOREST THEATRE CONCERTS**   **FREE**
Sundays, free concerts at 2pm at the Outdoor Forest Theater, Mountain View and Santa Rita. Presented by The Sunset Center with funding provided by the Mayor's Youth Fund. 626-1255.

June/July   **PARKFEST**   **FREE**
Musicians and performers, free hot dogs for the kids. Noon on Fridays at Devendorf Park, Ocean and Junipero. 626-1255.

June 6   **HMS PINAFORE**   **$$**
By Gilbert and Sullivan.Circle Theatre, Casanova btwn 8th & 9th. Pacific Repertory Theatre. 622-0100. www. pacrep.org.

June 24   **11TH ANNUAL ART & WINE FESTIVAL**   **FREE+$$**
Enjoy art throughout the gardens, with live music. Wine tasting and food. Fifteen local vintners, food samplings from Barnyard restaurants., $15.To benefit MCAP. 1-4pm at The Barnyard, Highway 1 to Carmel Valley Rd. 624-8886.

JULY

July-Oct   **FARMER'S MARKET AT THE BARNYARD**   **FREE**
Entertainment, food samples. Tuesdays, 2-6pm. 624-8886.

July 15-16   **DOG SHOWS AND OBEDIENCE TRIALS**   **FREE**
Del Monte Kennel Club All-Breed, Dog Shows & Obedience Trials. Free admission daily, parking $3 daily. Food available from Carmel Kiwanis. 8am-5pm at Carmel Middle School. Club, 333-9032, Ruth, 649-4280.

July 15-Aug 6   **CARMEL BACH FESTIVAL**   **FREE+$$**
A lively celebration of baroque music. Enjoy their "Discovery Series" of free events including open rehearsals, concerts for kids and families, lectures, brass concerts, and free ice cream. Volunteer to be a hostess or an usher to enjoy the concerts. Festival office at Sunset Center. Information: 624-2046, fax 624-2788, www.bachfestival.org.

AUGUST

Aug 11-Oct 15   **SHAKE-SPEARE FESTIVAL**   **$$**
Take-off on the Bard's tales - lots of fun. "Two Gentlemen of Verona," Circle Theatre, Casanova btwn 8th & 9th. Pacific Repertory Theatre. 622-0100. www. pacrep.org.

August 24   **PETER PAN**   **$$**
Directed by Walter deFaria. Outdoor Forest Theatre. Pacific Repertory Theatre. 622-0100. www. pacrep.org.

Aug 24-Sept 24   **PETER PAN MUSICAL**   **$$**
At the Outdoor Forest Theatre by the Pacific Repertory Theatre. 622-0100.

August 26   **FERRARI CONCOURS**   **FREE**
2nd Annual. The Ferrari Owners Club brings Ferraris to the Barnyard for the public to view, 3-6pm. 624-8886.

SEPTEMBER

Sept or Oct   GREAT SAND CASTLE CONTEST   FREE
39th Annual. No entry fee for this theme-based
contest within the boundaries of 10th and 12th
avenues. Anyone and everyone is invited to participate.

   The top prize is the Golden Shovel Award with
almost 30 lesser prizes awarded, including Advanced Soapbox and the Sour Grapes Award
(given to the best–or worst–whiners).

   Children, kindergarten thru high school, are
invited to enter contest for theme and logo competition. Held at Carmel Beach, end of Ocean
Ave. For more information, call 626-1255.

September   FESTIVAL OF FIRSTS $$
22nd Annual. 3 days, Sunset Center Theater, San Carlos at 9th. 624-3996.

September   FINE ARTS 5K RUN/WALK   Spectators FREE
Meet at 9am at Carmel Beach, Scenic Drive and Ocean Ave. 758-8406..

September   SEPTEMBER SALON $$
Colleagues of the Arts raises funds specifically to help financially disadvantaged
and gifted young people with artistic talent, who wish to develop their skills and/
or pursue careers in the arts. To volunteer, call 626-4029.

September 2-3   OUTDOOR ART FESTIVAL   FREE+$$
Enjoy fine-art exhibits and live music. Benefit for the Carmel Cultural Commis-
sion. Sunset Center, San Carlos & 9th. 624-3996.

Sept 8- Oct 15   SHAKE-SPEARE FESTIVAL $$
"Volpone" by Ben Jonson, Golden Bough Theatre, Monte Verde btwn 8th & 9th.
Pacific Repertory Theatre. 622-0100. www. pacrep.org.

September 24   CARMEL MISSION FIESTA   FREE
Mariachi dancers and singers, bagpipers, strolling musicians, children's games,
arts and crafts, farmers market, food vendors. 3pm live auction with Dan Green.
Bill Bates cartoons. Noon-5pm at the Mission, on Rio Road west of Highway 1.
Info and advance barbecue tickets: 624-1271.

Sept 29 - Oct 15   SHAKE-SPEARE FESTIVAL $$
Take-off on the Bard's tales - lots of fun. "A midsummer's Night Dream," Outdoor
Forest Theatre. Pacific Repertory Theatre. 622-0100. www. pacrep.org.

OCTOBER

October 1st week   MONTEREY WORLDMUSIC FESTIVAL $$
Sunset Center. 4th annual. 622-9595. www.montereyworldmusic.org.

October 5-21   CARMEL PERFORMING ARTS FESTIVAL   FREE+$$
The finest regional and national theatre, dance and music…and a few surprises…
in the intimate and historic theatres of charming Carmel. Free music, and recep-
tions at galleries, parks, and shopping centers in Carmel during the festival. Call
for places and times. Tickets $5-$40. 644-8383, 624-7675, fax 622-7631.
www.carmelfest.org.

October 14-15   THE ROBINSON JEFFERS' FESTIVAL   FREE+$$

Presented by the Tor House Foundation, beginning with a reception at Jeffers' home, Tor House, on Friday night, to honor festival speakers. This event is $5, or free to those with advance reservation for the Saturday seminars and banquet. Free Jeffers Poetry Walk on Sunday morning. Meet at Sunset Cultural Center for coffee and the walk ends with a brown bag lunch at noon on Carmel beach. 624-1813, 624-1840. www.torhouse.org.

October 29   19TH ANNUAL HARVEST FESTIVAL   FREE

Enjoy a fun, safe, family-oriented Halloween at The Barnyard. Trick-or-treat, pony rides, costume contest with prizes, hayrides, and entertainment. 1-4pm at The Barnyard, Highway 1 and Carmel Valley Road. 624-8886.

October 31   HALLOWEEN PARADE & BARBECUE   FREE+$$

Carmel's 84th Birthday. Costumed children parade from Junipero down Ocean to Monte Verde and back. 11am at Devendorf Park, barbecue at noon, adults $15, children $3. Free ice cream for the children. Entertainment by local band. Benefit the Mayor's Youth Fund. Tickets at City Hall or call 625-0450, 624-5039.

October 31   SUNDOWN BEACH FIRE   FREE

On Carmel Beach, 13th and Scenic Drive, at sundown with Taelan Thomas. For twenty years, local bohemians meet to share ghost stories, poems, readings and mythic tales. Bring log, soulful story, poem, or music to share. 659-3947.

DECEMBER

December   KINDERGARTEN ART SHOW   FREE

Pat Spencer's kindergarten class artwork show in the cafe area of The Thunderbird Bookshop in The Barnyard Shopping Village. 624-1803.

December 1   CARMEL LIGHTS UP THE SEASON   FREE

An open house at Carmel Plaza. Complimentary photos with Santa follows the tree lighting ceremony. 5pm at Devendorf Park, on Ocean Ave. between Junipero and Mission Streets. 624-0137.

December 2-3   22ND ANNUAL CHRISTMAS FESTIVAL   FREE

1-4pm each day. Music, carolling, entertainment, food and more. Benefit High School Padres. The Barnyard. 624-8886.

Redwings Horse Sanctuary

Sanctuary for horses. Stop in and enjoy the animals. They also offer educational courses. Open to the public 10am-3:30pm. Off Highway 1, just north of Point Lobos. For information, call Karen Neely at 831-624-8464.

Support The Performing Arts in Monterey County

Some of these organizations offer free performances, and all are run with the generous help of volunteers. Call for more information. www.culturalmonterey.org.

Monterey County Theatre Alliance

- California's First Theatre
  Scott & Pacific Streets, Monterey, CA 93940. 375-4916
- Carmel Ballet Academy & Dance Kids, Inc.
  P.O. Box 2586, Carmel, CA 93921. 624-3729
- Forest Theater Guild - also CCMC member.
  P.O. Box 2325, Carmel-by-the-Sea, CA 93921. 626-1681
- Magic Circle Center
  8 El Caminito Rd, Carmel Valley, CA 93924. 659-1108.
- Monterey Peninsula College Theatre
  980 Fremont St., Monterey, CA 93940. 646-4213
- Pacific Repertory Theatre - also CCMC member.
  P.O. Box 222035, Carmel, CA 93922. 622-0100
- Practically Perfect Productions
  P.O. Box 222846, Carmel, CA 93922. 649-1531
- Third Studio
  602 Larkin St., Monterey, CA 93940. 373-4389
- Unicorn Theatre
  320 Hoffman Ave., Monterey, CA 93940. 649-0259
- The Western Stage - also CCMC member.
  156 Homestead Ave., Salinas, CA 93901. 755-6816 or 375-2111.

Cultural Council for Monterey County

- Carmel Bach Festival, 624-2046
  Concerts at Sunset Center and Mission; Chapel in the Forest, P.B.
- Carmel Music Society, 625-9938
  All concerts at Sunset Center, Carmel.
- Chamber Music Society of the Monterey Peninsula, 625-2212
  All concerts at Sunset Center, Carmel.
- Great Performances, 977-1690
  Performances at Sherwood Hall, Salinas.
- Keyboard Artist Series, 624-7971
  All concerts at Sunset Center, Carmel.
- Monterey Blues Festival, 394-2652
  All concerts at Monterey Fairgrounds.
- Monterey County Symphony, 624-8511
  Concerts at Sunset Center, Carmel, and Sherwood Hall, Salinas.
- Monterey Jazz Festival, 373-3366
  All concerts at Monterey Fairgrounds.
- Mozart Society of California, 625-3637
  All concerts at Church of Religious Science, Monterey.
- Performance Carmel, 624-3996
  Concerts at Hartnell College Main Stage, Salinas.
- Portofino Presents, 373-7379
  Performances at P.G. Art Center, and Church of Religious Science.

Entertainment
Music & Dancing

◆ **Mission Ranch.** Dinner music, sing-along/Open Mic at piano bar. Tue-Thurs, 6-9pm, piano music, 9-midnight. Sunday brunch jazz, 10am-2:30pm. No cover. 26270 Dolores (behind Carmel Mission) off Rio Road. Wonderful pastoral views from the dining room. 1850 Farmhouse, opposite. Ranch was saved from development by Clint Eastwood, a frequent patron. 625-9040.

◆ **Highlands Inn.** Dancing 9-midnight Fri-Sat; piano jazz Mon/Wed, 6-9pm. No cover. Unbeatable ocean views. Carmel Highlands, Highway 1, four miles south of Carmel, 624-3801.

◆ **Cypress Inn.** Afternoon Tea, 2-4pm, reservations required. A Carmel tradition. Fee. Happy Hour, 5-7pm. Lincoln & 7th. 624-3871, 800-443-7443.

◆ **La Gondola.** Live music every Fri-Sat 5-8pm; piano bar until 11; Happy Hour daily 4-7pm. Dine late 7 days a week. 3690 The Barnyard, Highway 1 and Carmel Valley Road. No cover. 626-0430.

◆ **Lugano Swiss Bistro.** Dancing last Fridays 7-11pm. No cover. Under the windmill in The Barnyard, Highway 1 and Carmel Valley Road. 626-3779.

◆ **Caffé Cardinale Coffee Roasting Company.** Live music on Friday nights during the summer. No cover. Ocean Avenue and Dolores Street. 626-2095.

◆ **The Jazz & Blues Company.** The World's First All-Jazz Store. Official Monterey Jazz Festival off-site merchandise headquarters. Watch DJs at work playing your jazz favorites live on-air while you shop. 236 Crossroads Blvd. Call for entertainment dates and prices, 624-6432.

Music & Dancing Groups

◆ **Big Band Swing & Latin lessons** Sun 6 and 7pm, Carmel American Legion. Pre-registered intro, $5; ongoing, $8; drop-ins $10. 800/368-0415.

◆ **Greek Folk Dancing** at Sunset Center, Rm. 10, 9th and San Carlos. Beginners, Tues, 6:30pm, Intermediate and advanced, 7:30-9pm. No partner needed; all ages welcome. Darold Skerritt, Judy Lind, 375-2549. $4 night. September through June. http://members.xoom.com/xoros/. The Greek Village Dancers provide free entertainment at various Monterey Peninsula convalescent homes and hospitals and perform at the Greek Orthodox Church in Monterey, the Feast of Lanterns in Pacific Grove, and First Night® Monterey.

◆ **Argentine Tango** 7:30-9:30pm, Thurs, Carmel American Legion. Beginners welcome, no partner needed. $8. 372-4062.

◆ **Music Together**, cutting-edge music enrichment program for infants, toddlers, preschoolers and their parents & caregivers. Songs, chants, movement, instrument play, <u>free demonstration classes</u>. Sunset Center on San Carlos between 8th & 9th. 642-2424.

Theatre & Dance

◆ **'Dances of Universal Peace'** held 7-9pm, second Saturdays at the Community Church of the Monterey Peninsula on Carmel Valley Road, one mile from Highway 1. Participants will learn how to dance and chant in unison with guitar, drum, and flute music. No experience or partner is required; a $5 donation. Margot Edwards, 375-1974 or Pat Dally, 625-1136.

◆ **Carmel Music Society**. All concerts at 8pm at Sunset Center. <u>Students in grades 6-12 can attend free concerts</u> through the student ticket program which is funded by grants through local schools. 625-9938.

◆ **Pacific Repertory Theatre**. <u>Presents free performances at TheatreFest during the summer</u>. Live theatre at Golden Bough Theatre, Monte Verde btwn 8th & 9th; Circle Theatre, Casanova between 8th & 9th; Forest Theater, Santa Rita and Mountain View. Presents Spring Festival in March/April, Summer Festival May-July, and Carmel Shake-speare Festival, July-October. For details, contact Marcia Hardy at 622-0700.

◆ **Santa Catalina School** Drama Department, puts on <u>some free performances</u>. Call 655-9341 for dates and times.

◆ **Children's Experimental Theatre**. 624-1531.

◆ **Dance Kids, Inc.** 626-2980.

Movie Theater

◆ **Crossroads Cinemas**, <u>free refill on large popcorn and large drinks</u>. Highway 1 at Rio Road. Seniors and matinees before 6pm, $5.00. 624-8682 (call 777-FILM #118). www.cinemacal.com

Yoga Classes

◆ **Kundalini Yoga** class is ongoing, meets 7:30-9pm Wednesdays. Bring mat, wear loose clothes, eat lightly. Unitarian Universalist Church, 490 Aguajito Road, Carmel. <u>Donations accepted</u>. 659-2969.

◆ **Yoga Center** offers <u>free yoga classes</u> in July for kids 10-17. Ongoing Hatha Yoga classes. Yoga Center, Cottage 17, Sunset Center, San Carlos Street btwn 8th and 9th Avenues. 624-4949. www.carmelyogacenter.org

Day Spas

◆ **Le Spa** has complete spa packages and individual services–massage, facial, makeup, hand & foot therapy. Dolores btwn 7th & 8th. 620-0935.

◆ **Yonka Signature Day Spa**. Facials, waxing, electrolysis, massage, hair, makeup, pre-and post-op surgical. 118 Crossroads Blvd. 625-4410.

◆ **Skin Care By the Sea**. Facials, body care, waxing, makeup, bridal makeovers, etc. 3855 Via Nona Marie, Ste 108. 626-1614.

Parks & Recreation
Waterfront Activities

▲ **Carmel Beach**, west end of Ocean Ave., is a favorite beach for locals and visitors alike. White sand, beautiful sunsets, native cypress trees, walks, surfing, kites, sunbathing, and picnics. Fires allowed on the beach only south of 10th Avenue. No leash law for dogs on this beach or in city parks. Site of several city and private celebrations. 6am-10pm. 620-2000, 624-3543.

➤ **Monthly beach cleanup** by the Carmel Residents Association, from 10am-noon. Everybody is welcome to help clean up the beach. Volunteers should bring their own gloves. 624-3208.

▲ **Carmel River State Beach**, Carmelo Road. Take Rio Road off Highway 1, turn left on Santa Lucia St., then left on Carmelo Road and into parking lot. Also called "Carmel River Lagoon and Wetlands Natural Preserve." Trails,  shallow lagoon for children, wildlife viewing, restrooms. Dogs on leash. Dangerous surf. California Sea Otter Game Refuge continues from the Carmel River south to San Luis Obispo County. Stewart's Cove is at the north end. To the south is a wonderful view of Pt. Lobos, and you can follow a small land trail to Monastery Beach. 624-4909.

The east side of the marsh is a protected bird sanctuary. Species: willett, heron, gull, Canadian Goose, kite, harrier, swallow, hawk, teal, mallard, tern, egret and killdeer. South of the river there is access from Ribera Road, near the white wooden cross. Portolá Cross, on the hill, marks the approximate spot where Gaspar de Portolá erected a cross in 1769 to signal passing ships. Open 7am-10pm.

■ **Carmelite Monastery Chapel** and gardens are open free to visitors 7:30am-4:30pm daily. Cloistered nuns. Mass is 8am daily, except Thursday, and 9am on Sunday. 624-3043. www.carmelitemonastery.com sells items.

▲ **Monastery Beach**, across from the Carmelite Monastery, about 1.5 miles south of Ocean Avenue. No fee. Experienced scuba divers only. Unsafe for swimming or wading; wear shoes for walking on rocky sand. Open 7am-10pm; parking lot closes at sunset. Also park on highway. 624-4909.

City Parks

▲ **Devendorf Park**, corner of Junipero and Ocean Ave., across from Carmel Plaza. A large open grassy area surrounded with benches and shade trees. WWII memorial, fish pond, restrooms, and a bus stop adjacent. Site of community events.

▲ **Piccadilly Park**, Dolores St., between Ocean and 7th Ave. 6am-11pm. Small and quaint and the perfect place to sit on benches, read, or relax under the giant shade tree. Granite fountain, restrooms. Designated open space through the efforts of the Carmel-by-the-Sea Garden Club.

▲ **Vista Lobos**, on 3rd between Torres and Junipero. A small park with vistas of Point Lobos. A recreational facility is housed and managed by City staff. Outdoor tables, barbecue, benches. Free parking. 624-3543.

▲ **Forest Theater**, Mountain View Ave., is a 2-acre park that houses the first outdoor theater west of the Rocky Mountains. Where the Mission Trail Nature Preserve ends.

▲ **Forest Hill Park**, Scenic Rd. and Camino del Monte. 5¹/₂ acres. Children's play area, volleyball and basketball court, grills, trails, tennis court, picnic tables, a horseshoe pit, shuffleboard, restrooms. No close parking. There are World Exercise stations along the road, for a good workout. 624-3543.

▲ **Mission Trail Nature Preserve**, Rio Road across from the Carmel Mission Basilica and Museum. Other access: Mt. View and Crespi, 11th, Hatton Road. 35 acres. Trails, benches, playground, trees, and wildflowers, spring and winter. **Rowntree Arboretum**, a native garden, dominates. **Flanders Mansion** is next to the garden. Dogs are welcome except in the Arboretum, which has hitching  posts at each entrance. Open dawn to dusk. Brochures for self-guided tours are available at all park entrances and at the Visitor Center, Eastwood Bldg., San Carlos near 5th. 624-3543. The Flanders Foundation: 626-3826.

■ **New Hatton Canyon Park,** 34 acre park donated by the Monterey Peninsula Regional Park District. Enter at the NE corner of Albertson's parking lot, next to the Union 76 gas station on Carmel Rancho Boulevard. 659-5381.

Recreation Departments

▲ **Carmel Recreation Department**, San Carlos between 8th and 9th. The City provides programs and coordinates community activities through their offices at Sunset Community and Cultural Center. 626-1255.

▲ **Carmel Adult School**, 624-1714.

▲ **Carmel Youth Center** at 4th Ave. & Torres St., open 2-6pm Mon-Thurs; 2-11pm Fri; 3-10pm Sat, for middle and high school students. Ping-pong, billiards, recording studio, video games, snack bar, weight room. 624-3285.

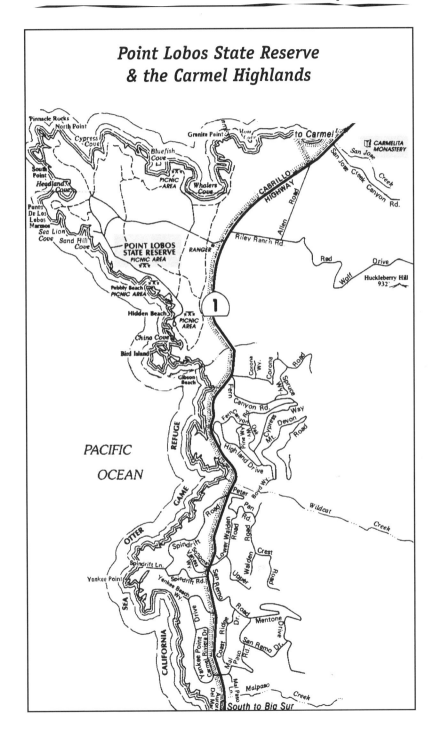

Point Lobos State Reserve
& the Carmel Highlands

Point Lobos State Reserve

...the greatest meeting of land and water in the world.

Visit this fabulous state reserve 3 miles south of Carmel on Highway One and discover for yourself the verity of landscape artist Francis McComas' words. You may park along Hwy 1 and walk in free. Open 9am-5pm daily, with extended hours during summer. 624-4909.

The crown jewel of California's state park system was called "the greatest meeting of land and water in the world" by landscape artist Francis McComas. R.L. Stevenson visited here in the 1840s and his *Treasure Island* is believed based on Pt. Lobos. Photography, painting, nature study, picnicking, diving and hiking, and spiritual contemplation are popular activities.

750 acres of underwater and 550 acres of ecological reserve filled with scenic trails, abundant wildlife and marine and terrestrial points of interest. Admission is $7 per car, $1 discount for seniors, and includes a trail map. Picnic tables, restrooms, telephone at main entrance. Docent talks and slide programs by previous arrangement. A perfect place to rest and meditate between Big Sur and Carmel. http://pt-lobos.parks.state.ca.us.

Trails include: Lace Lichen Trail and Sea Lion Rocks, 3 miles, easy; Whaler's Cove & North Shore, 2.5 miles, moderate; Lace Lichen & Cypress Grove Trail, 3 miles, easy; South Plateau Trail & Bird Rock, 3 miles, moderate.

Visit the Whaler's Cabin at Whaler's Cove and see many artifacts, including the 100 year-old diver's suit, left, used by earliest divers for abalone. Diving is permitted only in Bluefish and Whalers Coves; swimming at China Cove. An Underwater Reserve, the only underwater trail in the U.S., is accessed off Bluefish and Whaler's Cove. Reservations for divers: ptlobos@mbay.net or 624-8413.

More Recreation Fun

➤ **Tennis Courts.** In addition to the one court at Forest Hill Park, Del Monte and Junipero, several free tennis courts are available at Carmel High School and Carmel Middle School, after school and on weekends. 624-3543.

➤ **Labyrinth Walk:** This ancient ritual for meditation and creative insight is available free to the public in Woodhull Hall at the Community Church of the Monterey Peninsula, one mile east of Highway 1 on Carmel Valley Road. A 40' diameter permanent labyrinth will be built on church grounds patterned after the one located in Chartres Cathedral, France (1220) and Grace Cathedral, San Francisco (1997). A 36' portable labyrinth is available now. Call for dates: Donald Mathews, 373-7809 or 624-8595. To find more labyrinths: www.gracecathedral.org, click on "Veriditas."

➤ **Sierra Club, Ventana Chapter.** Free outings, call 624-1467. Meetings last Thursday of the month; call for meeting place and time. http://ventana.org. Chapter Office and Sierra Club Book Store, Las Tiendas Building, Ocean Avenue btwn Dolores and San Carlos. 624-8032, fax 624-3371.

➤ **Peninsula Walk Walk Walk Club** meets at 8am, Mon-Fri, at the Carmel Mission; free and open to all. All levels welcome. Learn race walking on Thursdays. Call 372-2592 to arrange time.

➤ **Hike-Walk-Talk** meets Thursdays, 9:30am, behind Brinton's in Carmel Rancho, Hwy 1 & Carmel Valley Road. 625-7632.

➤ **On the Beach Surf Shop**, Ocean & Mission St. offers free wax and stickers with any purchase. Surfboard museum: their walls are covered by surfboards dating back to the 1930s. 10-6 daily. 624-7282.

➤ **MBOC Beach Party**. Call for details of this free event. 242-7943.

Favorite Restaurants in Carmel

• Allegro Gourmet Pizzeria	Italian	3770 The Barnyard	626-5454
• Anton & Michel	European	Mission btwn Ocean & 7th	624-2406
• Bully III	American	Dolores & 8th	625-1750
• Caffe Napoli	Italian	Ocean near Lincoln	625-4033
• California Market	New American	4 mi S. on Hwy 1	622-5450
• Casanova	European	5th & Mission	625-0501
• Chevys	Mexican	123 Crossroads	626-0945
• Chez Christian	French	Ocean btwn Lincoln & Monte Verde	625-4331
• China Delight	Chinese	133 Crossroads	625-3367
• Club Jalapeño	Mexican	San Carlos btwn 5th & 6th	626-1997
• da Giovanni	Mediterranean	Lincoln btwn 5th & 6th	626-5800
• Flaherty's	Seafood	Dolores & Sixth	625-1500
• Flying Fish Grill	New American	Mission near Ocean	625-1962
• French Poodle	French	5th & Junipero	624-8643
• From Scratch	California cuisine	The Barnyard	625-2448
• Golden Buddha	Chinese 3678	The Barnyard	625-1668
• Grasing's	Californian	6th & Mission	624-6562
• Hanagasa	Japanese	8th near Mission	625-4470
• Il Fornaio	Italian	Ocean at Monte Verde	622-5100
• Kincaid's Bistro	French	217 Crossroads Blvd	624-9626
• La Boheme	French	Dolores & 7th Ave	624-7500
• Le Coq D'Or	French	Mission btwn 4th & 5th	626-9319
• Lugano Swiss Bistro	Swiss	The Barnyard	626-3779
• Merlot! Bistro	Californian	Ocean Ave & Lincoln	624-5659
• Mission Ranch	New American	26270 Colores	625-9040
• Nico	Mediterrean	San Carlos btwn Ocean & 7th	624-6545
• Pasqual's	American	Junipero btwn 5th & 6th	624-2200
• Polo Club	Pacific Rim	The Barnyard	626-0430
• Porta Bella	Mediterranean	Ocean btwn Lincoln &Verde	624-4395
• Rio Grill	Californian	Hwy 1 at Rio Road	625-5436
• Robata Grill	Japanese	3658 The Barnyard	624-2643
• San Souci	French	Lincoln btwn 5th & 6th	624-6220
• Simpson's	American	San Carlos at 5th	624-5755
• The Gem	American	San Carlos btwn Ocean & 7th	625-4367
• The Grill	American	Ocean Ave Btwn Dolores & Lincoln	624-2569
• The Oaks	Californian	One Old Ranch Rd	626-2533
• Toots Lagoon	American	Dolores near 7th	625-1915
• Village Corner	Mediterranean	Dolores at 6th	624-3588
• Village Pub	American	San Carlos btwn Ocean & 7th	626-6821

*Sorry, the Hog's Breath Inn closed its doors in 1999

Picturesque Carmel Accommodations

Bed and Breakfast Inns

		(831)	(800)	Rates
• Briarwood Inn	San Carlos	626-9056	999-8788	$115-250
• Carmel Fireplace	San Carlos	624-4862	634-1300	$85-195
• Cobblestone Inn	Junipero/7th & 8th		833-8836	$105-220
• Edgemere	San Antonio		624-4501	$100-160
• Forest Lodge	Ocean & Torres	624-7023		$149+
• Green Lantern	7th & Casanova	624-4392		$90-200
• Happy Landing	Monte Verde	624-7917		$90-165
• Monte Verde	Monte Verde	624-6046	328-7707	$99-155
• San Antonio	San Antonio	624-4334		$99-155
• Sandpiper Inn	Bay View/Martin	624-6433	633-6433	$95-235
• Sea View Inn	Camino Real	624-8778		$90-155
• Vagabond's House	Dolores & 4th	624-7738	262-1262	$85-165

Lodges–Inns–Motels

• Adobe Inn	Dolores at 8th	624-3933	388-3933	$116-364
• Best Western	San Carlos & 5th	624-1261		$75-160
• Candlelight Inn	San Carlos/4th & 5th	624-6451	433-4732	$125-219
• Carmel Country	Dolores at 3rd	625-3263	215-6343	$115-165
• Carmel Garden	4th & Torres	624-6929		$125-245
• Carmel Oaks	Mission & 5th	624-5547	266-5547	$59-249
• Carriage House	Mission & 4th	624-2711	533-2711	$58-148
• Coachman's	San Carlos at 7th	624-6421	336-6421	$68-250
• Cypress Inn	Lincoln & 7th	624-3871	443-7443	$110-285
• Dolphin Inn	San Carlos at 4th	624-5356	433-4732	$99-229
• Hofsas House	San Carlos & 4th	624-2745	221-2548	$75-180
• Lobos Lodge	Monte Verde	624-3874		$99-185
• Svendsgaard's	San Carlos at 4th	624-1511	433-4732	$95-219
• Wayside Inn	Mission at 7th	624-5336	433-4732	$95-259

Reservation/Concierge Services

• A Place to Stay		624-1711	847-8066	Free
• Resort II Me		642-6622	757-5646	Free
• WWW Consulting		659-7061	434-3891	Free

Use the web: www.carmel.ca.com and look in the lodging section.

At the Mouth of the Valley

Carmel Rancho Shopping Center

Shop 'til you drop! Albertson's Food & Drug, Yellow Brick Road Thrift Store, Bagel Bakery, Rite Aid Drug Store, Cornucopia Community Market & Cafe, Brinton's House and Garden Shop, and more. Center office, 624-4670.

The Barnyard Shopping Village

A village of fifty shops, international restaurants and fine galleries situated in rustic barns amid lush gardens. Over an acre of gardens, brick walkways and authentic California architecture. Shops for apparel, fine art, gifts, home accessories, books, records and jewelry. Free events include tours of the gardens every Sunday at noon in the summer with horticulturist Margot Grych. Farmer's Market, July-Oct, Tuesdays 2-6. Free parking. Village office, 624-8886. www.thebarnyard.com.

The Crossroads Shopping Center

In the summer, free music and dancing, Saturdays 1-3pm in the gardens. More than 90 boutiques and shops with apparel and shoes, jewelry and accessories, home accents, personal services, gifts and cards, specialty foods, entertainment, health and fitness. Open 10am-6pm daily. Tourist information, restrooms. Free parking. 625-4106. www.carmelcrossroads.com.

➤ **Cornucopia Community Market & Cafe**, 26135 Carmel Rancho Blvd. Occasional free events. Call 625-1454.

➤ **Bountiful Basket**, offers free International Olive Oil & Vinegar Tastings, with a detailed history, 10:30-5:30, Mon-Sat., 12-5pm, Sunday. 625-4457.

➤ **Restaurant 211**, local art displayed. 625-3546.

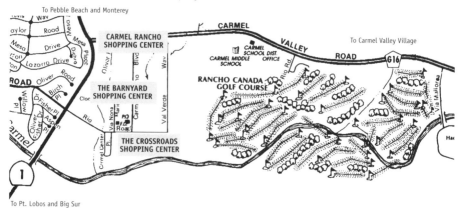

Carmel Valley

For a delightful day trip into the countryside, explore Carmel Valley with its rolling ranchland, expansive parklands, wine-tasting rooms, and a variety of shopping and entertainment opportunities. Carmel Valley Road intersects with Highway 1 just south of the Ocean Avenue exit to Carmel by-the-Sea. Follow Carmel Valley Road twelve miles east to Carmel Valley Village, a true country town with 283 days of sunshine a year, friendly inhabitants, and lots to see and do. Follow the numbers on the maps.

1 Encino de Descanso. Stone commemorating site where Indian carriers rested with their dead on the way to burial grounds deep in the valley.

2 Covey Restaurant. Live music, Fri-Sat, 6:30-9:30pm. No cover. Panoramic view of the valley. Quail Lodge Resort & Golf Club, Valley Greens Dr. 624-1581.

3 Free outdoor community concert by **The Monterey Symphony** at Quail Meadows adjacent to Quail Lodge, June 25, 2000. Info, call 624-8511.

4 Carmel Valley Racquet & Health Club. First personal training tennis lesson free. 27300 Rancho San Carlos Rd., 624-2737.

4a Santa Lucia Preserve. At end of Rancho San Carlos Road. 20,000 acre preserve of wooded canyons, redwood groves, bulrush marshes. Call Julie at 626-0608 to make hiking reservations. Free.

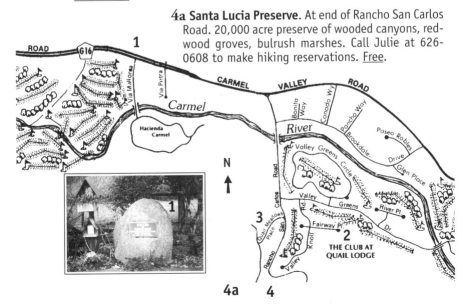

5 Valley Hills Shopping Center

An opportunity to stretch your legs and browse the shops: Baja Cantina Restaurant, Carmel Floral Company, Carmel Valley Antiques, Tancredi & Morgen Country Store, Hacienda Hay & Feed, Wagon Wheel Restaurant, Barbara's Bakery and Deli, Pacific Coast Catering. More shops at Mid-Valley.

◆ **Baja Cantina**. Bands on Friday, 7:30-10:30pm; jazz guitar on Sundays, 1-4pm. No cover. Other special events, such as Super Bowl Sunday, Hot Chili Nites. Call for dates and information, 625-2252.

● **Hacienda Hay & Feed**, flowers and a good selection of decorative stone and ceramic pots at near wholesale prices. 624-5119.

6 Earthbound Farm – Organic farming at its best; organic children's garden. Mon-Sat 9:30-6, Sun 10-5. Produce stand open to the public during the growing season, ending with a pumpkin patch at Halloween. Occasional free events, contests and demos. 625-6219. www.ebfarm.com.

6a Saddle Mountain & Carmel-by-the-Sea RV Park – Privately owned tent and trailer camping sites, hook-ups, showers at end of Shulte Road. Closed during the winter. 624-1617, 624-9329.

7 Farmer Joe's. Fruit, vegetable, and flower stand open daily during the summer months with a delectible variety of locally grown produce.

8 Carmel Valley Manor invites you in to see the local art on display. 8545 Carmel Valley Road. Daily 9am-5pm. 626-4711.

9 Chateau Julien – Free wine tasting, Mon-Fri, 8am-5pm. Sat-Sun, 11am-5pm. Free tours of the wine estate by reservation. 8940 Carmel Valley Rd. www.chateaujulien.com. 624-2600.

10 Griggs Nursery – Large nursery with shrubs, trees and flowers. Open Mon-Sat, 8am-5pm, Sun,10am-4pm. 9220 Carmel Valley Road. 626-0680.

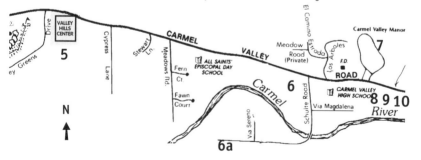

11 Mid-Valley Shopping Center

- **Robin's Jewelry**, designs by Robin Mahoney. Robin will give you a free magic wand with any purchase. 11^{ish}am-5pm, Tues-Sat, 626-4119.

- **Mid-Valley Antiques and Collectibles** has furniture, art, jewelry, toys, etc. Mon-Sat, 10:30am-5pm. 624-0261.

- **Deli Treasures**, deli, wine, catering, gift baskets. Mon-Fri, 7am-6:30pm, Sat 8am-5pm, Sun 9am-4pm. 624-9140.

- **Carmel Valley Coffee Roasting Co.**, espresso, latte, whole beans, etc. Mon-Fri, 7am-5pm, Sat-Sun, 7:30am-3:30pm. 624-5934.

12 **Trade Bead Museum & African Art Gallery**, free, upstairs, 27885 Berwick Dr. Collection of beads and original African Art. 624-4138.

13 **Paul Wilson Sculpture**, 27881 Robinson Cyn Rd. Unusual wood, stone, and concrete fountains and sculptures in the yard. 625-3112.

14 **Korean Buddhist Temple Sambosa**, 28110 Robinson Cyn Rd. You are invited to attend their Sunday services at 10am; see the beautiful altar. 624-3686.

15 **Oaks Lounge**. Jazz, Fri-Sat, 7-10pm. No cover. Carmel Valley Ranch Resort, 1 Old Ranch Road, 6 miles from Carmel, off CV Rd. 626-2533.

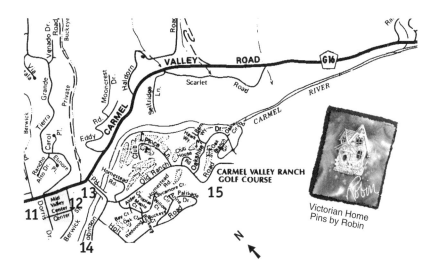

16 **Garland Regional Park**, 700 W. Carmel Valley Rd., 8.6 miles from Highway 1. Free admission; dogs are welcome. 4462 acres. Open year-round from sunrise to sunset. Carmel River flows at the entrance, near a visitor's center complete with maps and informative literature, docents and plant and wildlife exhibits. Day use activities include hiking, photography, horseback riding, nature study and educational field trips, landscape painting, walking & jogging, solitude, and limited mountain bike riding at the Cooper Ranch only. Picnic areas, restrooms. 659-4488.

▲ **Trails include:** Redwood Canyon River Trail, 3.5 miles, moderate; Lupine Loop with stone cliff and waterfall, 2.4 miles, easy. Call ahead for naturalist-led hikes, classroom programs and lectures: 659-6062.

▲ **Junior Rangers** meet every Wed 1-4 p.m. at Garland Park Visitor Center, 659-6062. **Friends of Garland Park**, free outings.484-9692.

▲ **MIRA**, Monterey Institute for Research in Astronomy, hosts a Star Party here, with telescopes available for public viewing plus Native American folk tales by the campfire. Free, call for dates, 659-2809.

17 **Boronda Adobe,** Boronda Rd., built in 1840 by Don José Manual and María Juana Boronda, maker of the original Monterey Jack Cheese. Now a private residence; drive-by only please.

18 **Los Laureles Country Inn & "The Restaurant"**. Former 1890's Del Monte Hunting & Fishing Lodge. Dinners: 5:30-9:30. Complimentary car service with dinner from the Carmel Valley area. Friday Open Mic. Live entertainment Sat 7-10 in the Saloon. Open 4pm to closing. Heated pool, $8 day, 11am-6pm; free to hospitality industry on Mondays. 313 W. Carmel Valley Rd. 659-2233. www.LosLaureles.com.

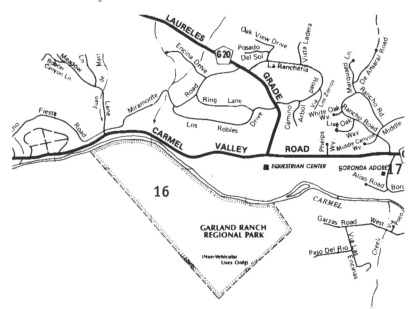

Carmel Valley Village #19

- **Carmel Valley Chamber of Commerce**, 13 W. Carmel Valley Rd., Wed-Thurs-Fri, 11-5pm, Sat, 11am-3pm. 659-4000.

- **Durney Vineyards** has a new tasting room in the Village, 69 W. Carmel Valley Rd. $3 wine tasting cost applied to any purchase. Open Mon-Fri, 11am-5pm, Sat-Sun, 10am-5pm. 659-6220. 1-800-625-8466.

- **Robert Talbott Vineyards,** 53 W. Carmel Valley Rd, Thurs-Sun, 11-5pm; free glass with tasting price. Mail order; gift shop. Emily, 659-3500.

- **Georis Winery.** 4 Pilot Road. Minimum half-bottle purchase. Thurs-Sun, 12-4pm. Call for information about special events. 659-1050.

- **Bernardus Winery,** 5 W. Carmel Valley Road, in the Village. Free white wine tasting, red $3. Daily 11am-5:30pm. 659-1900.

- ◆ **Plaza Linda Mexican Restaurant**. 9 Del Fino Place. Wed & Fri, Mexican music; Thurs, blues music, Sat, jazz, all 6:30-8:30pm. No cover. Authentic Mexican food. 659-4229.

- **LyonsHead Gallery** In a restored village pottery shop, with adobe patio, lush foliage and seating, flanked by 12 sculpted lion heads spouting water into a long trough. 12 Del Fino Place. 659-4192.

- **White Oak Grill** displays local art. Thurs-Mon, 11:30-2:30 for lunch, 6-8:30pm for dinner. 19 Carmel Valley Road, in the Village. 659-1525.

- **River Ranch Vineyards** tasting room at the White Oak Grill. Wine tasting Sat-Sun, 11:30am-4pm. 659-1525.

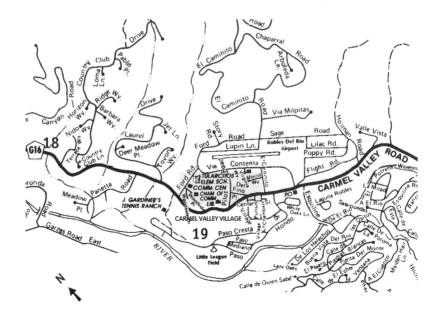

- **Magic Circle Center** An intimate 60-seat performing arts theater, 8 El Caminito Rd, 659-1108. Presents quality productions year around.

- **Carmel Valley Library**, 65 W. Carmel Valley Road. Tues-Thurs, 11am-8pm, Fri, 10am-5pm, Sat, 11am-5pm. Storytime Theater Fri at 10:30am, Homework Center, Tues-Thurs, 3-5pm for all students. Book Reading Group every Fri, 2:30-4pm, adults. 659-2377.

▲ **Carmel Valley Community Park and Youth Center** facilities include activity hall, swimming pool, horseshoes, volleyball court, gazebo stage, play area, barbecue pits, and open space. Free admittance. 25 Ford Road. 659-3983, fax 659-9373. Rentals: 659-5287. Pool: 659-2606.

▲ **Senior Programs** at Community Park. First Mondays, 11am-2pm. All seniors welcome, bring a friend. Free lunch, bingo, prizes. 659-2640.

▲ **Carmel Valley Branch of the Boys & Girls Club** of the Monterey Peninsula, Community Hall, 25 Ford Road. Mon-Fri, 9am-6pm. Sports, arts & crafts, computer club, movies. Free. Contact Jeff Magallanes, 659-2308.

- **Visual Pleasures Art Gallery** and Art Therapy Studio, 96 Calle de Quien Sabé. Janet Steinberg creates art to bring beauty, harmony and balance midst the chaos of life. Call before you come, 659-5940.

- **Artisan's Hand** A Truly Different Gallery Experience. Several local artists represented, including Kyra Goodyear, Barbara Sayre and William Schnute. 19 East Carmel Valley Road, in the Village. 659-2250, fax 659-2258.

On Cachagua Road East of the Village

1 Galante Vineyards. Free wine tasting by appointment, free tours, Sun-Fri, 11am-3pm. 18181 Cachagua Road. 415/331-1247.

2 Joullian Vineyard. Picturesque winery. Tasting Mon-Fri, 11am-3pm. 20300 Cachagua Road. 659-2800.

3 Carmel Valley Tennis Camp, 20805 Cachagua Road. Free T-shirt to camp participants. Kids: summer; Adults: spring and fall. 659-2615.

4 Cachagua Community Park and Los Padres Reservoir. Free admittance. Follow the signs from the Village to Cachagua, then to Nason Road and the Park. Fishing, ballfield, tot-lot playground, picnic facilities, swimming, row boats, hiking trails past **Los Padres Dam** into the **Los Padres National Forest**. Site of the annual Cachagua Country Fair each May. Open 9am-6pm daily. Dogs on leash or immediate voice command. Cachagua Com. Center, 659-8108. Visit www.wateroverthedam.org for info about The River Celebration.

5 AT&T Jamesburg Earth Station, past the Village on Cachagua Road, a 34-ton, 10-story antenna dish, focused on a satellite more than 22,000 miles away. Call 659-6100 to arrange a free tour.

6 Chews Ridge, 6 miles from Jamesburg, a small town east of the Village. A popular spot for camping and hiking, it is also the location for the MIRA Observatory and Oliver Observing Station.

■ **Oliver Observing Station** on Tassajara Road. 36-inch professional research telescope and mountaintop scientific research that runs on solar and wind power and collected rainwater. Considered to be best place for viewing in the continental U.S. because of the smooth airflow off the ocean, the 5,003 foot elevation and the dark Big Sur coast that stretches for miles. Call 883-1000 ext. 58 or e-mail: mira@mira.org to make reservations and get directions; also free booklet on MIRA.

7 Tassajara, Zen Buddhist Center. Known for its healthful waters and their restorative benefit, a few days at this retreat will also restore your spirit. Fee. Tassajara is operated as a Soto Zen Buddhist monastery, providing a meditation and work place for monks and students. Guests may participate from early May until the first week in September at five-day retreats, a series of workshops combining Zen practice with poetry, hiking, and yoga, or simply hot soaks in the bathhouse and delicious vegetarian meals. You'll want to explore the surrounding woods and swim in the warm water pool. Shared and private accommodations from stone rooms, cabins, and yurts are available. Day guests are permitted from 8am-5pm. Costs vary. Continue through Carmel Valley Village on Carmel Valley Road and turn right at Tassajara Road to Jamesburg and follow the signs. Fees range from $14 day use. Bring drinking water and bug spray. For reservations: 415-431-3771, 415-865-1895. For more information: call 415-431-4438, 831-659-2229, or write Zen Buddhist Center, Tassajara Reservation Office, 300 Page Street, San Francisco, 94102.

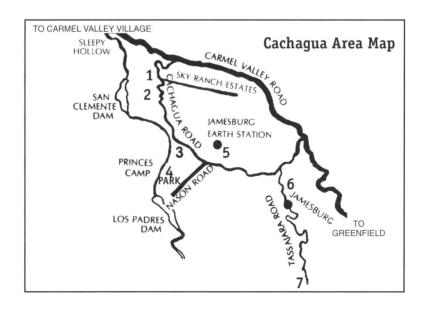

Calendar of Events

Year 2000 dates shown. Updates at www.montereycountyguide.com.
Please call in advance to verify as information is subject to change.

JANUARY

January 17   **A VILLAGE AFFAIR**   **$$**
Gourmet food and wine tasting, silent and live auctions to benefit Community
Valley Village Improvements. 5:30-8:30pm, Bernardus Lodge. Joan, 659-5099.

FEBRUARY

February 12   **AN EVENING AT THE BUCKEYE**   **$$**
Benefit for the CV Library by the Friends of the Library, 65 W. Carmel Valley Rd.
Buffet dinner, 6-9pm. Entertainment, 7pm. Live auction. Douglas, 659-4575.

APRIL

April to October   **CLASSIC CARS HOT CHILI NITES**   **FREE**
Every Thursday, begins and ends with daylight savings time changes. See 30-
100+ cars of local Stars: Hot Rods, Classic Cars, and Special Interest Cars. Special
$7 barbecue and live music. 6-9pm. Third Thursdays is free raffle and hats. Rhythm
and blues bands. Baja Cantina, 7166 Carmel Valley Road, in the Valley Hills Center, next to Quail Lodge. 625-BAJA (2252).

MAY

May   **GOAT RANCH TREK**   **$$**
Trekkers meet at the Rancho San Carlos main gate at 10am for carpools to site
where author Robert L. Stevenson was rescued by rancher Jonathon Wright in
1879. Wear long pants, walking shoes; bring water & snack. Maureen, 375-0195.

May   **OBSERVATORY TOUR**   **FREE**
Monterey Institute for Research in Astronomy (MIRA) invites you to experience their
popular free tours of the Oliver Observing Station on Tassajara Road, 1pm and
3pm. See their 36-inch professional research telescope and discover how their
mountaintop research runs on solar and wind power and collected rainwater.
Call 883-1000 ext. 58 or email mira@mira.org for reservations and directions.

May 14   **FLOWER SHOW**   **$$**
Hidden Valley, flower show and plant sale, 11-3. Joyce Stewart, 624-3671.

May 21   **RUMMAGE SALE**   **FREE**
Congregation Beth Israel, 5716 Carmel Valley Road. 624-2015.

JUNE

June 6   **MONTEREY SYMPHONY CONCERT**   **FREE**
Monterey Symphony presents their annual free outdoor community concert at
Quail Meadows adjacent to Quail Lodge. 11:30am gates open, concert at 1pm.
Gourmet food and beverages sold to benefit the Symphony and the SPCA. 624-
8511, fax 624-3837.

JULY

July 10 "GREAT BALLS OF FIRE" STREET DANCE & BARBECUE $$
Mid-Carmel Valley Volunteer Fire Department benefit at Mid-Valley Shopping Center. Barbecue, $10, at 6pm, dancing 8pm-midnight. 624-5907.

July 15-16 DEL MONTE KENNEL CLUB SHOW FREE
A comprehensive representation and competition of registered purebred dogs. Carmel Middle School, 8am-5pm. $5 parking. Info, 649-4280.

AUGUST

August STEELHEAD RESCUE FREE
The Carmel River Steelhead Assn annual steelhead rescues are usually conducted in the drying tributaries of the Carmel River on Sat mornings. Each session lasts about 4 hours. Call Jeff at 626-6586 for more information & to volunteer to help.

August 4-6 CARMEL VALLEY FIESTA FREE+$$
Arts and crafts, children's games, swim meet, dog & puppy show, and golf tournament, street dance, 10k run, pancake breakfast, food booths in the Village Park, noon-5pm Sat-Sun. Live music continuous from noon. Fri night barbecue at Trail & Saddle Club. Clowns and Fiesta Parade, Sat 11am. 659-2038, Chuck, 659-4502.

August 12 WINEMAKER'S CELEBRATION FREE+$$
25 Monterey, Carmel Valley and Salinas Valley vintners open their doors for a day of complimentary tasting, tours, and fun in the sun. Winemakers' Celebration at the Custom House Plaza Saturday, tickets $18, includes wine tasting, various exhibits, and a food fair prepared by many of the county's finest chefs, plus a souvenir wine glass. Special discounts on cases, tastings of rare wines. Visit A Taste of Monterey Wine Visitors Center on Cannery Row for more complimentary tasting. From 11am to 4pm. For complete information, call Monterey County Vintners and Growers Association at 375-9400; ask them to fax you a brochure.

August 17-19 BROOKS USA AUCTION $$
Classic car auction, Quail Lodge, Carmel Valley. Viewing August 17-18. Auction starts 5pm, Aug. 19. Valerie, 415-391-4000.

August 18 CONCOURSO ITALIANO $$
Honor Pininfarina and Ferrari Show Cars & Prototypes. special tribute to automotive leather craftsmen of Italy. Italian fashion show and opera, drive-by presentations, booths of classic car memorabilia, and a corral of non-Italian cars. You can see these lovely cars touring the Peninsula throughout the weeks before and after the event. 9am-4:30pm. Quail Lodge Resort and Golf Club, 8205 Valley Greens Dr. 624-1581, 425-688-1903. www.concorso.com

August 27 GARY IBSEN'S TOMATOFEST™ $$
The largest tomato tasting event in the nation featuring more than 200 tomato varieties at Quail Lodge. Music, children's garden project. 12:30-4:30pm, Tickets $40. Children under 12 free. Info: call 620-8830. Reservations: 626-2475, fax 622-9468. www.tomatofest.com.

SEPTEMBER

September 17-19   CARMEL VALLEY RANCHER'S DAYS   FREE
Cowboys compete for cash prizes at Carmel Valley Trail and Saddle Club, E. Garzas Road. Events include cutting competition, queen contest horsemanship, team roping, stock horse, simulated calf branding with whitewash, open team penning, kids' events. <u>Free admission to all events.</u> Wild boar barbecue, steak/chicken barbecue and snack bar; live music Saturday evening. Proceeds from entry fees and food sales benefit schools, 4 H clubs, fire stations and others. 659-9221.

September 18   "GREAT BOWLS OF FIRE" $$
Chili cookoff at Holman Ranch, 5-8pm. $15. To benefit the Carmel Valley Chamber of Commerce. 659-4000.

September 19   FALL FESTIVAL   FREE
Live music, kids' games, crafts, silent auction, farmers' market, country store, rummage sale and raffle prizes. Barbecue. An outdoor Mass at 10:30am, Festival following from noon to 5pm. Our lady of Mt. Carmel Church at 9 El Caminito, just up from Carmel Valley Road in the Village. 659-2224.

OCTOBER

October   SCENIC DRIVE   FREE
Take a scenic drive through the county at Halloween to see the fall colors and visit the pumpkin patches. Farmer Joe's Produce, Carmel Valley Road at Schulte Road, is open daily during the growing season. Decorative pumpkins fill the field next to the parking lot and the white wooden farm stand. Earthbound Farm's Farm Stand, 7230 Carmel Valley Road, open daily 9:30am to 6pm until Halloween. Hacienda Hay and Feed, 7180 Carmel Valley Road just past Earthbound Farms. Maze, petting zoo, and great pumpkins all month, 8:30am to 5:30pm. 624-5119.

October   TULARCITOS FALL FESTIVAL   FREE
Call for more information, 659-2276.

October 7   SOUL AND BLUES REVUE   FREE+$$
2-10pm at Hidden Valley Music Seminars, Carmel Valley Village. <u>Free seminars</u> on variety of instruments for musicians of all ages until 5pm. Show/barbecue following, $40, under age 21, $20. Net profits for local youth music programs. Gary Luce, 624-0101, Barry Harrow, 659-1234, or Jennifer Hill, 625-5137.

October 15   WILD CELEBRATION $$
2-5:30pm, to benefit the SPCA, Holman Ranch, 659-6054, 659-2640.

October 15   JEWISH FOOD FESTIVAL $$
Jewish Food Festival & Crafts Faire. Corned beef, kugels, blintzes, lox and bagels, matzo ball soup, chopped liver and cabbage rolls, rugelah, mandelbrot, strudel and cheesecake. Music, entertainment, wandering storytellers, strolling musicians, cooking demonstrations, synagogue tours and more. Crafts booths and exhibits offering jewelry, art, clothing, and other handmade items with a Jewish theme or made in Israel. 10am-3:30pm. <u>Free entrance to seniors over 65 and children under 12.</u> $3 adults, $1 teenagers. Congregation Beth Israel, 5716 Carmel Valley Road. Park at the Carmel Middle School for <u>free shuttle bus</u>. 624-2015, 624-8272.

October 28   ALL SAINTS' FALL FESTIVAL   FREE
Carnival booths, costume parade, karaoke, haunted house, train rides, cake walk,

drawings. Barbecue. <u>Free ice cream</u>. 11am-3pm, All Saint's Episcopal School, 8060 Carmel Valley Road. 624-9171.

October 28   **"HOWL-O-WEEN"**   **Spectators FREE**
"Costume Competition for Man's Best Friend" presented by Del Monte Kennel Club. Costume competition for you and your dog. All ages welcome to participate. Prizes $10 to enter dog competition (register 8:30-9:30am); $3 to enter the costume contest. CV Community Center, 25 Ford Road. Ruth Edwards, 649-4280 or 333-9021.

October 31   **COSTUME PARTY**   **FREE**
Live music, complimentary limousine rides at 9pm, prizes, drink specials. Hosted by Carmel Valley Ranch and Baja Cantina, Treats for the kids. 7166 Carmel Valley Road, 3.5 miles from Highway 1. 625-2252.

October 31   **TRICK-OR-TREAT**   **FREE**
Mid-Valley Shopping Center has free candy for those in costume. 5.5 miles up Carmel Valley Road from Highway 1.

NOVEMBER

November 5   **LIFE'S GREATEST LUXURIES**   **$$**
Car raffle, wine, jazz, food, to benefit Special Olympics. Holman Ranch. 659-6054.

November 23   **THANKSGIVING DINNER**   **FREE**
Carmel Valley Community Thanksgiving Dinner for all residents, 1-4pm, Carmel Valley Community Center and Cachagua Community Center. The dinners are free and all Carmel Valley residents are invited. <u>Volunteers are needed</u> on Nov. 24, 25 and 26 to help with food preparation, serving, and cleanup. For reservations or information, call 659-2640.

DECEMBER

December 2   **CHRISTMAS TREE LIGHTING**   **FREE**
Community gets together to light up the tree, 4-5pm, Carmel Valley Community Park in the Village. 659-2640.

December 9   **SANTA FLY-IN**   **FREE**
Santa Claus arrives at the Carmel Valley Airport, 11am, followed by a Christmas Parade to the Community Youth Center. 659-3983.

Central Coast Birding Trail

Good birding is one of the Central Coast's finest recreational features. When birding, please respect private property and be careful not to disturb birds. Help us preserve the habitats for birds and other wildlife.

• **Elkhorn Slough Estuarine Sanctuary** - Great Blue Heron and Great Egret rookery, waders, shorebirds. ducks. All year. Take Dolan Road off Hwy 1 next to Moss Landing power plant, drive east to Elkhorn Road and turn north for 2 miles to sanctuary entrance on the left. 728-2822.

• **Moss Landing Wildlife Area** - Nesting Caspian and Forser's terns, avocets. Fall through early spring. Drive 2 miles north on Hwy 1 from Moss Landing Harbor to the entrance road on your right, about 1/4 miles past Struve Rd.

• **Moss Landing State Beach and Harbor** - Cormorants, loons, grebes, scoters, Greater Scaup, egrets, stilts, avocets. Fall through early spring. Continue past the Moss Landing Bridge 1/2 miles to Jetty Rd. Turn left into the Park.

• **Salinas River Wildlife Area** - Northern Harrier, Gadwall, avocets, stilts, Snowy Plover, shorebirds, gulls and terns, pelicans, fall rarities. Fall-winter. 12 miles north of Monterey, take Del Monte Blvd. exit, northwest 0.7 miles to parking area at the end of the dirt road.

• **Toro Regional Park**- Townsend's and Hermit Warblers, Brown Creeper, Pygmy Nuthatch, Fox Sparrow. Winter. Off Hwy 68 at Jacks Peak Drive.

• **Jacks Peak Regional Park** - Townsend's and Hermit Warblers, Brown Creeper, Pygmy Nuthatch. Winter. Off Hwy 68 at the Monterey airport

• **Monterey Harbor and Recreation Trail** - loons, grebes, scoters, cormorants, Harlequin Duck, Pigeon Guillemot, gulls. Winter, early spring. Along the water from Seaside to Pacific Grove.

• **Pt. Pinos and Crespi Pond** - Virginia Rail, Sora, ducks, geese, gulls, warblers, Black Oystercatcher, turnstones. Fall-winter. On Ocean View Ave at the northern tip of the peninsula.

• **Carmel River and Lagoon** - Vagrant passerines, Chestnut-backed Chickadee, Wrentit, Wilson's Warbler. Fall-winter. Hwy 1 and Rio Rd. in Carmel. Best access is behind the Crossroads center north of Hwy 1 bridge.

• **Pt. Lobos State Reserve** - Western Gull, cormorants, Pigeon Guillemot, Black Oystercatcher, Brown Pelican, Dark-eyed Junco. All year. Hwy 1 south of Carmel 2 miles.

• **Garland Ranch Regional Park** - Hutton's Vireo, Nuttall's Woodpecker. Spring-summer. Carmel Valley Rd 9 miles east from Hwy 1.

• **Pinnacles National Monument** - Prairie Falcon, Plain Titmouse, Rock Wren, Costa's Hummingbird. Spring-summer. Hwy 101 to Soledad and follow signs.

• **Chews Ridge and China Camp** - Mountain Quail, Flammulated Owl, Solitary Vireo. Spring-summer. Follow Carmel Valley Road east out of Carmel 24 miles to Tassajara Rd, turn right for 9 miles to the saddle at Chew's Ridge; China Camp is 1.5 miles beyond the ridge.

Compliments Monterey Peninsula Audubon Society, 831/645-6617.

Carmel Valley Restaurants & Accommodations

Restaurants

• Baja Cantina	Mexican	Valley Hills Center	625-2252
• Bon Appetit	French	In the Village	659-3559
• CV Coffee Roasting Company		Mid Valley Center	624-5934
• Deli Treasures	American	Mid Valley Center	624-9140
• Jeffrey's Grill	California	Mid Valley Center	624-2029
• Oak Deli	California	In the Village	659-3416
• Rancho Cañada Golf Club	CaliforniaC.V. Road		624-0111
• River Rock Deli	American	In the Village	659-5052
• Running Iron	American	In the Village	659-4633
• Salt & Pepper Cafe	American	In the Village	659-0605
• Sole Mio	Italian	In the Village	659-9119
• Taqueria del Valle	Mexican	In the Village	659-1373
• Wagon Wheel	American	Valley Hills Center	624-8878
• White Oak Grill	French	In the Villae	659-1525
• Wills Fargo	American	In the Village	659-2774

Lodges–Inns–Motels

		(831)	(800)	Rates
• Acacia Lodge	20 Via Contenta	659-2297	367-3336	$79-152
• Bernardus Lodge	C.V. Road	659-3247		call
• Blue Sky Lodge	10 Flight Rd.	659-2256	733-2160	$55-105
• Carmel River RV	27680 Schulte Rd.	624-9329		call
• C.V. Lodge	8 Ford Road	659-2261	641-4646	call
• C.V. Ranch	1 Old Ranch Rd.	625-9500	422-7635	call
• Hidden Valley Inn	102 West C.V. Rd.	659-5361	367-3336	$79-186
• JGTennis Ranch	114 C.V. Road	659-2207	453-6225	call
• Los Laureles Country Inn	C.V. Road	659-2233		call
• Robles Del Rio	200 Punta del Monte	659-3705	833-0843	call
• Stonepine	150 East C.V. Rd.	659-2245		call

Spas and Inns with Spas

• Spa at Bernardus Lodge	415 Carmel Valley Rd	659-3131
• The Golden Door Spa	1 Old Ranch Rd.	625-9500
• Quail Lodge and Golf Resort	8000 Valley Greens Dr.	624-1581

Pictured opposite: Garland Park, photo by Carmela Fay

North Monterey County

Marina Sculpture Center

Salinas River Wildlife Refuge

Lazzerini Farms, Hwy 1, Moss Landing

Marina

1. City Hall, 211 Hillcrest Avenue, 831-384-3715
2. Police Station, 384-7575
3. Community Center, 384-5225
4. Fire Department, 384-7575
5. Visitor Information, 384-9155 – www.marinachamber.com

Shopping Centers

- El Rancho, 350 Reservation Road
- Marina Landing, 150 Beach Street
- Marina Square, 265 Reservation Road
- Marina Village, Vista Del Camino/Reservation
- Seacrest Plaza, 279 Reservation Road

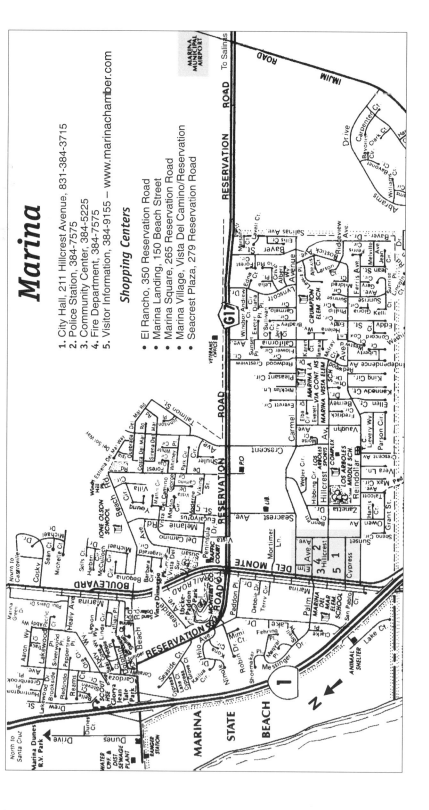

Marina Municipal Airport

Marina Municipal Airport, east on Reservation Rd. off Highway 1, left on Imjim, is alive with activities. In addition to the activities shown, Marina is seeking volunteers to provide services at the airport: tree trimming, weed abatement, litter removal and painting, between 8am-5pm, Wed-Sun. Information, call the city clerk's office at 384-3715, ext. 7101.

■ **Monterey Sculpture Center** has 45-min. Free guided tours from 10:30am-4pm, Mon-Fri. Left, welding monumental bronze by sculpture artist Betty Saletta and preparing piece for patina. Right, foundrymen pouring molten bronze into ceramic shell molds. Free 10 acre Sculpture Habitat and Nature Walk at entrance to airport. Walk through oak groves to see a changing exhibit of famous sculptures; bring a picnic to enjoy. Christine, 384-2100.

➤ Free Airplane Rides – Youth Orientation Flights at Marina Airport. **Young Eagles Program** of Chapter 204 of The Experimental Aircraft Association. Local pilots and aviators take up kids ages 8-17 for a free 15-20 minute ride that may include hands-on experience. The  "Young Eagles Rally" is all part of a worldwide endeavor to fly 1 million kids by 2003, the 100the anniversary of the maiden flight of Wilbur and Orville Wright at Kittyhawk. Adult permission is required. Flights are four times a year at 10am on Saturdays. There are other chapters at airports around the country - check in your hometown for this free orientation to the joy of flying – and free airplane rides. For info, 373-6587. www.eaa.org

S. Johnston '82

➤ Free **Air Faire** at the Marina Municipal Airport. Oct. 14, 2000. Aircraft displays, antique & classic automobiles, hot rod & muscle cars, airplane & helicopter rides, food, vintage airplane fly-bys. 9am-5pm. 582-0104.

Calendar of Events

Year 2000 dates shown. Updates at www.montereycountyguide.com.
Please call in advance to verify as information is subject to change.

April 22 **MARINA 5-MILER** **Spectators FREE**
Meet at Vince DiMaggio Park, 8:30am, to register. 9am: children 11 and under, free 1-mile fun run, 4K walk. Adults: 5 mile run, $15-$20. Children's Easter Egg Hunt after the run. Free drawing. Dj entertainment by KWAV. Benefit for city recreation programs. Free soda and ribbons. 3200 Del Monte. Margie, 384-4636.

May 5-7 **WIND FESTIVAL** **FREE**
Kites, balloons and lots of fun. Held at the Marina State Beach and at the Marina Airport. Call for information, 384-5121.

June & Sept **MARINA MOTORSPORTS SWAP MEET** **FREE**
7am at Marina Airport, Reservation Road. Free admission and parking. Car show and drawing by Salinas Valley Rodders and Salinas Valley Classic Car Club. Music, go-kart races, food. 384-1200.

August **YOUTH PAGEANT & TALENT SHOW** **FREE**
Annual. Marina residents only. Medals and savings bonds awarded. 384-0615.

September 2 **LABOR DAY PARADE & CELEBRATION** **FREE**
24th Sanctioned Annual Parade starts at 11am from Reservation Road and Crescent. After parade there will be a trophy award, food, music and entertainment at Vince DiMaggio Park. 3rd Annual car show 11am-4pm. Robert, 384-1512.

October 14 **OCTOBER AIR FAIRE** **FREE**
Marina Air Flying Club show at the airport, 9am-4pm. Fly for 10¢/lb. 883-9680.

October 1-31 **YOUNG LIFE PUMPKIN PATCH** **FREE balloons**
Pick your own among scarecrows, cartoon characters and bigger-than-life pumpkin carriages. Free balloons on weekends. 9am-5:30pm in October. Nonprofit youth organization. Call to verify location, Grace, 422-6441, 757-5813.

October 21 **10K RACE/WALK AT FT. ORD** **FREE**
20th Memorial for Giulio DePetra, founder of the Monterey Peninsula Walk Walk Walk Club. Call Hansi Rigney for time and place, 626-6602.

December **AMATEUR RADIO KIDS DAY** **FREE**
Marina Amateur Radio Contest Station invites kids to visit the station at 599 DX Dr. Call for reservations 384-3715 or 905-6652.

December **CHRISTMAS TREE LIGHTING** **FREE**
Entertainment, refreshments and Santa Claus treats for the children. 6pm at Marina Village Shopping Center, 265 Reservation Road. 384-0425.

December **MRWMD RECYCLED ART FESTIVAL** **FREE**
Sculptures and artwork created by local artists from reused objects and materials. Monterey Regional Waste Management District, 14201 Del Monte Blvd., two miles north of Marina. Mon-Sat, 8am-4:30pm. 384-5313.

December 25 **POTLUCK CHRISTMAS DINNER** **FREE**
Marina Community Hall, 221 Hillcrest Ave. Attendees are asked to bring a favorite dish to share, and place settings. People who can't bring food are asked to volunteer their time. The dinner is free and open to everyone. 394-4445.

Restaurants, Markets & Entertainment

- **Asian Market**, Korean & Japanese, 3056 Del Monte Blvd., 384-3000.
- **Bamboo Pavilion**, Chinese, 265 Reservation Road, 883-2265.
- **Cafe Pronto**, Italian, 330 Reservation Road, 883-1207.
- **Danang Market**, Asian, Del Monte Blvd., 384-8303.
- **Ho Wah Restaurant**, Chinese,3116 Del Monte Blvd. 384-7951.
- **Marina Club**, 204 Carmel Ave. No cover. Karaoke Fri-Sat, 9-1. 384-7632.
- **Marina Village Restaurant**, American, 215 Reservation Road. 384-4711.

Library & Bookstores

- **Marina Library**, 266 Reservation Road, Suites K and L, 384-6971. Hours: Tues, 10am-6pm, Wed-Thurs, 12-8pm, Fri-Sat, 10am-5pm. Closed Sun-Mon. Preschool storytime, Tues-Thurs, 2:30-5pm. Homework Center, Tues-Thurs, 2:30-5pm. **North County Bookmobiles**, phone for schedule, 663-2292.

- **Athena's Book Shop**, 265 Reservation Road. Athena, a mix of German Shepherd and Norwegian Elkhound, holds court, greeting visitors with one of her fuzzy teddy bears in her mouth – oh, and they have a good selection of books, too. Great place to browse. Mon-Sat, 10-8; Sun, 11-6. 883-9323.

Beach Garden Project Calendar 2000

Since 1992, volunteers from the Beach Garden Project have grown and planted over 63,000 dune seedlings into the Monterey Bay Dunes from Monterey State Beach to Salinas River State beach. People of all ages are welcome to join the activities: collecting seeds from native dune plants, germinating the seeds, and transplanting seedlings into the dunes. 659-1263.

Outplantings of Seedlings, 10am-noon

Jan 1	Seaside State Beach
Jan 8	Monterey State Beach
Jan 15, 22, 29	Ft. Ord Dunes State Park
Feb 5	Carmel River Beach
Feb 12	Monastery Beach, Carmel
Feb 19	Marina State Beach
Feb 26	Del Monte Beach, Tide Ave.

Bluff Lettuce

The late Fran Ciesla, courtesy of Ted Ciesla

Seed Collection/Dune Walks, 10am-noon

Aug 12	Marina State Beach
Aug 19	Salinas River State Beach (Molera Rd)
Aug 26	Carmel River Beach
	(Carmelo Ave. & Scenic Drive, Carmel)

Propagation Workshops, 10am-noon

Sept 2,9,23,30	Marina Ranger Station (61 Reservation Rd)
Sept 16	Carmel River Beach (Carmelo Ave. & Scenic Drive, Carmel)

Parks & Recreation

▲ **Marina State Beach**, off Highway 1 at Reservation Road. 170 acres. Dolphins, pelicans, whale watching in season (Dec-Mar), kite flying, sand dunes, boardwalk, fishing, hang-gliding, cafe, observation deck, surfing. Dangerous surf for wading or swimming. Dogs o.k. on beach, not on dunes.

▲ **Marina Dunes Open Space Preserve**, is located off Dunes Dr. just north of Marina State Beach. Most of these 10 acres of coastal dunes are being restored as endangered species habitat for the snowy plover, Smith's blue butterfly, and others, with coastal pedestrian access to the beach. Foundations of an old sand processing plant are still visible. Walking, jogging, dog-walking, exercise, photography, contemplation, fishing, family activities, sunbathing, surfing, and hang-gliding. This site provides a relatively quiet and under–utilized access that has not yet been "found" by the crowds. Stay on designated paths and respect dune restoration and habitat closure signs. Open dawn to dusk. 384-7695, 659-4488.

▲ **Glorya Jean Tate Park**, Abdy Way and Cordoza Ave. 4 acres. Ballfield, community building, multiuse field, picnic area, playground, rentable rooms, restrooms. Field use by reservation only. 384-4636.

▲ **Locke-Paddon Park**, on Reservation Road near Del Monte Avenue. Unique vernal ponds, remnant salt marshes created 12,000 years ago in the last glacial retreat, are now a wildlife habitat. Original wetland wildlife preserve. Shoreline trail, picnic tables, restrooms. 384-4636.

▲ **Los Arboles Sports Complex**, Reindollar and Vaughn avenues.6 acres. Ballfield, community building, trails, multiuse field, tennis, volleyball, restrooms. Snack bar. Field use by reservation only. 384-4636.

▲ **Vince DiMaggio Park**, Del Monte Blvd. and Reservation Rd. 1 acre. Community building (once the United Methodist Church sanctuary), is used for recreation department activities and has rentable rooms. A popular family picnic and playground site. 384-4636.

Bicycling Information

▲ **Bicycle path** along the beach goes north to Castroville, south to Pacific Grove. Call 384-9155 for other bike paths. **Community Center**, 211 Hillcrest Ave., conducts <u>free bicycle and helmet safety programs</u>. Call 384-5225. <u>Free air and maps</u> at **BoyerSports**, 721 Neeson Road, 883-6644.

Golf Clinic

▲ Free golf clinics with a PGA professional for **Fairway Partners**, the Salvation Army Monterey Peninsula Corp.'s junior golf program. Kids 7-17. Bayonet/Black Horse Golf Course at Ft. Ord driving range. Rides from Seaside available. Call for reservations: 899-4911 ext. 25.

Recreation Centers

▲ **Marina Senior Center**. Free ballroom dancing on Wednesdays, 12:15-2pm. For a modest fee, play bingo on Fridays from 12:15-3pm. Many more activities for seniors, call 384-6009.

▲ **Shea Gymnasium**, 4480 Col. Durham Road (Old Ft. Ord) is open for residents 14 and older to play basketball, Tues-Fri, 3-6pm (Fri 8pm), Sat, 10am-6pm, and Sun, 2-6pm. Registration required for free supervised sports activities Sat, 10-2pm. 899-6270.

▲ **Zaruk "Tak" Takali Teen Center**, 304 Hillcrest Ave., near Los Arboles Middle School, free big-screen TV, games and sports, 3-7pm weekdays. Special events like pizza parties, video nights and field trips. 884-9542.

▲ **Youth Center**, 211 Hillcrest Ave. is open Mon-Fri, 2-6pm, closed weekends and holidays. Variety of activities: ping-pong, pool, foosball, box hockey, tetherball, a merry-go-round, swings and a slide set. Portable basketball goals are available. Two playgrounds at Olson and Crumpton Schools are open after school, Mon-Fri, until 5pm, and supervised by staff. Afterschool youth sports leagues throughout the year. Monthly Activity Calendars can be picked up at playgrounds or the youth center. Programs are free. To register, call 384-4636 in the am or 384-3715 ext. 7203, 1-5pm.

More Marina Attractions

➤ **Western Hang Gliders**, located at Marina State Beach, offers free ground school for hang-gliding, open dawn to dusk, 384-2622.

➤ **Marina Dunes R.V. Park**, 3300 Dunes Dr. Exit Highway 1 at Reservation, west, to Dunes Dr., right. All camping sites are attractively landscaped for privacy and beauty. All sites have picnic table; some have cable TV and most have water/electric/sewer. Laundry room, restrooms with hot showers, store, recreation room. Privately owned. 384-6914, fax 384-0285.

➤ **Dunes Restoration, Beach Garden Project**. Volunteers needed to out-plant seedlings for revegetation of sand dunes. Call Joey, 659-1263.

➤ **Ocean Outreach Volunteers** conduct a training course for volunteers who wish to lead beach clean-up programs, assist with community festivals, and much more. 2222 East Cliff Dr. Suite 5A, Santa Cruz. 462-9122.

➤ For great bargains, visit Monterey Regional Waste Management District's Resale Shop, **Last Chance Mercantile**, 14201 Del Monte Blvd., 2 miles north of downtown Marina. Hours: Mon-Sat, 8am-4:30pm. 384-5313.

➤ **Skydive Monterey Bay**, 3261 Imjim Road. Wear comfortable clothes and just show up – they supply the training and equipment. Reservations are recommended but not required. Skydives daily, weather permitting. www.skydivemontereybay.com. 384-3483, 888-229-5867.

Moss Landing & Elkhorn Slough

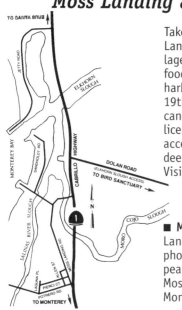

Take Highway 1 north of Monterey to Moss Landing, a New England type fishing village with storefronts, rusting boats, seafood restaurants, antique shops, and a busy harbor, once a thriving whaling station and 19th century shipping port. Wind surfing, canoeing and kayaking, boat ramp, fishing licenses and supplies, restrooms, wheelchair accessible. Port opens onto the 7,500-foot-deep submarine canyon of Monterey Bay. Visitor Information, 633-4501.

Attractions

■ **Moss Landing Post Office**, 8042 Moss Landing Road. Lobby contains historical photos and articles about the first European settlers, whalers, and the founder of Moss Landing, Captain Charles Moss. Open Mon-Fri, 9am-5pm, Sat 9-12.

■ **Phil's Fish Market**, Sandholdt Road. Moving down 2 doors in early 2000. The last remaining cannery, now a very popular restaurant and fish market. Bring your own pot to take home flavorful cioppino. Watch the sea critters in open tanks. Buy T-shirts with famous recipes. Open daily in the summer, 8:30am-8:30pm. Winter: Mon-Thurs, 10:30-6pm, Fri-Sat, 10:30-8pm. 633-2152.

■ **Monterey Bay Aquarium Research Institute**, 7700 Sandholdt Road. Research arm in the Marine Sanctuary for the world-famous Monterey Bay Aquarium. Call for date and time of their Educational Open House. 775-1773. To view day's research: www.mbari.org.

■ **Antique Stores**, an eclectic collection on Moss Landing Road, take you back to yesteryear. Browsing the shops is definitely a fun way to spend an afternoon and take home that inevitable souvenir. Several restaurants in the area will satisfy your appetite too.

■ **Fisherman's Memorial** at **Harbor Community Park** is dedicated to local fishermen who lost their lives at sea. Small park near the bridge with benches and picnic table.

Waterfront Activities

▲ **Salinas River State Beach**, on Potrero Rd. off Hwy 1. Hiking and equestrian trails, wildflowers, fishing, fires at the north end only. Undercurrents make swimming unsafe. **Salinas River National Wildlife Refuge**, south of beach, shelters brown pelicans, least terns and snowy plovers. Small ponds are remains of Salinas River. 384-7695.

▲ **Elkhorn Slough National Estuarine Research Reserve**, NE of Moss Landing, 1700 Elkhorn Road, 2 miles north of Dolan Road. 1400 acres. Five miles of trails meander through this estuary area which is an important nursery area for fish, sharks and rays, and home to over 200 species of birds including herons, egrets, and brown pelicans. Rays and sharks can be spotted in the slough's shallow waters in midsummer. Guided trail walks 10am and 1pm weekends, wildflower walk 9am Fri. Day-use fee $2.50. Closed Mon and Tue. Free Visitor Center with interpretive exhibits, trail maps and brochures. Hikes include: Long Valley Five Fingers Loop, 2.3 miles, easy; South Marsh Loop, 3.3 miles, easy. Special Mother's Day celebration in May and Estuary Day in mid-September. Be a volunteer docent! www.elkhornslough.com, 728-2822/728-5939.

▲ **Kirby Park**, off Elkhorn Road, midway down the slough. Fishing, boating, birding. **Nature Conservancy Preserve** is reached through the park. Wheelchair accessible, on-site guided tours and nature study, 728-5939.

▲ **Zmudowski State Beach** north of Moss Landing, turn on Struve Road and follow the signs to Giberson Road. 175 acres. A popular fishing and surfing spot where the Pajaro River meets the sea. Swimming, picnic, walks. Extends south to Moss Landing State Beach. Sand dunes and wetlands, equestrian trail, restrooms. 384-7695, 649-2836.

▲ **Moss Landing State Beach**, Jetty Rd. off Hwy 1, south of Zmudowski. $3/car. Surfing, wind-surfing, kayak, canoe, surf fishing, hiking, horseback riding, birdwatching, wooden pier, jetty. Restrooms. Overnight camping. 384-7695.

▲ **Moss Landing Wildlife Area**, off Highway 1, dirt access road is north of Struve Rd. 649-2870.

Surfin' and Slough Sleuthin'

➤ **Elkhorn Slough Safari**, a 2-hour cruise on a 27' pontoon boat with Captain Yohn Gideon. View playful sea otters, harbor seals and birds. Naturalist guide and activities for kids. Adults $24, under 14 $18. Reservations. www.elkhornslough.com. For more info, call 633-5555.

➤ Surfing is good at Moss Landing. Visit the **Moss Landing Surfshop** at 7544 Sandholdt Road for custom made surfboards and private lessons at reasonable prices. Call Richard, 633-6123.

➤ **Tom's Sportfishing**, 633-2564.

Entertainment & Restaurants

◆ **Maloney's**, guitarist, 6-9 Fri, live jazz, 6-9pm, Sat, no cover. 724-9371.

◆ **Moss Landing Inn**, music, Fri-Sat 9-1, Sun 4-7, no cover. 633-9990.

◆ **Phil's Fish Market**, live music, 2nd & 4th Mondays, 7-8pm. 633-2152.

◆ **The Whole Enchilada**, Mexican, Hwy 1 & Moss Landing Rd. 633-5398.

Calendar of Events

Year 2000 dates shown. Updates at www.montereycountyguide.com.
Please call in advance to verify as information is subject to change.

May 6   **ELKHORN NURSERY OPEN HOUSE**   **FREE**
10am-3pm. Free tours, hiking, artists, falconer, and free food. Beautiful slough views. Hwy 1 directly across from the Beacon Gas Station in Moss Landing at Struve Road, go one mile through the strawberry fields. Jean, 673-1207.

May 14   **MOTHER'S DAY CELEBRATION**   **$$**
Elkhorn Slough Reserve, 10am-4pm. Pack a picnic and bring mom and the family to the slough to see the egrets, herons and sharks. $2.50 day use fee. Free treats & flowers for mom, strawberry shortcake, live music, crafts and nature walks. 1700 Elkhorn Road, 5 miles inland from Moss Landing. Marian, 728-2822.

July 30   **ANTIQUE STREET FAIRE**   **$$**
30th Annual. 8am-5pm. 200+ vendors and over 20 permanent shops. Pancake Breakfast 7am, fish fry 11am. Admission $2, children under 12 free. Free parking. No dogs. Moss Landing Chamber, 633-4501. www.monterey-bay.net/ml.

Sept 16   **CLEAN UP ELKHORN SLOUGH**   **FREE**
9am to noon, Kirby Park on Elkhorn Road. Free T-shirts for the first 75 volunteers. Bring your friends, boots or kayak and see the slough for free. 622-7651.

October   **PUMPKIN PATCHES**   **Scenic Drive**
Springfield Farms, Highway 1 just south of Moss Landing, open 8:30am-5pm. 633-8041. Dominic's, Highway 1, 2 miles north of Moss Landing.

October   **MARINE LABS OPEN HOUSE**   **FREE**
With touch tanks, seminars, videos, fish printing, puppet shows, current research, fresh seafood, algae pressing, dune and beach walks, kids' activities and more. Featuring their resident sea lions, Beaver, Sake and Nemo. Sat 11am-5pm, Sun 10am-5pm. New location: Water Tower Hill above the Castroville Cemetery on Moss Landing Road. No pets please. For more information, call MLML at 755-8650 or visit http://color.mlml.clastate.edu/www/.

October 6-8   **MONTEREY BAY BIRD FESTIVAL**   **FREE+$$**
Bird banding, bird songs and calls, photography, shorebirds, gulls, native plants, raptors. Live music, exhibits, food, special demonstrations. 10am-5pm. 728-3890, 728-2822. E-mail esf@elkhornslough.com. Website: www.elkhornslough.org. Fee birding classes: 633-5555. Elkhorn Slough free on annual Clean-up Day.

Oct 13-14   **ELKHORN NURSERY OPEN HOUSE**   **FREE**
10am-3pm. Hiking, birding, picnic facilities. Posters and plant sale. Beautiful slough views. Hwy 1 directly across from the Beacon Gas Station in Moss Landing at Struve Road, go one mile through the strawberry fields. Jean, 673-1207.

Aromas

June 4   **GARDEN TOUR**   **$$**
8th Annual. 10am-4pm. Sponsored by Aromas 4-H, a self-guided tour through private gardens and a tour of the orchid greenhouses at the Rod McClellan Company. Pancake Breakfast, 7:30am, and a Marketplace at the Grange, 11am-4pm: plants, produce, garden art and food. Tour maps, $10 donation. 726-1344.

July 4   **POPS & ROCKS INDEPENDENCE DAY CONCERT**   **$$**
Nonprofit benefit by advance ticket at Graniterock's A.R. Wilson Quarry. BBQ, fireworks. Free parking. Wheelchair accessible. 768-2007 or 888-ROCK100.

● **Monterey County Free Library**, in the Old Firehouse Market Building at Carpenteria near Blohm. Storytime Thurs 10am. Homework Center, Wed 2-6, Thurs 1-5. Open Wed-Fri 2-6pm, Thurs-Sat 10-12 & 1-5pm. Free summer reading program for all ages. Friends of the Aromas Library need volunteers to assist the librarian, patrons on the Internet and students at Homework Center. 726-3240.

● **Aromas Grange**, part of the Grange movement which began in the U.S. in 1867 by Oliver Hudson Kelley, who conceived the idea to heal the wounds of the Civil War and improve the economic and social position of the farm population. Pancake breakfast, 4th Sun, 7-11am, $3.50, children $2. Drop into Joane Ingram's realty office at 388 Blohm Avenue for colorful local info; 726-0100.

▲ **Royal Oaks County Park**, between Aromas and Prunedale on Maher Road off Echo Valley Road. 122 acres. The oldest park in the county, established in 1966. Softball diamond, tennis courts, basketball court, horseshoe pits, trails, volleyball standards, and picnic areas. Short trails, average .5 miles. Call 755-4895 for picnic reservations (up to 300). 663-2699.

Prunedale

Visitor Information 831-663-0965

Calendar of Events

Year 2000 dates shown. Updates at www.montereycountyguide.com.
Please call in advance to verify as information is subject to change.

June 24-25 **AMATEUR RADIO FIELD DAY** **FREE**
NPGS Amateur Radio Club demonstrates the latest in radio communications using generators, solar, wind and bettery power. Discover ham radio and get radio-active 11am at Manzanita Park, Castroville Blvd. 384-0705.

August 20 **FUN DAY AT MANZANITA PARK** **Spectators FREE**
Castroville Blvd., off San Miguel, between Highways 101 and 156. Free children's Fun Run, 8:30am. 10K/5K runs and 5K walk, softball tournament. Fund-raiser for Manzanita Sports Complex. Info: Diane Carrillo, 663-2108.

November 13 **HOUSEHOLD CAT PET SHOW** **$$**
Lots of fun. Enter your cat or kitten. Great for kids. Prunedale Grange on Moro Road. $3 adults. 372-7018.

More to See and Do

◆ **The Office**, at intersection of Hwys 101 & 156. Line dancing instruction, Country western instruction, karaoke, live music, no cover. 663-4047.

● **Monterey County Public Library**, 17822 Moro Rd. Preschool storytime, ages 2¹/₂-5yrs, Wed 11am. Homework Center, grades 1-12, Mon-Wed, 3-6pm. Mon 1-9, Tues-Wed 10-9, Thurs-Sat 10-5. 663-2292.

➤ **Mobilastics, Gymnastics**, 10161 Reese Circle. Free trial class in gymnastics to first time students. Kung Fu for kids, Martial Arts Aerobics, Step Aerobics and Tai Chi. Events include a Show Day in September, a Halloween Party in October, and Summer Camp. 663-6028.

▲ **Manzanita Park**, Castroville Blvd. 464 acres of gently rolling hills sprinkled with manzanita, oak, and pine. Quiet, scenic trails are shared by hikers and horses in this multi-use nature center. Softball fields. Food for sale in the snackbar adjacent. Spectacular views of all of North County. 663-2699. Batting cages open Mon-Fri 2pm-dusk, Sat 8-dusk, Sun 10-4. 663-1206.

Pájaro

● **Monterey County Free Library**, 29 Bishop St. In the historic landmark Porter-Vallejo Mansion, right. Storytime (bilingual) Thurs, 11:30am. Homework Center, grades 1-12, Tues & Thurs 10-1 & 2-6, Sat 1-5. 761-2545.

● **Casa de la Cultura**, community center fun by Sister Rosa Dolores Rodriguez. <u>Provides music lessons and other free services.</u> 763-0702.

➤ **Pájaro Valley Golf Club**, a lush 18 holes with scenic views. Open to the public, an historic course since 1926. Call for info: 831-724-3851.

Accommodations in Marina, North County

● **Motel 6**, 100 Reservation Rd. Marina. 384-1000. $42

● **Marina Beach Travelodge**, 3290 Dunes Drive, Marina. 883-0300. $59+

● **Marina Beach Inn**, 3270 Del Monte Blvd, Marina. 384-1010. $59+

● **El Matador Hotel**, 420 Reservation Road, Marina. 384-5121. $55+

● **Marina Dunes RV Park**, 3330 Dunes Drive, Marina. 384-6914.

For a beautiful 4-color brochure listing unique and wonderful adventures in North Monterey County, with many free opportunities, write to:

North Monterey County-Marina Chamber of Commerce 211 Hillcrest Avenue, Marina CA 93933. Telephone 888-428-0627.

Castroville

Visitor Information 831-633-6545

Founded in 1863 by Juan B. Castro, Castroville is the second oldest town in Monterey County. The artichoke crop, introduced in 1920, made the

town famous. It is now the third largest cash crop in the Salinas Valley, making Castroville the official "Artichoke Center of the World." The annual **Artichoke Festival** draws visitors from all over the world to see the fascinating thistle. Marilyn Monroe was the first Artichoke Queen in 1947. Each year there's more music including a swing band, country music and a mariachi band; antique and classic automobiles and hot rods; Marilyn Monroe T-shirts, buttons, and other memorabilia. Castroville is busy sprucing up the town with a beautification plan for $25 million worth of improvements over the next decade. Tickets $5, kids $2. For more information, write: Castroville Festivals, Inc. P.O. Box 1041, Castroville, CA 95012-1041. 831-633-2465.

Castroville Attractions

■ **Giant Artichoke Restaurant**, 11261 Merritt St. See everything artichoke, including a giant 12' statue in front. One million people are rumored to have had their picture taken here. Open Mon-Thurs, 7am-4pm, Fri-Sun, 7am-9pm. 633-3204.

■ **Bing's Diner**, 10961 Merritt St., a "900 Series" streetcar built in the 1920s, used in Oakland, and converted to a diner in Castroville in 1950. Locals claim it's named after Bing Crosby who ate here during his early years of travel to Monterey County. Open 6am-8pm for breakfast, lunch and dinner. Try their famous ribs. 633-0400.

■ **La Scuola Ristorante**, 10700 Merritt St. This Italian restaurant is located in Castroville's original schoolhouse. Decor includes historical pictures of early Castroville. Open Tues-Sat, 11:30-2pm for lunch and 5-9pm for dinner. Sat 5-9 for dinner only. Closed Sun-Mon. 633-3200.

■ **Central Texan Barbecue**, 10500 Merritt. Well-known for generous portions of delicious barbecue. Closed Tuesdays. 633-2285.

● **Castroville Public Library**, 11266 Merritt St. Open Tues-Thurs 12-8, Wed 10-6, Fri-Sat 10-5. Homework Center for grades 1-12, open Tues-Thurs, 3-6pm. 633-2829.

▲ **Castroville-Marina Bike Trail**, newly opened trails for bike enthusiasts take riders from the shore inland. Call 633-6545 or 384-9155.

▲ **Crane Street Park**. Castroville's newest park opened in February, 1999. Tot-lot playground, picnic table, and a small barbecue pit, a large grassy area, and a view of Castroville's artichoke fields.

▲ **North County Recreation**, Castroville Community Center, 11261 Crane St., has many classes for kids and teens. 633-3084.

Calendar of Events

Year 2000 dates shown. Updates at www.montereycountyguide.com.
Please call in advance to verify as information is subject to change.

May 20-21 ARTICHOKE FESTIVAL FREE+$$
Castroville Community Center, 10am. Entertainment, car show, live music, an artichoke-eating contest, arts and crafts, food, celebrity chefs cooking demos, a parade, and the coronation of the Artichoke Queen. Robert Steen, 633-2465.

November 23 THANKSGIVING DINNER FREE
12-4pm at Castroville Community Center, 1126 Crane St. (behind Catholic church). Santa will have toys for children. 633-3084

Old Monterey
& Fisherman's Wharf

Fisherman's Wharf

Museums of Art

Historic Adobes

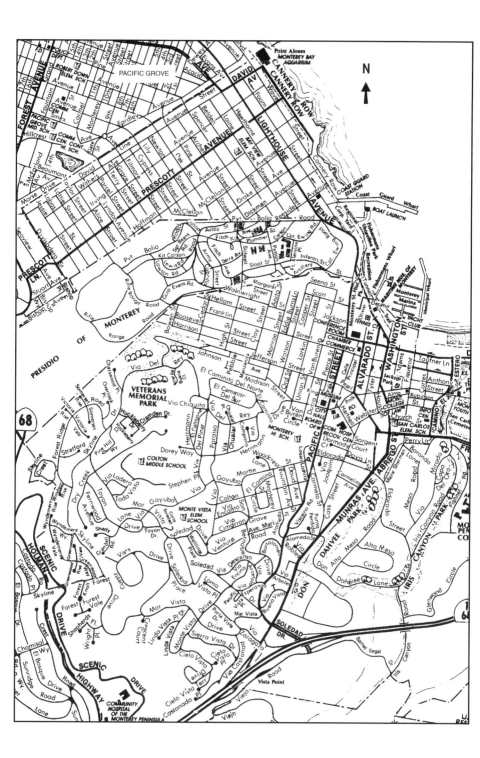

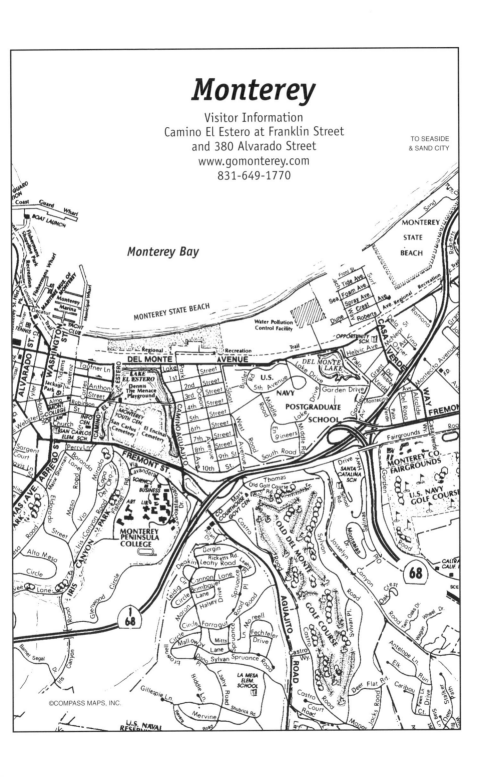

Monterey

Visitor Information
Camino El Estero at Franklin Street
and 380 Alvarado Street
www.gomonterey.com
831-649-1770

TO SEASIDE
& SAND CITY

Monterey Bay

MONTEREY STATE BEACH

MONTEREY
STATE
BEACH

Water Pollution
Control Facility

DEL MONTE AVENUE

LAKE
EL ESTERO

Dennis
The Menace
Playground

U.S.
NAVY

POSTGRADUATE
SCHOOL

DEL MONTE
LAKE

MONTEREY
YOUTH CEN.

El Encinal
Cemetery

San Carlos
Cemetery

FREMONT ST.

SCIENCE
BUSINESS

ART LIB.

MONTEREY
PENINSULA
COLLEGE

MONTEREY CO.
FAIRGROUNDS

U.S. NAVY
GOLF COURSE

Fairgrounds

SANTA
CATALINA
SCH

OLD DEL MONTE

GOLF COURSE

LA MESA
ELEM.
SCHOOL

U.S. NAVAL
RESERVAL

©COMPASS MAPS, INC.

68

68

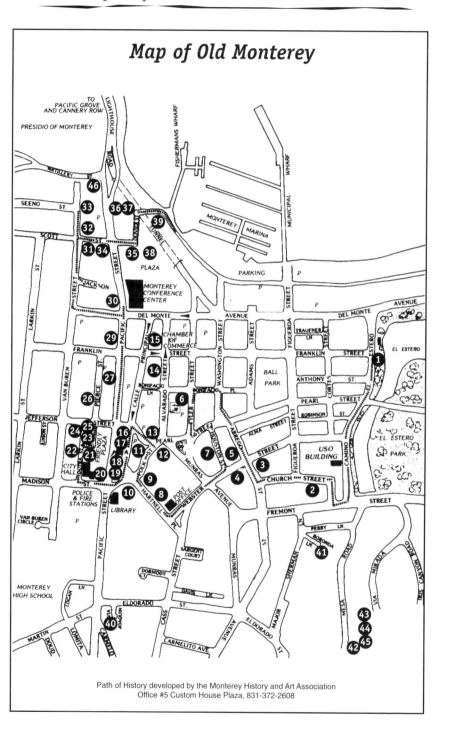

Map of Old Monterey

Path of History developed by the Monterey History and Art Association
Office #5 Custom House Plaza, 831-372-2608

Historic Sites Walking Tour

1. First French Consulate (P)
2. Royal Presidio Chapel (N, SHL #105)
3. Casa Madariaga (P)
4. Casa Pacheco (P)
5. Casa Abrego (P)
6. Estrada Adobe (P)
7. Stevenson House (SHL #352, MSHP)
8. General Fremont's Quarters (P)
9. First Federal Court (P)
10. Stokes Adobe (P-Restaurant)
11. Casa Amesti (P)
12. Cooper Molera Adobe (MSHP)
13. Alvarado Adobe (SHL #348, P)
14. Casa Sanchez (P)
15. Osio-Rodríguez Adobe
16. Larkin House (N, MSHP, SHL #106)
17. Sherman Headquarters (P)
18. House of the Four Winds (P, SHL #353)
19. Casa Gutiérrez (SHL #713, MSHP)
20. Brown-Underwood House (P)
21. Colton Hall & Old Jail (SHL #126)
22. Casa Vásquez (SHL #351)
23. Gordon House (P)
24. Casa Alvarado (P)
25. Casa de la Torre (P)
26. Casa Jesus Soto (P)
27. Casa Serrano (*)
28. Capitular Hall (P)
29. Merritt House (P-Merritt House Inn)
30. Casa Soberanes (SHL #712, MSHP)
31. Perry House
32. Doud House
33. Old St. James Church
34. California's First Theatre (SHL #136, MSHP)
35. Casa Del Oro (SHL #532, MSHP)
36. Old Whaling Station (P)
37. First Brick House (MSHP)
38. Pacific Building & Memory Garden (SHL #354, MSHP)
39. Custom House (Maritime Museum Of Monterey, N, MSHP)
40. Casa Joaquin Soto (P)
41. Casa Boronda (P)
42. Casa Buelna (P)
43. Casa de Castro (P)
44. Casa Bonifacio (P)
45. Casa de Doud (P)
46. Vizcaino-Serra Landing Site (SHL #128)

Cooper Molera Adobe

LEGEND
(N) National Historical Landmark
(SHL) State Historical Landmark
(MSHP) Monterey State Historic Park
(P) Private Residence, not generally open to public
(*) Monterey History & Art Assn. Headquarters
P Off-Street Parking
(Residents-apply for a free parking permit at City Hall)

CALIFORNIA STATE PARKS

The Path of History in Old Monterey

For outdoor lovers, romantics, artists and shoppers, there is an infinite array of possibilities in Monterey. The bustling, seaside town is best known for Fisherman's Wharf, Cannery Row, and its collection of historic buildings. The Path of History walking tour will take you through these buildings and gardens, past art galleries and museums, the eateries and shops.

From Monterey State Parks: **The Path of History** includes 46 unique nineteenth century historic structures, maintained by the Monterey History and Art Assn., the State of California Department of Parks and Recreation, and the City of Monterey. You may follow the line on the map to see all 46 structures, or begin the selected walk below at the Custom House Plaza; it takes about 90 minutes. Numbers in parenthesis indicate their position on the map and their date of construction. There are gold markers on the sidewalk, illustrated tiles in four languages and descriptive signs to guide you. Free admission noted, others by guided tour from the Stanton Center and Cooper-Molera Adobe. The gardens are always open. Watch a free video at the Stanton Center before you go.

■ **Stanton Center & Custom House Plaza(Map#39),** site of the Monterey Visitors and Convention Bureau, State Historic Park Visitor's Center, State Park History Theatre, and the Maritime Museum. Free film: 17-minute Monterey history film every 20 minutes, 10am-5pm. Gift shop with local items and books, 649-7118. Walking tours depart from here hourly, $5 for all. A free self-guided kids' treasure hunt daily in the foyer. **The Maritime Museum**, Monterey's fishing history artifacts collection, and Monterey History & Art Headquarters, is free several times a year, including FirstNight®. Free symposiums with marine themes occasionally offered. Adults $5, seniors, teens, military $3, children 6-12 $2, and under 5 free. 10am-5pm, closed Thanksgiving, Christmas and New Year's. 373-2469. www.mbay.net/~mshp. Volunteer to be a "Watchstander," call 372-2608 ext 14.

■ **Pacific House & Garden (#38)** (1847) Built for the storage of U.S. military supplies, it has also been a hotel, law office, church, ballroom, and newspaper office. It now houses the **Monterey Museum of the American Indian** and a new visitor center/museum, open early 2000. Visit the Memory Garden behind the Pacific House, created in 1928 and one of the loveliest of the historic walled gardens.

Each year, the Merienda, celebrating the founding of Monterey in 1770, takes place in the Pacific House garden pictured to the right. Descendents of original families gather with local dignitaries. Often the Spanish Consulate sends a delegation. La Dueña and La Favorita, dressed in period costumes, are chosen to reign over the traditional Spanish/Mexican festivities.

■ **Custom House & Garden (39)** (1827), Custom House Plaza. Free admission, 10am-5pm daily. During California's Mexican era, the Monterey Custom House presided over Mexico's only port of entry on the Alta California coast, opened to foreign trade in 1822. It was here that Commodore John Drake Sloat raised the American flag in July of 1846, claiming over 600,000 square miles of territory for the United States. Gardens reflect the Mexican era with specimen succulents, cacti and other drought-tolerant plants.

■ **First Brick House & Garden (37)** (1847), Heritage Harbor. Free admission, 10am-5pm daily. Briefly inhabited by its builder, Gallant Dickenson, this building represents the kiln fired brick construction method brought to California by settlers in the early American period.

■ **Whaling Station & Garden (36)** (1847), Decatur Street, Heritage Harbor. The Old Whaling Station boasts Monterey's only remaining whalebone sidewalk, a reminder of one of the town's most important industries from 1850-1900. The charming adobe and its gardens are now under the stewardship of the Junior League of Monterey County.

■ **Casa Del Oro & Garden (35)** (1845), **Picket Fence,** Scott and Olivier Streets. Free admission, Thurs-Sun, 11am-3pm. Used as a general store by 19th century businessmen David Jacks and Joseph Boston, the Casa del Oro is open again as the **Boston Store**, operated by the Historic Garden League. Volunteer to help them with the restoration of Monterey's gardens on first Tuesdays and third Saturdays, 9-11am, at various state-owned properties: second Wed 9-11am at Doud House, Scott and Van Buren. Bring gloves, clippers, rake, etc. Call for Tues and Sat locations, 649-6825. The Boston Store, 649-3364. Pleasant gardens including scented herb garden.

■ **First Theatre & Garden (34)**
(1844), Scott and Pacific Streets. Free admission, Wed-Sat, 1-5pm. Jack Swan's saloon became a theatre when he let the NY Volunteers, assigned to Monterey at the end of the Mexican War, put on plays. The Troupers of the Gold Coast have been presenting 19th century melodramas here since the 1930's. Call for times, 375-4916.

■ **Mayo Hayes O'Donnell Library**
(1876), 155 Van Buren Street. Free admission, Wed, Fri-Sun, 1:30-3:45pm. This little red church was the first Protestant Church in Monterey. It is now a library of "Californiana" and owned by the Monterey History and Art Association. Take a book, settle into a chair with a comforting view of the bay, and absorb some Monterey and California history. Friendly docents answer questions and find books. Brochures and maps available.

■ **Casa Soberanes & Garden (30)**
(1842), 336 Pacific Street. With its thick walls, interconnecting rooms, cantilevered balcony and lovely garden, Casa Soberanes tells the story of life in Monterey from its Mexican period beginnings to recent times. Terraced borders of abalone shells, antique bottles and a whalebone grace the garden created in 1907. The gardens are always open to the public and tours for the interior of this adobe are included on the twice yearly public tours of the adobes. See Calendar of Events. Call for more information, 373-2469.

■ **Osio-Rodríguez Adobe (15)**, 380 Alvarado St., built in the early 1840s by Jacinto Rodriguez, a delegate to California's first Constitutional Convention in 1849, now houses the Chamber of Commerce and **Visitors Center & Gift Shop**. Mon-Fri, 8am-5pm 649-1770.

■ **Casa Serrano (27)** (1843), 412 Pacific Street.  Free admission, Sat-Sun, 2-4pm. It was originally started by Thomas Larkin in 1843, and purchased and finished by Don Florencio Serrano, one of the first school teachers, in 1845. On fourth Saturdays of each month, chat with docent Diana J. Dennett, local author and 9th generation descendant of an early Monterey family that came with Father Serra in 1770. Dennett is pictured at right with Señor Camilo Alonzo-Vega, Consul General of Spain, in 1998 at the Presidio of San Francisco, with her enchanting and historical book, *Tell Me More Ancestor Stories, Grandma!*, available at the Boston Store, the National Steinbeck Center, and local bookstores.

■ **Larkin House & Garden (16)** (1834), 510 Calle Principal. This adobe built during Monterey's Mexican period by Thomas O. Larkin, American merchant and U.S. Consul to Alta California, has stood witness to intrigue, business deals, and lively social occasions. Today its early 19th century rooms hold antiques from many parts of the world. Walled garden from 1842 was replanted as an English-style garden in the 1920s with yew, magnolia, redwood, rose arbor, fuschia, rhododendron and foxglove.

■ **Casa Gutierrez (19)** (1846), Madison and Calle Principal. Tucked away alongside other buildings, Casa Gutierrez is one of the few remaining adobes built in the simpler Mexican style which once lined Monterey's streets. Presently, the structure is not open to the public.

■ **Colton Hall (21)** (1849), Pacific Street at Madison. Free admission, daily 10am-5pm. Built and finished as a town hall in March by Walter Colton, by September it was the site of a convention called by Governor Riley to draft California's first Constitution, a copy of which resides inside. It served as Monterey County seat and Court House until 1872. Between 1873 and 1897, it was

a grade school. In 1949, the City of Monterey established the **Colton Hall Museum**, dedicated to the history of the City. A museum attendant is available for tours and information. Full-size bronze grizzly bear sculptures by sculptor Kris Swanson are tentatively set to be unveiled here on Sept. 9, 2000, the sesquicentennial of California's statehood. Peek through the bars of the **Old Monterey Jail** (1854) just behind the museum. Sesquicentennial festivities are planned throughout the year; call for info, 646-5640.

■ **Cooper-Molera & Garden (12)** (1827), Polk and Munras Streets. The former home of John Rogers Cooper, a New England sea captain who came to Monterey in 1823, and three generations of the Cooper family. He changed  his name to Juan Bautista Rogerio Cooper, his citizenship to Mexico and his religion to Catholic, married into the Vallejo family. The large complex includes an exhibit room, carriage display, period garden and farm animals. The two-acre period garden was planted in the 1980s by the Old Monterey Preservation Society. Chickens, a rooster and sheep freely wander in the Victorian flower garden, vegetable garden and fruit orchard. A museum store is open daily, 10am-4pm, winter, and 10am-5pm, summer (Memorial Day through end of Daylight Savings). Special garden tours of Cooper-Molera Adobe, Stevenson and Larkin House gardens from May through Sept, 2nd and 4th Tues & Sat, 1pm, $2. 649-7118.

■ **Stevenson House & Garden (7)** (1840), 530 Houston. Reading more like a Robert Louis Stevenson tale of travel and romance than real events taking place in Monterey, the story of Stevenson's courtship of Fanny Osbourne, his future wife, comes alive amid period settings and displays of Stevenson memorabilia. Stevenson lived here briefly in 1879. A large Victorian garden hidden behind a high wall is a peaceful oasis with benches, an old Ficus and Angel's Trumpet vine. Free admission on Nov. 14, noon-3pm, on Robert Louis Stevenson's Unbirthday. Docents, Scottish pipers in the garden and Stevenson himself! 649-7118.

■ **Royal Presidio Chapel (2)** (1794), 500 Church. Free admission, 8:30am-6pm daily. Oldest structure in Monterey and an example of Spanish Colonial Architecture. San Carlos Gift Shop, 373-6711.

■ **First French Consulate (1)** (1848) On Camino El Estero, near Franklin St., former home of the first French Consulate in California, now is one of Monterey's **Visitor Centers**. Here you will find a knowledgeable staff, maps, brochures, and postcards. Open Mon-Sat, 9-5, Sun 10-4. Gardens shown below.

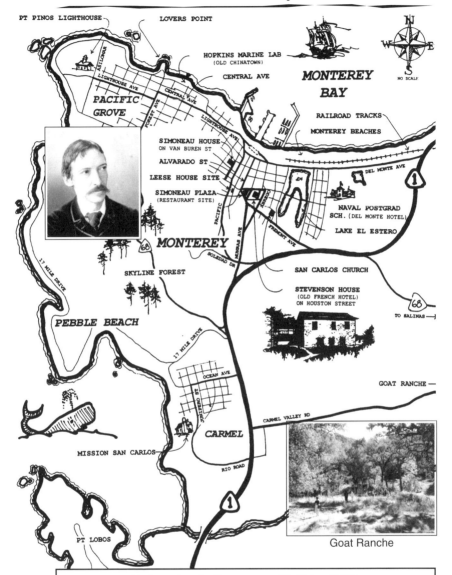

PT PINOS LIGHTHOUSE

LOVERS POINT

HOPKINS MARINE LAB
(OLD CHINATOWN)

CENTRAL AVE

MONTEREY
BAY

NO SCALE

PACIFIC
GROVE

LIGHTHOUSE AVE

CENTRAL AVE

FOREST AVE

LIGHTHOUSE AVE

RAILROAD TRACKS

MONTEREY BEACHES

SIMONEAU HOUSE
ON VAN BUREN ST

ALVARADO ST

LEESE HOUSE SITE

SIMONEAU PLAZA
(RESTAURANT SITE)

DEL MONTE AVE

NAVAL POSTGRAD
SCH. (DEL MONTE HOTEL)

LAKE EL ESTERO

PACIFIC

MONTEREY

MUNRAS AVE

SOLEDAD DR

FREMONT AVE

SKYLINE FOREST

17 MILE DRIVE

SAN CARLOS CHURCH

STEVENSON HOUSE
(OLD FRENCH HOTEL)
ON HOUSTON STREET

TO SALINAS

PEBBLE BEACH

17 MILE DRIVE

OCEAN AVE

JUNIPERO ST

CARMEL

MISSION SAN CARLOS

RIO ROAD

CARMEL VALLEY RD

GOAT RANCHE

PT LOBOS

Goat Ranche

Robert Louis Stevenson Visit in 1879

In August of 1879, RLS came to Monterey following Fanny Osbourne, whom he later married in San Francisco. Map shows sites in Monterey that he visited and commented on in his letters and "The Old Pacific Capitol," an RLS essay first published in 1880. The Goat Ranche tours are usually on the 2nd or 3rd Saturday in May. Open House at the Stevenson House is the last weekend in August to celebrate his arrival in Monterey on Aug 30, 1879. Maps may be purchased at the Stevenson House, Cooper Store and Colton Hall. $1.50 donation goes to pay for interpretive panels at Simoneau Plaza. Compliments of the RLS Club, P.O. Box 2562, Monterey, CA 93942.

Special Adobe Activities

➤ Each year certain adobes participate in two public tours in early spring and at Christmas; 2000–April 15, and Christmas in the Adobes, Dec. 7 & 9.

➤ Casa Serrano, Cooper-Molera, Memory Garden, Perry House, Doud House and the Mayo Hayes O'Donnell Library are available for private parties. For more information, call Linda Jaffee, Executive Director Monterey History and Art Association, 625-6103 or 649-7118.

Volunteer Opportunities with Monterey State Parks

➤ **Monterey State Historic Park Docent Training Class** will be Sept. 29, 1999, 6-9pm. Topics include California history, Monterey's historic buildings and gardens, tour techniques and presentation skills, living history, period clothing, school programs, and more. Call 647-6204 for information and to receive an application. For more information, see the Monterey State Historic Park web site at: www.mbay.net/~mshp/.

➤ **Old Monterey Preservation Society** (OMPS) is the nonprofit Cooperating Association with Monterey State Historic Park whose purpose is to provide educational and interpretive programs and activities, give support for various interpretive projects, and foster preservation of Old Monterey. You can help when you join for $10 which entitles you to free entrance to scheduled tours of the Adobes, invitation to programs, docent training, workshops in costumes, crafts and living history, and special events. 647-6226.

Other Interesting Places

■ **Naval Postgraduate School**, off Del Monte Ave., was originally the Del Monte Hotel built in 1887 by Charles Crocker. The Hotel was part of a 20,000 acre complex which included all of Pebble Beach and hundreds of acres of rare botanical gardens and recreational facilities. **Eagles Eye Art Gallery**, Rm#24, is in the basement of Hermann Hall, and open free Mon-Fri, 11:30am-3pm, featuring local watercolors. Check out the murals around the building and the Jo Mora art in the La Novia room. Ask at the quarterdeck in Hermann Hall for a key to the viewing tower and enjoy a spectacular 360-degree view of Monterey and the bay. The **Roman Plunge** swimming pool is open summers Tues-Fri,

11am-3pm, Sat-Sun, noon-5pm. Fees vary, call 656-2275. **Del Monte Lake** offers walking paths and bird watching. Visitors may take a free self-guided walking tour of the building and grounds which includes the **Arizona Garden** with a very large collection of cactus and succulents. The

original garden required three train cars of succulents from Sonora, Mexico. Pick up a free map in Hermann Hall, the main building. Free concerts on the lawn Memorial Day, 4th of July, and Labor Day weekends, plus other free events. Call for dates and times, Public Affairs Office, Mon-Fri, 8am-4:30pm, 656-2023, 656-1049.

■ **State Theatre**, 417 Alvarado. Opened in 1926 as the Golden State Theatre, one of several beautiful theatres built on the Monterey Peninsula during the early 1900s. Of these, the Golden State Theatre was the largest and grandest and today it is the only one left. It was designed by the Reid Brothers architectural firm of San Francisco which also designed the Fairmont Hotel, the Cliff House and the Music Pavilion in Golden Gate Park, plus the Hotel del Coronado in San Diego. The architecture follows a medieval Spanish theme complete with tapestries, wrought-iron chandeliers, colorful heraldic shields and old ornamentation. The auditorium is designed to give the impression of a Castilian courtyard. A nonprofit group, The State Theatre Preservation Group, has been formed to promote and facilitate the restoration of the theatre to its original 1926 appearance. To help, call 373-7678. Visit their webiste: www.stpg.com.

■ **St. John's Chapel**, 1490 Mark Thomas Drive, between Del Monte Golf Club and the Hyatt Regency. This historical church will be open September 9, 10am-3pm, for tours during their annual Bargain Hunt which features antiques, collectables, art, books, clothing, toys, crafts, and much more. Coffee, sandwiches, baked goods and jams, and friendly smiles. 375-4463.

■ **Monterey Airport**, Highway 68 & Olmstead Rd. Art-at-the-Airport. "Wood Wings" sculptures through March 30, 2000, thereafter at airport office of Million Air. Enjoy watching the planes take off and land while dining at the **Golden Tee Restaurant**, 206 Fred Kane Drive, 373-1232.

$3 Gift Certificate

Join In the Fun of
LYCEUM LEARNING
Call 372-6098 for a free Catalog of
Classes or visit
www.lyceum.org

Lyceum of Monterey County

Educational programs on science and nature, arts and crafts, sports and hobbies, computers, humanities and life skills in various locations throughout the county. Free on special occasions. Mon-Fri, 9am-4:30pm. Call for a free catalog and more information: 372-6098, fax 372-6065. 1073 6th Street.

Fisherman's Wharf & Commercial Wharf #2

"Everything for family fun!" A stroll down the wharf brings exciting sights and sounds to your senses. Browse the shops, sample free salt water taffy and clam chowder at Old Fisherman's Grotto. Watch the harbor seals, pelicans, cormorants and sea gulls. Take in a whale watch cruise or do some deep sea fishing. Artists are sketching portraits and musicians are strolling among the crowds.

Public Art At the Wharf

Pietro Ferrante, 1969. Robert H. Hoge (1904-1998). Bronze. Gift from Ferrante family, placed at current site in 1989.

Santa Rosalia, 1979. Richard Lutz. Bronze. Donated to the city by the Italian Heritage Society.

Sabu Shake, statue of beloved local businessman.

There's always something going on at Fisherman's Wharf and Commercial Wharf #2. See the boats enter and leave the harbor. Watch fishermen bring in the day's catch and buy the freshest seafood available. There's a variety of excellent restaurants and The Wharf Theatre for after dinner entertainment. For more information and a <u>schedule of free entertainment and events</u>, call the Fisherman's Wharf Assn., 373-0600.

➤ **The Wharf's General Store**, 14 Fisherman's Wharf, is open 7 days a week, 9:30am-10pm. *It's the place you're bound to find something you just can't live without!* Receive one <u>free hour of parking</u> when you show this book. 649-4404. www.twgs.com.

➤ **Harbor House Gifts**, 1 Fisherman's Wharf, is open daily at 10am. Collectibles, valuables, and a little something special for everybody. 372-4134.

➤ **Hawaiian Chieftan**, pictured here. The Tall Ships may dock at Fisherman's Wharf for <u>free public tours</u> in October. Call 800-200-LADY for dates.

Enjoy These Special Discounts

➤ <u>$5 off/person on fishing trips. $2 off on whale watching trips</u>
Angelo Shake Monterey Sportfishing and Whale Watching Cruises
96 Old Fisherman's Wharf
800/200-2203, 831/372-2203, www.montereysportfishing.com

Benji Shake Monterey Baywatch Cruises
90 Old Fisherman's Wharf
831/372-7153, www.montereybaywatch.com

➤ <u>$1 off/person on Glass Bottom boat tours</u>
Sea Life Tours/Glass Bottom Boat
90 Old Fisherman's Wharf
831/372-7151, www.sealifetours.com

➤ <u>$5 off/person on fishing trips.</u>
<u>$2 off on whale watching trips</u>
Randy's Fishing and Whale Watching
66 Old Fisherman's Wharf
831/372-7440, www.randysfishingtrips.com

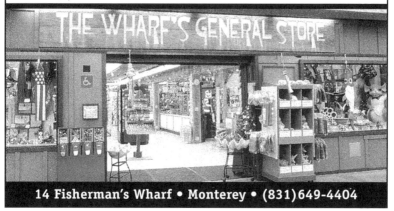
Marine Mammals on the Beach

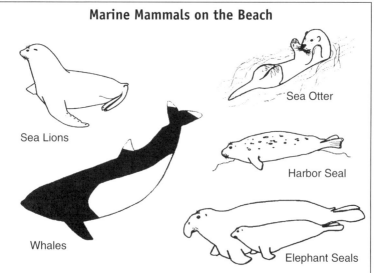

Sea Otter

Sea Lions

Harbor Seal

Whales

Elephant Seals

Observe these creatures from a distance—it's the law. If you see that one is injured or in danger, call 911 if people are involved; otherwise, for seals, sea lions and cetaceans (alive only) call the Marine Mammal Center at 633-6298 or 646-5534 (evenings & weekends); sea otters, call the Monterey Bay Aquarium at 648-4840 (dead or alive). Drawings by Milos Radakovich.

Browsing the Shops in Old Monterey

■ While visiting the adobes, you'll have plenty of opportunities to window shop: Christopher Bell Collection, Chivalry Bath Shoppe, Do Re Mi Music & Video, Dudley Doolittle's Travel Shop, The First Noel, A&J Gallery, Aiello Jewelers, Alvarado Mart, The Art Show, Avalon Beads, The Consignment Gallery, Nomad's Fine Rugs, Dick Bruhn's Menswear, Levin Camera Gallery, The Bachelor Shop, Bay Books, Burlwood Gallery, Gasper's Jewelers, Green's Camera World, Hats & Caps, Hellams Tobacco Shop, Pieces of Heaven, Troia's Market, and more. Old Monterey Business Assn., 655-8070. Info: 648-5360.

■ **Del Monte Shopping Center**, Munras Ave. at Hwy 1. Open air center with lush and whimsical gardens. Free summer music series July through September. Over 80 shops and restaurants, and 6 screen theater. 372-2705.

Soda, Pizza & Ice Cream

➤ **Savor Monterey Market**, 1280 Del Monte Ave., offers a free 20 oz soda with purchase of any sandwich. Deli: 7am-6pm, Market 8am-8pm. Wine tasting noon-7pm. 642-0708.

➤ **The Santa Lucia Market**, 484 Washington St., serves up bite-size samples of free pizza every day, and free sushi samples Friday. 333-1111.

➤ Come into **Carmel Creamery**, 459 Alvarado St., for a free taste of their gourmet ice cream. You'll be so glad you did - it's out of this world! Open 11-8 daily (Fri-Sat, 11-10). 372-4720.

Public Marketplaces

■ **Monterey Bay Certified Farmers Market**, 2:30-6pm Thursdays at Monterey Peninsula College lower lot, 980 Fremont St. Certified organic produce, honey, bread, and much more. Free food samples. 728-5060.

Old Monterey Market Place

■ **Old Monterey Market Place**, Alvarado Street from Pearl to Del Monte, is lined with over 100 vendors every Tuesday, 4-7pm winter, 4-8pm summer. Go to the Market, it's a great way to get outdoors, learn about the city and its people, and be entertained at the same time. Free food samples, demonstrations and live entertainment. Featuring the Baker's Alley on Bonifacio Place with fresh breads, pastries, pizza. Fresh fish, flowers, produce, herbs, honey, arts, crafts, clothing, food to go. Children's events, Bookmobile 6-7 p.m. (first Tuesday at 6:15: stories, songs and finger plays for all ages). Santa visits early December. 655-2607.

■ **Monterey Fairgrounds Flea Market**, March to December, last weekend of month, 7am-4:30pm. $1 admission. 2004 Fairgrounds Rd. 372-5873.

Art Galleries

● **Monterey Museum of Art at Civic Center**, 559 Pacific St. Open Wed-Sat, 11am-5pm, Sun 1-4pm. Regular admission is $3 general, $1.50 students and military, under 12 free. Free to the public on third Thursdays, 5-7pm, with entertainment and refreshments. Features Monterey and California art, photography, Asian art and international folk art; lectures, films and workshops. The docent program teaches art enthusiasts how to guide children and adults through the exhibitions, plus take part in field trips and lectures. Call 372-5477. www.montereyart.org.

● **Eagles Eye Art Gallery**, Rm#24, in the basement of Herrman Hall, Naval Postgraduate School. Mon-Fri, 11:30am-3pm. Local artists. 372-3565.

● **Christopher Bell Studio**, 200 Alvarado St. 10am-7pm daily. Sculpture, fountains, other artworks. 649-0214.

● **Spa on the Plaza**, 201 Alvarado St. Local art. 7am-9pm daily. 647-9000.

● **Venture Gallery Coop**, 260 Alvarado St. 10am-6pm daily. 372-6279.

● **Alvarado Gallery**, Monterey Conference Center. Mon-Fri, 9:00am-4:30pm.

● **Burlwood Gallery of Monterey & LeBlanc Gallery-Metal Sculpture**, 271 Alvarado St., 10am-6pm daily. 372-7756. also at 1299 Del Monte Ave. 372-4008.

● **LALLApalooza**, 474 Alvarado St. Mon-Fri, 11am-10:30pm, Sat-Sun, 4pm-12:45am. Dan Koffman originals in a restaurant setting. 645-9036.

● **Levin Gallery Inc.**, 408 Calle Principal. 9:30am-5pm, or by appt. Mon-Fri. Photography - Westons, Ansel Adams and others. 649-1166.

● **A Woman's Wellspring**, 575 Calle Principal. Tues-Fri, 10am-6pm, Sat 9am-3pm. Women's art. 649-2320.

● **Morgan's Coffee & Tea**, 498 Washington St. Open daily, 6:30am-10pm. Call for calendar of events. Saturday events for children. 373-5601.

● **Monterey College of Law Art Gallery**, 404 W. Franklin. 373-3301.

● **Gold Leaf Frame Design**, 620 Munras Ave. Tues-Sat, 8am-5pm. Local artists. 649-3520.

● **Thomas Kinkade Gallery**, 692 Del Monte Shopping Center. Mon-Fri, 10am-9pm, Sat 10am-7pm, Sun 11am-5pm. 657-1210.

● **Marsh's Oriental Art & Antiques**, 599 Fremont St. Wed-Sat, 9:30am-4:30pm. 372-3547.

● **Monterey Peninsula College**, 980 Fremont. Art gallery showcases student art from the college and from local high schools. Call for dates and times of free art shows and receptions, 646-4200.

● **Monterey Museum of Art at La Mirada Adobe**, 720 Via Mirada off Fremont Blvd. Located in an adobe built in the 1800s, this museum is surrounded by rose gardens, the Peden Rhododendron Garden, picturesque stone walls, and a beautiful view of the bay. Museum is open Thurs-Sat, 11am-5pm; Sunday 1-4pm. Always free admission to the gardens. 1st Sundays are free to the public, guest musicians from 1:30-3:30pm, and complimentary hors d'oeuvres. 372-3689. Annual Monte Carlo Night, last Saturday in Feb, features gaming, live music, and silent auction; admission charge. 372-5477.

● **Mezzanine and Upstairs Galleries** at the Monterey Peninsula Airport Terminal, 200 Fred Kane Drive, 8am-10pm daily. 624-7910.

● **Upstairs Gallery**, Fisherman's Wharf. 12-5pm daily. Local artists and others. 372-1373.

● **Balesteri's Wharf Front**, #6 Fisherman's Wharf. 9:30-8pm daily. Amazing collection of wood and metal, natural handcrafts and art. 375-6411.

● **Sea N Tree Gallery**, #15 Fishermans Wharf. Antique reproductions, local art, sculpture, glass, handcrafts. 9am-9pm daily. 649-6222.

● **Santa Catalina School Gallery**, 1500 Mark Thomas Dr. Local artists. Mon-Fri, 9am-5pm, Sat-Sun, 11am-5pm. 655-9300.

Become a Docent at the Monterey Museum of Art

As a volunteer you will find it a rewarding experience. You may spend a few hours a month sharing the exhibitions with the visitors, providing groups of adults or school children with an appreciation of both fine and decorative arts, and personally experience a program of art education through visits to other museums and studios and in presentations by artists. You will also enjoy a wealth of activities available to you as a member of the Monterey Museum of Art.

If you are interested in this opportunity for voluntary service in one of the nation's premier small city art museums, please call the Museum at 372-5477.

Public Art in Monterey

Clockwise from top left, at the **DoubleTree, Portolá**, 1986, Fausto Blazques (b. 1944), bronze, dedicated by King Juan Carlos I of Spain in 1987; parking lot mural of jazz musicians, Washington St.; **Two Cougars**, 1910, Arthur Putnam (1873-1930), bronze cougars as top decoration on the Berthold Monument in the Friendly Garden; parking lot mural on Pacific St. of early Monterey buildings.

Not shown: bronze fountain at the Custom House Plaza, "The Planetary Tidepool," by Monterey Bay Sculptors.

This mural painted on the side of the Fire and Police Station building on Pacific Street at Madison depicts life in Monterey under Mexican rule and shows El Cuartel, the former military barracks and government headquarters. Painted by Monterey County teens in the "One Voice" Mural Project.

A Self-Guided Tour of Public Art

A colorful pamphlet prepared by Colton Hall Museum and Cultural Arts Commission, with the location of more public art displays in Monterey, is available at the Visitors Center, 380 Alvarado Street.

Monterey Public Library

Monterey Public Library, 625 Pacific St., 646-3932, Reference 646-3933, Bookmobile 646-3710. Mon-Thur 9am-9pm, Fri 9am-6pm, Sat 9am-5pm, Sun 1-5pm. California's first public library, it was organized as a subscription library in 1849. Free library card with proof of local residence. Check out <u>free books, art prints, magazines, CDs, books on tape, video and audio cassettes. Free access to the Internet</u> from five work-

stations. Visit the California Room for an extensive collection of Cali Comfortable chairs and a polite, knowledgeable staff. Web site a monterey.org/lib/lib.html has Kid's Page. Internet services or to Friends of the Monterey Public Library, contact Library Directo Simpson, 646-5601, e-mail: simpson@ci.monterey.ca.us.

Free Youth & Children's Programs

Pajama Storytime, last Tuesday, 7pm, ages 3-7 and family.
Baby & Me, last Friday 10am, babies to age 2, siblings 2-5, adults.
Old Monterey Marketplace - 6:15pm first Tuesday, look for Bookmobile on Alvarado Street at Pearl. All ages.
Preschool Storytimes, Tue-Wed, 11am, ages 3-5.
Toddler Storytime, Wed 10am, 2 year-olds. One child on one adult lap.

Other children and adult activities also, call 646-3949. Persons with disabilities who require assistance to attend programs, please contact the Administrative Office at 646-5603.

2000 Meeting Calendar for Literary Circle

It's a monthly book discussion group, not a club, facilitated by Stuart and Paula Walzer. <u>Free and newcomers are always welcome</u>. Meets Thursday, 7-8:45pm, in the Community Room, with these selections on these dates:

January 27	*The Hours* by Michael Cunningham and *Mrs. Dalloway* by Virginia Woolf
February 24	*The Reader* by Bernard Sclink
March 30	*The Turn of the Screw* by Henry James (offsite)
April 27	*National Poetry Month* – bring poem to read & discuss
May 25	*The Poisonwood Bible* by Barbara Kingsolver
June 29	*The House of Mirth* by Edith Wharton
Sept 28, Oct 26, Nov 30 – Titles not selected.	

All selections are currently in print and may be borrowed from the library or purchased at local book stores. Some selections may require special order, so contact your bookseller early. Call 646-3477 for books Sept-Nov.

Bookmobile Schedule, Tentative Jan-June 2000

Casanova/Oak Knoll: Casanova Plaza Apts.. (800 Casanova)...alternate Wed 10:30-11:30; Casanova/Oak Knoll Park Center Preschool...alternate Tues 11-11:30; Lerwick Dr...every Fri 4:30-5:45; Ralston Dr. near Casanova Ave...alternate Wed 5-5:45.

Deer Flats: Deer Forest Drive near Deer Flats Park...Thurs 4:45-5:45.

Del Monte Beach: Surf Way near Sea Foam...alternate Tues 4:45-5:45.

Downtown: Old Monterey Market Place, Alvarado St. at Pearl...every Tues 6-8pm. (Nov-Mar, 6-7pm only)

East Downtown/El Estero: Youth Center Preschool, Pearl St., between Camino El Estero and Camino Aguajito...alternate Fri 11-11:30.

Fisherman's Flats: Via Isola at Trapani Cir...every Thurs 3:30-4:30.

Glenwood Circle: Park Lane #200...every Fri 1-2:30; Glenwood Cir.... near Kimberly Place #300...alternate Sat 1:45-2:30.

La Mesa Village: Leahy Rd., between Shubrick and tennis courts...every Wed 1-4:15.

Monte Vista: Monte Vista Center...alternate Sat 11:15-12; Mar Vista Dr. between Via Gayuba & Toda Vista...alternate Fri 3-4.

Montecito: Hannon St. at Montecito Ave...alternate Tues 4:45-5:45; Montecito Pk., Montecito Ave., between Dela Vina and Ramona...alternate Sat 11:15-12:15.

New Monterey:

Archer Park, on McClellan St. near Archer...alternate Fri 3-4

Archer Park Preschool...alternate Tues 11-11:30

Bay View School...alternate Tues 11:35-12:30

Grace St. between Withers & David...alternate Wed 5-5:45

Hilltop Park Center, 871 Jessie, at Withers...every Tues 3:15-4:15

Hilltop Park Preschool...alternate Fri 11-11:30

Oak Newton Park on Newton St. at McClellan...alternate Sat 3-3:45

Oak Grove: 2nd St. at Park Ave. by El Estero Apts...alternate Sat 2:45-3:45

Old Town: Portola Vista Apts, Del Monte between Pacific and Van Buren...alternate Wed 10:30-11:30.

Villa Del Monte: Encina Ave., between Palo Verde & Del Robles...alternate Sat 1:30-2:15.

For more information, exact dates of alternating stops (or a complete daily schedule), or to request a particular item, call 646-3710.

Local Bookstores

● **The Book Tree.** Books of uncommon interest for discerning readers...local authors. Mon-Fri 10am-5:30pm, Sat 10am-2pm. 118 Webster St. 373-0228.

● **Monterey Bible Bookstore.** Oldest bookstore on the Monterey Peninsula, founded in 1951. Providing Bibles, books, music, and gift items. MST bus passes. Mon-Sat 10am-5:30pm. 487 Alvarado St. 375-6487.

● **Old Monterey Book Co.** Wed-Sat 11am-5pm. 136 Bonifacio Place. e-mail: montbook@mbay.net. 372-3111.

● **The Bookhaven.** 10am-10pm daily. Book searches, storytelling, reading and study group access. 559 Tyler St. 333-0383.

● **Waldenbooks Kids.** 222 Del Monte Center. Mon-Thurs, Sat, 10-9, Fri 10-10, Sun 10-6. 373-0987.

● **Bay Books.** Free lectures, bookclub, speakers and events regularly scheduled. Call for dates and times. Coffeehouse with comfortable browsing, large selection and friendly service. Locally-baked cakes, muffins and freshly-roasted coffees and espresso. Sun-Thurs 7:30am-10pm, Fri-Sat 7:30am-11pm. 316 Alvarado. 375-1855.

● **Monterey Institute of International Studies Book Store.** Mon-Fri 8:30-5, Sat 10-2. 434 Pacific Street, 647-8288. Free lectures; call 647-4100.

Lectures, Classes, Books

● Free "Ark for Kids", music, crafts, games plus dinner, ages 4-11, Tues 6-7:45pm. **Monterey United Methodist Church**, Soledad Dr. 375-8285.

● **Gentrain Society of the Monterey Peninsula** presents speakers at 1:30 first and third Wed, Lecture Forum 102, MPC. Free. 373-7254.

● Free classes for adults at **Monterey Adult School.** Call 899-1615.

● **Monterey College of Law**, 404 W. Franklin Street, presents free lectures. Call for dates and times, 373-3301.

● **MPC** offers free gardening classes in various communities around the county for anyone age 21 and older. For information, call 646-4058.

➤ **Own-A-Book Annual Book Drive**, sponsored by **The Herald** each November. Donate your clean, gently-read books for children from birth to 14 years. Call 649-4409 for drop off points, to participate, or be a recipient.

➤ **Book Club Resources**: **AARP**'s "Book Talk" is at www.aarp.org/booktalk. **Oprah's Book Club** is at www.oprah.com/bookclub/bookclub.html. And **Great Books Foundation** is at www.greatbooks.org.

➤ **National Family Literacy Day** is Nov 1. Call 1-877-326-5481 to learn how to enroll or volunteer for literacy programs year around. www.famlit.org.

KUSP 88.9 FM

National Public Radio
for the Central Coast

Sunnyvale

Saratoga

Santa Clara

npr SM

MORNING EDITION

Felton

Scotts Valley

Santa Cruz

FRESH AIR WITH TERRY GROSS

Morgan Hill

Capitola

ALL THINGS CONSIDERED

Aptos

Gilroy

THIS AMERICAN LIFE

Watsonville

San Juan Bautista

CAR TALK

Castroville

WEEKEND EDITION

Marina

Hollister

and

Seaside

more

Carmel

Monterey

CLASSICAL MUSIC

Salinas

WORLD MUSIC

Highlands

Carmel Velley

JAZZ

Gonzales

BLUES

Soledad

CELTIC

Palo Colorado
Canyon

LOCAL PUBLIC AFFAIRS

Greenfield

For a FREE Program Guide CALL
831-476-2800 or 1-800-655-KUSP

Big Sur

88.9 FM throughout Santa Cruz, Monterey and San Benito counties.
Hollister 89.1 • Downtown Santa Cruz 89.3 • Los Gatos/Saratoga 90.3
Palo Colorado Canyon 91.3 • Big Sur Coast 105.9
TCI cable Santa Cruz 88.7 • AT&T cable Monterey 91.3   King City

Calendar of Events

Year 2000 dates shown. Updates at www.montereycountyguide.com.
Please call in advance to verify as information is subject to change.

JANUARY

January   DINE OUT FOR DAFFODILS $$
30+ restaurants will donate a portion of their sales to benefit local cancer patients. Call 372-4521 for list.

January 14-30   WHALEFEST 2000   FREE+$$
Celebrate as gray whales take their annual migration from Alaska to Baja California and back. An estimated 15,000 to 20,000 whales pass by Monterey Bay, south and northbound. Pick up your passport and schedule of Whalefest 1999 events at the Monterey Association of Cultural Institutions (MACI) booth in Custom House Plaza on Saturday the 15th at 10am. Also Saturday, free educational and entertaining hands-on exhibits and activities related to whales, continuous live music, cool whale stuff; free admission to the Maritime Museum. Live Dixieland music at the plaza throughout the day and continuous live music at Fisherman's Wharf. California Gray Whale Migration continues through March. 372-2203, 644-7588. www.monterey.com.

January 20-23   MONTEREY SWINGFEST $$
Swing dance workshops, contest and open dancing. 805-937-1574.

FEBRUARY

February 12   A DAY OF ROMANCE IN OLD MONTEREY $$
10am-2pm. Experience four living history reenactments of love stories in Monterey State Historic Park's most renowned homes - Stevenson, Larkin House, Diaz Adobe and Cooper-Molera Adobe. Food, music and period dances. 647-6204. www.mbay.net/~mshp.

February 12-13   A WHALE OF AN ART SHOW   FREE
Contemporary arts and crafts, 10-5pm at Custom House Plaza, near Fisherman's Wharf. Classical music entertainment. Gourmet coffee, fine paintings, handmade paper, jewelry, ceramics, wood, clothing, accessories, photography. 625-0931.

February 26   JOHN STEINBECK'S BIRTHDAY PARTY   FREE+$$
Free exhibits, entertainment, music and lectures at the Aquarium and free birthday cake at the rail car on the recreation trail, near the carousel. Fee events include walking tours of Cannery Row and Doc Ricketts Lab and a bus tour of Steinbeck country in Salinas. 372-8512, fax 375-4982.

February 26-27   EAST OF EDEN CAT SHOW $$
Annual feline show in the Salinas Room (agriculture building) at the Monterey Fairgrounds. 150+ felines. $5 general, $3 seniors, $2 children/students. 372-7018. Benefits the Monterey County SPCA.

MARCH

March   MONTE CARLO NIGHT $$
Gaming to benefit the Monterey Museum of Art. 372-5477.

March 2-5   **DIXIELAND MONTEREY**   **FREE+$$**
20 years of national and international bands of traditional Dixieland jazz. Early
Bird Dance Party at DoubleTree on the 2nd. Events all weekend at Fisherman's
Wharf, Monterey Conference Center and the DoubleTree. 443-5260, 888-349-
6879. www.dixiejazz.com/monterey.html.

March 5-7   ART, CRAFTS, & ALL THAT DIXIELAND JAZZ   FREE
Eighty artists and crafts people with paper art, paintings, photography, stone-
ware, leather, sculpture in glass, metal and wood, wearable art, jewelry, lamps,
garden accessories, toys. Custom House Plaza, near Fisherman's Wharf, 10am-
5pm. Carmel Art Guild, www.dixiejazz/monterey.html, 625-0931.

March 8   COLTON HALL BIRTHDAY   FREE
Living history, birthday cake and punch. Open House 2-4pm at Colton Hall Mu-
seum, Pacific Street between Madison and Jefferson. 646-5640.

March 18   SEA OTTER CLASSIC CYCLING FESTIVAL   FREE
Road cycling and mountain biking. $6 per vehicle park entrance fee. Family ac-
tivities include interactive games, a huge expo and great food. Saturday ride 10
miles through the rolling green, wildflower covered hills. Enjoy refreshment stops
and the chance to win great prizes. Laguna Seca, Highway 68, east of Monterey.
www.seaotter.org. 373-1839, fax 373-1089, 650-306-1414.

March 18   CUTTING DAY AT FRIENDLY PLAZA   FREE
44th Annual. Plants and cuttings from the historic garden. Come early!

March 23   TASTE OF OLD MONTEREY $$
4-9pm at Ferrante's in the Marriott. Food and entertainment; a fun-filled epicu-
rean extravaganza of downtown's international delights. Sponsored by The Old
Monterey Business Assn., 655-8070.

March 25-26   MONTEREY BAY SPRING FAIRE   FREE
Crafts faire, live Pacific Repertory Theatre, Actors-in-the-Adobes, and a Human
Chess Game with a theme. Custom House Plaza. www.pacrep.org, 622-0700.

March 25-26   SPRING HOME SHOW $$
New items for the home: roofing, flooring, security systems, patios, sunrooms,
spas, saunas, tile, marble, custom closets. Wildlife education program and prod-
uct demonstrations. Barbecue, live entertainment. Admission $3, children under
12 free. Sat 10am-6pm, Sun 10am-5pm. Monterey Fairgrounds. 800-237-0551.

March 30-April 2   MONTEREY WINE FESTIVAL $$
24th Annual. Various Peninsula locations. Free cooking demonstrations with the
finest chefs working their culinary magic. Call for locations and times. "New Release" Party, wine tasting, big bottle auction, wine brunch, workshops. Tickets
from $10-$150. 800/656-4282, 656-9463, fax 649-4124, www.montereywine.com.
More wine info: www.wine.brats.org/

APRIL

April 1   BABY AND CHILD FAIRE $$
Monterey County Fairgrounds. Call for more information, 375-1953.

April 7-9   HIGH SCHOOL JAZZ COMPETITION   FREE
30th Annual Monterey Jazz Festival High School Jazz Competition at the Fair-
grounds, starting Fri at 8pm; 2 performances each, Sat & Sun. 373-3366.

April 13-15   FOUNDATION OF AM SHOW HORSE   FREE+$$
Monterey County Fairgrounds. lower grounds. 805-969-9812

April 15   **HISTORIC ADOBES TOUR**   **FREE+$$**
53rd Annual event in the historic downtown adobes, 12am-7pm. Living history, food, entertainment. FREE to children under 16, adults $10. Tickets at Bay Books, Cooper Store, Maritime Museum. Monterey History and Art Assn, 372-2608.

April 15-16   **SEAFOOD AND MUSIC FESTIVAL**   **FREE**
Fresh seafood, live music and crafts. Washington St, Del Monte to Pearl. 10am-5pm. Old Monterey Business Assn., 655-8070.

April 20   **COASTAL COUNTRY DANCING**   **$$**
Dance workshops, contest and open dancing at the Hyatt. 805-937-1574.

April 22   **EARTH DAY**   **FREE**
Various activities in Monterey County. Watch newspapers and support the earth.

April 22   **EASTER EGG HUNT**   **FREE**
Easter Saturday hunt for pre-schoolers through third graders. Bring a basket and look for over 5,000 eggs and 100 golden prize eggs. 10am. Frank Sollecito Ballpark, 777 Pearl St., 646-3866.

April 22-28   **NATIONAL TV TURNOFF WEEK**   **FREE**
Stop by the Monterey Public Library for free stickers, bookmarks, etc. 646-3934.

April 29   **INTERNATIONAL DAY**   **FREE**
Graduate students from around the world present food, dancing, crafts and educational displays. Naval Postgraduate School. 12-4pm. 656-2186.

MAY

May   **ANNUAL WAG 'N WALK**   **Spectators FREE**
Breakwater Cove. Watch people with their leashed dogs walk the 2 to 4 mile course along the Recreational Trail at Shoreline Park. Benefit for the SPCA. $50 pledge to walk. 373-2631 ext. 231, 422-4721 ext. 223.

May   **ART IN THE GARDENS**   **FREE+$$**
At La Mirada. Sumptuous food, guest speakers, artists painting and selling works of art amidst La Mirada's exquisite garden. Call for details, 372-5477.

May   **STUDENT ART MONTH**   **FREE+$$**
Museum of Art, 559 Pacific Street, exhibits young artists in all media–photography, paintings, sculpture. Artists from over 25 county middle schools. 372-5477.

May thru June   **PACIFIC RIM SCULPTURE SHOW**   **FREE**
In the Cooper-Molera garden. Exhibit of contemporary sculpture from the Pacific Rim Sculpture Group. An interesting blend of the old with the new. 649-7118.

May thru Sept   **HISTORIC GARDEN TOURS**   **$$**
$2 to tour the gardens learn about plant lore, identification and uses at the Cooper-Molera, Stevenson House and Larkin House. Tues-Sat, 1pm. 647-6204.

May 5   **COOPER-MOLERA ADOBE**   **Seniors FREE**
All adobes will be open free to Seniors 55+. Refreshments will be served at Cooper-Molera, 11am-1pm. 525 Polk St. 649-7118.

May 13   **GARDEN DAY AT COOPER-MOLERA ADOBE**   **FREE**
Free refreshments and an opportunity to see the adobe gardens in full bloom and to buy cuttings from the garden. 9am-1pm. Bring containers and any plants, bulbs or softwood cuttings to exchange. Free seedling trees from the Monterey Parks Dept., 525 Polk St., 649-7118.

May 13-14   SCOTTISH/IRISH FESTIVAL AND GAMES   FREE+$$
33rd Annual. Scottish athletic events, historical reenactments, Highland & Irish
step dancing, Celtic music, crafts, food, drinks and more! Tickets $9-$14. Monterey
Fairgrounds. Free Caber Parade at 5:30pm, Friday, May 12, on Ocean Ave. at
Devendorf Park, Carmel. Celtic Concert Friday, too. Call for time and place. http:/
/www.Montereyscotgames.com. 484-0111, 626-3551, 484-2834.

May 19-21   MONTEREY SPRING HORSE SHOW   FREE
Monterey County Fairgrounds. lower grounds. Jumping, roping, team penning,
barrel racing, music, cowboy poetry, bbq, country dancing. 625-3333.

May 20-21   NASCAR WINSTON WEST SERIES $$
Laguna Seca Raceway. Order tickets on-line at www.laguna-seca.com.

May 27-28   GREAT MONTEREY SQUID FESTIVAL   FREE+$$
Entertainment, educational displays, cooking demonstrations, and arts and crafts.
Call for prices. Monterey County Fairgrounds. 649-6544. www.montereysquid.com

May 29   CONCERTS ON THE LAWN   FREE
Concert at 2pm by the Monterey Bay Symphony at the Naval Postgraduate School.
Public is also invited to the rehearsals at 10 and 12. Free tours of the former Del
Monte Hotel and Arizona Cactus Garden. Ice cream and hats for sale. 656-3346.

JUNE

June   TALL SHIPS IN THE HARBOR   FREE+$$
Due to retrofitting, Tall Ships may not visit the Monterey harbor in 2000. Call for
update and Santa Cruz dates, Nautical Heritage Society, 800-432-2201.

June-July   LOS NIÑOS DE MONTEREY   FREE
Week long sessions for school children at the Cooper-Molera. 649-7118.

June 3   MONTEREY MERIENDA $$
Monterey History & Art Assn. celebrates founding of Monterey in 1770. 372-2608.

June 9-11   SIDEWALK FINE ARTS FESTIVAL   FREE
Sidewalk Show on Alvarado Street. 10am-5pm. Handcrafted ceramics, paintings
and sculpture. Old Monterey Business Assn., 655-8070.

June 10   CHOCOLATE ABALONE DIVE   Spectators FREE
Watch divers search for 500 numbered chocolate abalone and win prizes. Break-
water Cove. Diver entry fees: $20-$23. 375-1933.

June 17   ROCK AND ART FESTIVAL $$
Monterey County Fairgrounds. Call for more details, 372-5863.

June 23-25   MONTEREY BAY BLUES FESTIVAL   FREE+$$
Continuous entertainment from 10:30am to 10:30pm at Monterey Fairgrounds.
Merchandise booths and great food. For more information, call Bonnie Adams at
394-2652. Tickets $20 to $100 for a 3 day festival pass. FREE Pre-Blues Festi-
val in early June at local club, call 649-6544.

June 23-25   "SWING BY THE SEA" $$
Swing dance workshops, contest and open dancing at the Hyatt. 805-937-1574.

JULY

July   CALIFORNIA BREWMASTERS' CLASSIC $$
Restaurants and caterers provide gourmet food and nonalcoholic beverages.

More than twenty breweries pour microbrews and answer questions. Tasting until 9:30pm, complimentary pilsner glass to first 600 arrivals. Dance, silent auction, gifts. 6:30pm at DoubleTree Hotel. Benefit for KAZU Public Radio. 375-7275.

July   JUNIOR OLYMPIC TRACK AND FIELD Spectators FREE
Parade at 10am followed by track and field events and a traditional awards ceremony with medals, ribbons and gold certificates for the Playground Program children, ages 5-14. Ice cream bars at the end for everyone! Monterey High Football Stadium at the end of Larkin Street. 646-3866.

July 1-2   CRAFTS FAIRE   FREE
Crafts faire, live Pacific Repertory Theatre, Actors-in-the-Adobes, and a Human Chess Game with a theme. Custom House Plaza. www.pacrep.org, 622-0700.

July 1-23   THEATREFEST   FREE
17th Annual event over four weekends. Pacific Repertory Theatre's annual gift to the communities of the Central Coast includes Fairy Tales Theatre, Actors in the Adobes, Arts & Crafts, Music, Human Chess Game, International Foods at Custom House Plaza. Support their Theatre Season March-October at the Golden Bough, Circle Theatre and Forest Theatre. Box office 622-0700. www.pacrep.org.

July 3   CONCERT ON THE LAWN SERIES   FREE
Free concert at 2pm by the Monterey Bay Symphony at the Naval Postgraduate School. Free tours of the former Del Monte Hotel and Arizona Cactus Garden. Bring a picnic lunch; ice cream and hats for sale. 656-2023.

July 4   ANNUAL SALMON DERBY   FREE+$$
Monterey Bay Salmon & Trout Project, Monterey Bay Veterans, noon-9pm. Cash & raffle prizes. Open to the public; stay to watch the fireworks from the Breakwater Cove Marina. Volunteers are always needed to help with the physically-challenged at Salmon Derby, Rock Cod Derby, and at Laguna Seca. John, 646-8324.

July 4   FOURTH OF JULY CELEBRATIONS   FREE
After military units raise American flags in downtown Monterey, the annual parade will run from 10-11am on Alvarado Street and Calle Principal. Alcohol-free Big Little Backyard Barbecue at 11am-5pm at City Hall, Pacific Street at Madison. Nonstop music, games, entertainment. Bring picnic or purchase food from nonprofit vendors. 20 minute fireworks at 9:15pm off Commercial Wharf#2. Choreographed to music on KWAV 97FM. 646-3866, 646-3427. Volunteers needed, call 646-3719.

July 4   7TH ANNUAL LIVING HISTORY FESTIVAL   FREE+$$
Features and old fashioned 4th of July with events sponsored by the State of California. Activities include children's games and crafts from the 1840s, and guided tours inside historic buildings, where people from the past will make history come alive. Tickets are limited. 647-6204. www.mbay.net/~mshp/

July 5   MONTEREY BEACH CLEANUP   FREE
Time to clean the beach again. Meet at 9am at Monterey Beach near Wharf#2. Call to register or just show up. 646-3719.

July 7-9   HONDA CHALLENGE $$
AMA National Superbike Series at Laguna Seca. 648-5111, 1-800-327-SECA.

July 8   SLOAT'S LANDING   FREE
Ceremony commemorating the landing of Commodore Sloat in Monterey, and the U.S. claiming of California from Mexico. Presidio of Monterey. Sponsored by the Monterey History and Art Assn. 372-2608, 373-2469.

July 22-23   **CRAFTS FAIRE**   **FREE**
Crafts faire, live Pacific Repertory Theatre, Actors-in-the-Adobes, and a Human
Chess Game with a theme. Custom House Plaza. www.pacrep.org, 622-0700.

July 28-30   **MONTEREY NATIONAL HORSE SHOW**   **FREE**
Jumping, roping, team penning, barrel racing, stock horse class and cutting class,
musical entertainment, cowboy poetry, barbecue, country-western dance, and
silent auction. Pattee Arena at the Monterey Fairgrounds, 372-5863, 769-9255.

AUGUST

August   **GREAT TOMATO CONTEST AND PARTY**   **FREE**
Vote on the best tomatoes around. Last year over 150 varieties were represented.
3-7pm. Monterey Fairgrounds, 375-4505.

August   **TURKISH ARTS & CULTURE FESTIVAL**   **FREE**
Turkish art, crafts, music, folk and belly dancing, children's activities. Sat-Sun
11am-6pm. Festival free, post festival concert/dance $15-$20. Custom House
Plaza. www.turkiye.net. 646-1916.

August 12-13   **CELEBRATION SIDEWALK SALE**   **FREE**
Arts, handmade crafts and downtown merchants. 10m-5pm on Alvarado & Mall.
655-8070.

August 15-20   **MONTEREY COUNTY FAIR**   **FREE+$$**
Food, entertainment, competitive and commercial exhibits, livestock, floriculture,
4-H, carnival rides and more. Specials and discounts include:

● Tues. 15th - $1 off admission, 12-1pm, with canned food donation.

● Tues. 15th - Senior's Day. 65+, $1 off admission & special activities.

● Wed. 16th - Kids under 12 admitted free to enjoy a variety of activities and
entertainment designed just for them at Munchkin Meadows, with fun and safe
rides, magic shows, singalongs, hands-on entertainment.

● Thurs. 17th - Special Friends' Day for individuals faced with physical and mental
challenges. They are invited to enjoy the fair with free admission, 372-5863.

● Free admission every day for those in military uniforms.

● $1 and $3 off coupons available at local bookstores and merchants.

● The Fair Xpress Bus Tour brings
performers to cities two days before
the Fair; including: Goldie the Scare-
crow, Elvis and McGruff the Crime
Dog. They entertain onlookers and
hand out Fair admission discount
coupons. For locations, 372-5863.
Craig Riddell, publicist, at right.

● Free shuttle service, provided by
MST, is available from the Del Monte
Shopping Center parking lot.

● Fair hours: Tue-Fri, noon-11pm, Sat 10am-11pm, Sun 10am-10pm.
www.montereycountyfair.com. 372-5863. See you at the Fair!

August 18-19   MONTEREY SPORTS CAR AUCTION $$
Cars on display in the Custom House Plaza at noon on both days. Open to the public with an entrance fee. Auction at the DoubleTree Hotel at Fisherman's Wharf. Call for information, 800/211-4371.

August 18-20   HISTORIC AUTOMOBILE RACES $$
Races for seven groups, broken down by years (pre-1928 sport and racing cars through 1981 championship cars). 400 historic racing Ferraris, Alfa Romeos, Porsches and Cobras. Tickets $25-$40. Volunteer opportunities. Laguna Seca on Highway 68. www.laguna-seca.com. 800/327-SECA.

August 26   R.L.S. ANNIVERSARY   FREE
Storytelling, Scottish music, Stevenson House tours and un-birthday cake with costumed docents, actors, writers, musicians and refreshments. Sponsored by the California State Parks, the Robert Louis Stevenson Club of Monterey and the Old Monterey Preservation Society. Stevenson House, 530 Houston St. Call for times and to make reservations for these one0half hour tours, 649-7118.

SEPTEMBER

September   DISCOVERY DAY   FREE
Hands-on science activities for youth of all ages, 10am-3pm at the Naval Postgraduate School. Call for date. 656-3346.

September 2-3   ANNUAL GREEK FESTIVAL   FREE
Live traditional music and costumed dancing. Food booths will serve Greek salads, mousaka, lamb and beef gyros, barbecued chicken, baklava and drinks. Arts and crafts, children's games (a mini-carousel), drawing. Benefit for building of a new church and other charities. Sat-Sun, 11am-7pm, Mon 11am-4pm, Custom House Plaza. Presented by Saint John the Baptist Greek Orthodox Church of Monterey County, 424-4434.

September 2-3   6TH ANNUAL REGGAEFEST $$
Reggae music, food and crafts. 10am-10pm. Children 10 and under free with paid adult. Monterey Fairgrounds. Information: 394-6534. Tickets 372-5863.

September 2-4   PERUVIAN PASO HORSE SHOW   FREE
"A Rolls Royce Ride, a Really Classy Horse Show." Sat-Sun 9am-5pm. Special evening performance Sunday 6:30-9pm: champagne challenge, costumes, special demonstrations. Monterey Fairgrounds. 484-2849.

September 4   CONCERT ON THE LAWN SERIES   FREE
Concert by Monterey Bay Symphony at Naval Postgraduate School at 2pm. Come early and bring a picnic lunch. Orchestra rehearsal at 1pm is open to the public. Free tours of the former Del Monte Hotel and Arizona Cactus Garden. 656-2023.

September State Historic Park Docent Training Class

Four Wednesday evenings and two Saturdays, 10am-1pm. Topics include California history, Monterey's historic buildings and gardens, tour techniques and presentation skills, living history, period clothing, and much more. Call 647-6204 for dates, information and to receive an application.

September 8-10   GRAND PRIX OF MONTEREY $$
Featuring the Shell 300 CART. FedEx Championship Series. Volunteer opportu-
nities. Laguna Seca Raceway. www.laguna-seca.com. 800/327-SECA.

September 9-10   FESTA ITALIA SANTA ROSALIA   FREE
To honor fishermen of this community and to keep the Italian culture alive. Pro-
cession from San Carlos Cathedral through downtown Monterey to Custom House
Plaza with children dressed in colorful Italian traditional dress, a float carrying
Santa Rosalia, queen and princesses, Grand Marshall and wife, Monterey High
School Band, Peace Makers Drill Team, Presidio color guard. 2 day National
Bocce Ball Tournament with 60 teams and a $3,000 prize. Italian food booths,
dancers doing traditional Italian dances and arts and crafts fair. Free admission
to the Maritime Museum. Blessing of the Fleet. Sat-Sun, 10am-5pm. 49-6544.

September 15-17   MONTEREY JAZZ FESTIVAL   FREE+$$
The longest continuously running jazz festival in the world. 43rd year. 6pm-mid-
night Friday, 12:30pm to midnight Saturday, and noon-midnight Sunday. Monterey
Fairgrounds. www.montereyjazzfestival.org. 373-3366, 372-5863, 800-307-3378.
Tickets $12-$27. Free jazz around town.

September 16   COASTAL CLEANUP   FREE
16th Annual. You've been enjoying those free beaches all year and now's the
time to show your appreciation, 9am-noon. Ask Jean Scott about the Adopt-A-
Beach Program. Call 384-0617 for locations.

September 21   INTERNATIONAL DAY OF PEACE   FREE
U.N. Declaration–watch the newspapers for opportunities to celebrate peace with
others in the community and around the world. Dan Koffman, 375-2026.

Sept 22-Oct 1 1ST ANNUAL MONTEREY BAY INT'L FILM FESTIVAL $$
Ambitious plan to present 135+ independent films on a dozen screens over a 10-
day period; workshops, lectures, panel discussions, parties. www.MBIFF.org

September 22-24   CHERRY'S JUBILEE   FREE+$$
Restored hotrod and other classic car owners get together to celebrate with par-
ties, dancing, food and souvenir booths. Free viewing: More than 800 restored
classic cars cruise Monterey and settle on Cannery Row for a "Show and Shine"
Friday 5-10pm; cars parade and are judged for "People's Choice Awards" at
Steinbeck Plaza, with live blues band. Saturday and Sunday the cars cruise the
track at Laguna Seca. The annual event is a fund-raiser for the Salinas Valley
Memorial Hospital. Laguna Seca is free to children younger than 6, otherwise $8
for teens and adults, seniors $5, and $2 children 6-12. Volunteer opportunities.
Laguna Seca Recreation Area, Highway 68. www.laguna-seca.com. 759-1836.

Sept 23-24   C.V. GEM & MINERAL SHOW & SALE   FREE+$$
Monterey County Fairgrounds. Call for more information, 384-8815.

OCTOBER

October   FAMILY FUN DAY   FREE
Entertainment, theater, martial arts, gymnastics, dance and computer design
throughout the day. Hands-on activities for children, cultural and dramatic pre-
sentations, prizes every hour, food available. MPC, 980 Fremont.646-3760. Spon-
sored by Community of Caring Monterey Peninsula, dedicated to improving life.

October 6   JOHN COOPER LANG DAY   FREE
Special day for the disabled, honoring John, a descendant of Capt. John Rogers
Cooper, the New England sea captain who first occupied the Cooper-Molera
Adobe in 1827. Tour at 11am. Public invited to picnic & enjoy gardens. 647-6204.

October 7   **MCAP AIDS WALK**   **Spectators FREE**
Registration-breakfast at 8:30am at Monterey High School (Hermann Drive). Walk through downtown, along the recreation trail to Lovers Point in Pacific Grove for awards at 11:30. Food, music, prizes, massages, children's activities. Return shuttles available. 394-4747. Also in Santa Cruz: start in San Lorenzo Park, circular route along West Cliff Drive and return to the park, 408/427-3900.

October 13   **CALIFORNIA CONSTITUTION DAY**   **FREE**
Anniversary Celebration of California's 1849 Constitution, presented by City of Monterey, Colton Hall Museum, and Cultural Arts Commission. Reenactment by local thespians. Reception and refreshments. 6pm at Colton Hall Museum on Pacific Street. Reservations required. 646-5640.

October 13-15   **VISA SPORTS CAR CHAMPIONSHIPS**   **$$**
American le Mans Series, Laguna Seca Raceway. 1-800-327-SECA.

October 21-22   **ROTA PSYCHIC FAIR**   **$$**
10am-6pm at Monterey Peninsula College, 980 Fremont St. Psychics, healers, readers, music, merchandise. 648-1003. www.voyagertarot.com.

October 21-22   **FALL HOME SHOW**   **$$**
New items for the home: roofing, flooring, security systems, patios, sunrooms, spas, saunas, tile, marble, custom closets. Wildlife education program and product demonstrations. Barbecue, live entertainment. Admission $3, <u>children under 12 free</u>. Sat 10am-6pm, Sun 10am-5pm. Monterey Fairgrounds. 800-237-0551.

October 28   **MAKE A DIFFERENCE DAY**   **FREE**
One-day community service project for local residents to help clean up, repair city parks and enjoy a free picnic. Register by calling the city volunteer program at 646-3719. Walk-in registration on the day will also be accepted. 9am-1pm. For other communities, call 800/776-9176. Always 4th Saturday in October.

October 31   **HALLOWEEN ACTIVITIES**   **FREE**
Del Monte Shopping Center, Highway 1 at Munras, costumed kids can Trick or Treat from 4-6pm. Chris, 373-2705.

Self-guided tours of **El Encinal Cemetery**, Fremont Blvd. and Aquajito Blvd. Brochures will be available from 8am-4pm that day at the office between Pearl and Fremont at El Estero. Look for headstones of Ed Ricketts, Flora Adams (Woods), cartoonist Jimmy Hatlo, actor Steve Cochran. 646-3864.

The **Monterey Police Department**, 351 Madison, and three **Fire Departments**: Pacific and Madison Streets, 500 block of Hawthorne, Dela Vina & Montecito, will give away 22" glow-in-the-dark bands from 3:30pm until they run out. Call School Resource Officer Ken Shen, 646-3808.

NOVEMBER

November   **SOUTHWESTERN INDIAN SHOW**   **FREE**
Jewelry, sand paintings, sculptures, kachinas, baskets, prints, art, rugs, pottery, gift items. Fri 5-8pm, Sat 11am-7pm, Sun 11am-5pm. Monterey Fairgrounds. 372-5863.

November 4-5   **CRAFTS FAIRE**   **FREE**
Crafts faire, Custom House Plaza. www.pacrep.org, 622-0700.

November 5   **BOOK FESTIVAL**   **$$**
4th Annual Meet authors, attend seminars, enjoy live music at the Fairgrounds. 10am-6pm. 375-1855, 624-1803.

November 11   VETERAN'S DAY ACTIVITIES   FREE
Marine Corps Detachment at the Presidio of Monterey will hold a U.S. Marine Corps Birthday Proclamation ceremony at 10am at Custom House Plaza. A pass in review and retreat ceremony at 4:15 at the Presidio of Monterey's Soldiers Field will honor U.S. veterans of all wars. An open house at the Edge Club, Bldg. 221 on Patton Ave. The public is invited to attend.

November 25   THANKSGIVING COMMUNITY DINNER   FREE
Thanksgiving Day Dinner for anyone who doesn't want to be alone on the holiday. Or help serve Thanksgiving dinner to those in need. Call ahead or just show up. Monterey Fairgrounds. 372-5863.

DECEMBER

December   ARTISTS' MINIATURES   FREE+$$
Large body of small scale works–collage, oils, watercolors, sculpture, pen and ink–represent artists from around the county. Each miniature will have its own drawing. Patrons indicate the artist of their choice. Call 372-5477.

December   HOLIDAY HELPERS CAMPAIGN
5th annual. Volunteers help grant special wishes from local seniors through Christmas Day. Sponsored by Community Care, Magic 63 radio and KION Channel 46. To receive list of wishes you can help fulfill, call Wendy at 633-4444.

December 1   MONTEREY TREE LIGHTING CEREMONY   FREE
Apple cider and refreshments are served after choral groups and bands and the 35' live fir tree is lighted. Santa Claus will be there to greet the children. In case of rain, ceremony will be held inside Colton Hall. 6:30-8pm, Colton Hall Museum, 351 Pacific Ave., 646-3866.

December 3   HOLIDAY ARTS & CRAFTS FESTIVAL   FREE
Entertainment, local artists and vendors, refreshments, a visit from Santa. 10am-4pm, Monterey Sports Center Gymnasium, 301 E. Franklin St. Monterey Recreation and Community Services Department. 646-3866.

December 7, 9   CHRISTMAS IN THE ADOBES $$
Candlelight luminaria, period decorations, musical entertainment, costumed volunteers, variety of refreshments in more than 20 adobes. Docents and military guard await your pleasure, 5-9pm. Tickets at Cooper-Molera store and Bay Books. Tickets are limited and reservations are encouraged. www.mbay.net/~mshp. 649-7118 (or 647-6226 after Oct. 15).

December 8-10 MONTEREY COWBOY POETRY & MUSIC $$
2nd Annual. Poetry, songs, storytelling by the best. 372-8520. www.cowboyjack.com.

Dec 8-31   SPECIAL CHRISTMAS FESTIVITIES $$
Free for members and children under 12, $3 for nonmembers. Special exhibitions, miniature works of art, and decorated trees. Monterey Museum of Art, 599 Pacific Ave., 372-5477.

December 8   LA POSADA   FREE
A traditional Christmas candlelight parade which reenacts the search of Mary and Joseph for lodging via the Larkin House, Stokes Adobe and Colton Hall. 6:30pm. at the Monterey Conference Center. For the whole family. Bring a candle or flashlight, sing Posada songs and Spanish Christmas carols. 646-3866.

December 9   **SANTA'S ARRIVAL**   **FREE**
Visits and activity on Alvarado Street at the Old Monterey Market Place, 5pm.
Free pictures with Santa, 5-7pm, by Green's Camera.

December 10   **"BRIGHTEN THE HARBOR"**   **Spectators FREE**
Lighted boat parade begins at 5pm from the U.S. Coast Guard Pier, to Lovers
Point and returning to the Monterey Harbor. Free to watchers on shore or in
boats, $25 entry per boat entry; forms at the Harbormaster's office, or call 645-
1980. Proceeds to the Monterey Peninsula Youth Sailing Foundation. Refreshments and trophies afterwards at the pier. Drawings for prizes. 393-0303.

December 25   **CHRISTMAS COMMUNITY DINNER**   **FREE**
Noon-3pm, everyone is welcome, sponsored by community businesses and individuals. Free food, entertainment and clothing for attendees as well as a visit
from Santa and toys for the kids. Volunteers needed to donate items and time;
call Barbara May, 375-8179. Monterey Fairgrounds. 372-5863, 373-3720.

December 31   **FIRST NIGHT® MONTEREY**   **FREE+$$**
Millennium theme, 3pm to midnight. A non-alcoholic New Year's Eve celebration
including music, entertainment, dancing, food and art exhibits. Over 100 groups
from opera to rock, folk dancers to poets, actors to clowns. Mission is to strengthen
our families and unite our community through the arts.

Downtown Monterey is closed to traffic and cultural events take place on the
street and inside the businesses. Buttons to admit to inside events $10, under 5
free. Plenty of things to see and do on the street. Support the arts and enjoy all of
the entertainment.

Free parking at Del Monte Shopping Center and shuttle service to downtown. All
bus service will be free, 2pm-2am, to anyone wearing a First Night button. Free
shuttle service for all passengers–button or not–between Del Monte Center and
the Monterey Transit Plaza from 1pm-12:30am. Call 899-2555 for extra free routes.

Call the Volunteer Center of Monterey to help: 800-776-9176. Volunteers receive
admission to the event and a free T-shirt. www.firstnightmonterey.org. 373-4778.

Dec/Jan   **THE CALIFORNIA CHALLENGE**   **FREE**
Designated driver program. Local clubs participate by offering free entry and free
sodas to designated drivers who fill out a RADD card available from participating
establishments or downloaded from www/ubl.com/radd. 724-0649.

Pet Psyc Youth Programs, Inc.

Companion animals used as
potential healers in non-tradi-
tional therapy. One of several
programs to help Monterey
County youth. Shown here are
Gregory Lodes and Leila Coo-
per with two of the more un-
usual house pets. Call founder
Terri Austin for more informa-
tion, 649-6283. You can help
with your donation to P.O. Box
2711, Monterey, CA 93942.

Entertainment
Music, Dancing, Karaoke and Pub Games

◆ **The Crown Anchor**, British pub and restaurant, outside patio. Free Quizgo trivia game, Wed 8:30pm. Happy Hour, Mon-Fri 4-6:30pm, special drink prices. 150 W. Franklin St. 649-6496.

◆ **Characters Sports Bar & Grill**. Drink and food specials, 5-6pm. In the Marriott, 350 Calle Principal. 647-4023.

◆ **Long Bar**. Sun-Thurs, live music, danding. Fri-Sat, dancing to Good Vibration DJs. Private parties, catering. No cover. 180 E. Franklin. 372-2244.

RISTORANTE ITALIANO
COCKTAILS
DINNER
JAZZ
301 Alvarado St. / Monterey
831-649-8151

◆ **Cibo Ristorante Italiano**. Live jazz, Sun-Thurs, with a variety of international musicians Fri-Sat. Happy Hour, Mon-Fri, 5-7pm. No cover. 301 Alvarado. www.cibo.com. 649-8151.

◆ **McGarrett's' Club**. Fri-Sat-top 40 disco. Mon-Ladies Night, Wed-Country Western, Thurs-Modern Dance. Cover varies. 321 D Alvarado at Del Monte Ave., upstairs. Hospitality employees always get in free. 646-9244.

◆ **Viva Monterey.** Live DJ music & dancing 7 nights a week, 9:30pm-1:30am. No cover. Billiards. 414 Alvarado St. Open 4pm-2am. 646-1415.

◆ **Britannia Arms**. Karaoke-Wed. Live music every Fri-Sat, 9:30pm-1:30am. No cover. Late night dining. 8 TVs. 444 Alvarado St. 656-9543.

◆ **The Mucky Duck**. Dancing Thurs-Sat, 9pm. No cover. Happy Hour, Mon-Fri(live music Tues&Fri), 4:30-6:30pm. Discounted drinks and appetizers. Fireplaces, darts, cribbage, chess, piano bar. 479 Alvarado St., 655-3031.

◆ **Knuckles Historical Sports Bar**. Free munchies, free parking, children welcome. Mon-Fri 4pm-1am, Sat 10am-1am, Sun 9:30am-1am. 372-1234.

◆ **Cafe Monterey**. Jazz piano, Tues-Thurs 7-10pm; jazz band, Fri-Sat 5:30-midnight. Jazz jam session last Sun, 2-6. No cover. At the Hyatt Regency, 372-1234.

◆ **El Indio**, Mexican restaurant. Happy Hour, Mon-Fri from 4-6pm with $2 Margaritas and $2 Drafts. FREE appetizers 5-6pm. Del Monte Shopping Center. 375-4446.

◆ **Casa Cafe & Bar**. Live music, no cover, Fri-Sat 7-11pm. Mon-Fri 4:30-6:30pm, free hors d'oeuvres, cocktails at Happy Hour prices. Casa Munras Garden Hotel, 700 Munras Ave. 375-2411.

◆ **The Safari Club**. Large screen. Mon-Fri 5-7pm, free hors d'oeuvres, Happy Hour beer prices. The Bay Park Hotel, 1425 Munras Ave. 649-1020.

◆ **Duffy's Tavern & Family Restaurant**. Big screen TV. Happy Hour Mon-Fri 4-6pm. Lunch & dinner delivery, Mon-Fri. 282 High St. 372-2565.

◆ **Wharfside**. Joe Lucido, jazz guitar, Fri 6:30-9:30pm. No cover and complimentary hors d'oeuvres. Fisherman's Wharf. 375-3956, fax 375-2967.

◆ **London Bridge Pub**. Seamus Kennedy will perform four times in 1999. April, June, July and October. No cover. Call for days and times. Free Celtic Jam, first Sundays at 6:30pm. Wharf #2. 655-2879.

◆ **Monterey Joe's**. Happy Hour Tues-Sun, 3:30-7pm. Discount food and drinks. 149 N. Fremont St., 655-3355.

◆ **Good Vibrations DJs**. Free entry at various Monterey "hot spots" when Good Vibrations DJs perform. Call for schedule or to book, 647-9234.

Dance Groups

◆ **Dance lesson** free at the Monterey Peninsula Dance Association. Dances every Friday, 7-10pm. 71 Soledad Drive, Mon-Fri, 11am-9pm, 648-8725.

◆ **Line Dancing**, free Mon & Wed, 6-8:30pm at the American Legion, top of Jefferson Street. 646-3039.

◆ **American Dancesport Academy**, 540 Calle Principal. 375-5533.

◆ **Scottish Country Dancing and others** at Monterey Youth Center, Senior Center, Archer Park. Free. Call Mtry Recreation Dept, 646-3866.

◆ **Contra Dancing,** 1st and 3rd Saturdays, 7:30pm, at the YMCA, 600 Camino El Estero. $7. www.nuthouse.com/contra/. 479-4059.

Dinner & Coffeehouse Entertainment

◆ **El Palomar**. Live Mexican music with dinner, Sat-Sun, 6:30-9pm. 724 Abrego St. 372-1032.

◆ **Morgan's Coffee and Tea**. Musical acts, some free. Saturday children's programs. 498 Washington St., 373-5601. Recorded schedule, 655-6868.

Movies and Theatre

◆ **Galaxy Six Cinemas**. Free refill on large popcorn and drinks. Seniors (55+), children, and matinees before 6pm, $5. Regular $7.50. 280 Del Monte Shopping Center, 655-4617 (777-FILM x135). www.cinemacal.com.

◆ **State Theater**. Free refill on large popcorn and drinks. Seniors (60+), & matinees before 6pm, $5. Regular $7.25. 417 Alvarado St, 372-4555.

◆ **MPC Theatre Company**. Children ages 5-17, accompanied by adult, are admitted free. Season tickets $45. MPC box office, 646-4213.

◆ **Osio Cinema**. Osio Plaza, 350 Alvarado. Art films. $5 matinee (before 6pm) $7.75 eves. 644-8171. Bergman Café has indoor & outdoor seating.

Play and Pray Together

◆ Join the Monterey **Community Band**, directed and conducted by Dick Robins. Free. Performs at the City's Christmas Tree Lighting Ceremony, Spring Concert, and other community events. No auditions but you must be able to read music and provide your own instrument. Weekly rehearsals: Mondays, September through June, 7:15pm-9:15pm, Monterey High School Band Room (lower parking lot, off Martin Street). Sponsored by the Monterey Recreation and Community Services Dept. Call Cindy Vierra 646-3866.

◆ **Taize Services**. Free. A candlelight service for prayer and meditation draws on the music and style of worship in Taize, an ecumenical Christian community in France. Instruments accompany the congregation in simple, chant-like prayerful song. Silent meditation and reflection. Infant care is provided (0 to 3 yrs.) Held 7:30pm, second Fridays, at the First Presbyterian Church of Monterey, 501 El Dorado, alternating months with St. Angela's in Pacific Grove. Other churches participate during Lent. 373-3031.

◆ **Life in the Arts**. Local arts program created by Marie Wainscoat to promote local visual and performing artists and encourage children to pursue arts education. Offers some Free concerts. Call 883-1331 for info.

◆ **Creating the Arts**. Series at Santa Catalina School. Free. Call 655-9310.

Jonathon Lee at the Big Sur Marathon

Jonathon Lee is one of Monterey's most beloved musicians. He volunteers every year to play at the International Big Sur Marathon and thousands are thrilled at his inspirational music on the edge of the Pacific Ocean. Jonathon is also available for day and evening functions. Two free offers for *Your Personal Guide* readers: Buy a CD and get a free autographed photograph of Jonathon Lee – or – book and prepay a major event, such as a corporate meeting, wedding or concert, and receive a complete autographed set of Jonathon's CDs. Expires 7-1-00. 525 Hartnell St., 800-533-8233, fax 648-3333. www.redshift.com/~jlm.

Waterfront Parks & Activities

▲ **El Estero Park and Lake**, Aguajito Road and Del Monte Avenue. 45 acres. Dennis the Menace Playground is the City's most popular and most famous, being the result of creative efforts donated by Hank Ketcham, creator of the Dennis the Menace comic strip, local sculptor Arch Gardner, and the Monterey Peninsula Jaycees. Unusual playground equipment includes a real steam engine, Dennis the Menace sculpture and climbing structure, umbrella tree, the Thing, giant swing ride, balancing bridge, lion drinking fountain, suspension bridge, giant slide, the maze, giant roller slide, moon bridge, circular slide and bell tower, coil spring with slide, and adventure ship. Harry Greene Island, a bird refuge in the middle of the lake, is named for the father of modern Monterey. Lake fishing (license required), barbecue/picnic, walking paths, benches, youth center, playing field, dance studio, boat concession and snack bar. Restrooms. Open 10 to dusk. 646-3866. Group picnic area 646-3866. Ballpark 646-3969. Snack Bar 372-8446. Youth Center 646-3873. Boating concession, paddle boats, 375-1484.

▲ **Skate Park**. A new skateboard park, opened in late 1999, is located in the turnaround area of the parking lot behind Frank E. Sollecito, Jr. Ballpark and Dennis the Menace Park, on the edge of the lake.

▲ **Fisherman's Shoreline Park**. Starts at Fisherman's Wharf, west to the Coast Guard Pier. Dogs on leash on the trail. 5 acres of grassy areas and bay view benches. Fine view of the wharf and boats in the marina. Gulls, pelicans, otters, seals, cormorants, paths to shore. Walk onto the Coast Guard Pier to see the many sea lions at the end. Open dawn to dusk. 646-3866.

▲ **Ed Rickett's Underwater Park**. Extends from the breakwater to Hopkins Marine Station. Named for renowned marine biologist. Exceptional diving.

▲ **Monterey State Beach** Wharf#2 east to Seaside, along the Recreation Trail and part of Monterey's Window on the Bay. Handicapped access. Fishing from pier, diving, kayaking, swimming, hiking, biking, volleyball and kite flying. Wading, sunbathing, picnics, restrooms at the wharf. Dogs on leash. Dawn to dusk. To reserve the volleyball court, 646-3866.

▲ **Monterey Bay Park** adjacent to the beach. 4.1 acre turf and landscaped areas. 5 sand volleyball courts, picnic and BBQ. Reservations: 646-3866.

▲ **Monterey Recreation Trail** in Monterey hugs the bay from Seaside city limits to the Aquarium; pedestrian and bicycling trail that spans the coastline 18 miles from Pacific Grove to Castroville. Always open.

▲ **Peter J. Ferrante Park**, at Encina and Palo Verde off Casa Verde Way. 1 acre league/softball diamond. Bleachers, BBQ, tot play equip. 646 3969.

Other Fun Activities at El Estero Park

➤ **Monterey Peninsula Walking Club** meets at the parking lot Sun 9am for "Fun Walk" Public is invited. Different levels of walkers. Variety of walks. Call Will Lyon for more information, 375-5732.

➤ **Volunteer gardeners** meet 9am to noon, Tues and Thurs, in the French Consulate building, Franklin and Camino El Estero. Tools provided. To join the fun, contact the Monterey Parks Department, 755-4899.

➤ **The Walking Society** meets 7pm Wed in parking lot on Del Monte Avenue at Camino Aguajito for congenial walks on the Rec Trail. 641-9643. Non-smoking adults welcome.

More Ways to Have Fun at the Beach

➤ **Tidepooling**. Pick up a free High-Low Tide Book at any Longs Drug Store for a year's worth of high and low tide times, plus a wind chill factor table, times of sunrise and sunset, a highway and shore map from Pt. Año Nuevo to Lucia, phases of the moon, and 2 recipes for clam chowder. There are two Long's Drug Stores on the Monterey Peninsula: 686 Lighthouse Ave., New Monterey, and 2170 Fremont St., Monterey.

➤ **Tips for Tidepooling**: Remain with your group–don't go off alone. Don't fool around on the rocks. Walk slowly and carefully as the rocks are very slippery. Wear tennis shoes. Don't get trapped by the rising tide. Waves can knock you down, so always watch for them. Don't bring glass containers in the tidepool areas. Don't pry animals from the rocks. Return animals to the same area from which you removed them. Return each rock to the exact spot you took it from. Sea animals don't like being stepped on or having fingers poked at them. Leave empty shells on the beach–they may be some animal's future home. Remember that all tidepool life is protected by law. (Courtesy Monterey Visitor and Convention Bureau)

➤ **Breakwater Cove Marina,** at the Coast Guard Pier, has two concrete ramps for your boats or kayaks, restrooms, benches, restaurants. 646-3950. Another free boat ramp is at the Harbor Master's Office near Wharf #2.

➤ July 5 is always **Monterey Beach Cleanup Day**. Call 646-3719.

➤ September 16 is the **Annual Monterey Bay Coastal Cleanup** at the following beaches: Asilomar State Beach, Bay Street, Carmel Beach, Carmel River, Coast Guard Pier, Fort Ord, Garrapata, Kirby Park/Elkhorn Slough, Lovers Point, Marina State Beach, MacAbee Beach, Molera, Monastery Beach, Monterey Dunes, Monterey State Beach, Moss Landing, Naval Postgraduate School, Pfeiffer, Rocky Shores, Salinas River, Seaside State Beach, Spanish Bay, Tioga Road, Wharf #1, Wharf #2, Zmudowski. Volunteers will collect and document debris found in the ocean, on beaches, inland waterways and dunes. Volunteers will also receive free items. Call 800-Coast4U.

Other Free City Parks

▲ **Larkin Park**, at the northern ends of Monroe and Clay Streets. 1 acre. Everything you need including a basketball court. Busy and noisy. Restrooms.

▲ **Veterans Memorial Park**, Jefferson St. and Skyline Dr. 50 acres hiking trails, picnic areas, playing fields and restrooms. RVs to 21'. 40 primitive campsites $15/ vehicle/night; hikers & bikers, $2/ night. Access to **Huckleberry Hill Nature Preserve**, 81 acres, trails, bay views. 646-3865. Batting cage at right, fields & bay views below.

▲ **Via Paraiso Park**, corner of Via Paraiso and Martin streets. 10.6 acres. Barbecue, picnic area, baseball diamond, large play area, tennis courts, basketball and volleyball. Trees and trails, clean restrooms. 646-3866.

▲ **Quarry Park**, on Via Del Pinar near Via Gayuba. 10 acres. Hiking trails.

▲ **Friendly Plaza**, Jefferson & Pacific. 2 acres. Lawn, benches, fountain, rose garden, and ornamental plantings at Colton Hall historic site.

▲ **Jacks Ballpark**, Franklin & Figueroa Streets, downtown. 3.7 acres. Ballfield & bleachers, night lighting, tot play area, restrooms. 646-3969.

▲ **Whispering Pines Park**, Pacific & Alameda. 3.1 acre group use with amphitheatre, BBQ, restrooms. Reservations, 646-3866.

▲ **Don Dahvee Greenbelt**. Munras Avenue btwn Del Monte Center and El Dorado St. 35.8 acres. Trails, bike paths, picnic table. Dawn to dusk.

▲ **Iris Canyon Greenbelt**, at Fremont & Iris Canyon Road. 32. 1 acre natural greenbelt area.

▲ **Lagunita Mirada**, at Fremont and Iris Canyon. 1 acre hillside Rhododendron garden with ornamental bridge and shaded pathways.

▲ **Montecito Park**, at Montecito and Dela Vina. 1 acre. Play equipment, BBQ, half court basketball, restrooms.

▲ **Casanova-Oak Knoll Park**, corner of Ramona and Euclid avenues. 1.3 acres. Fenced and nicely-maintained. Large barbecue area, grassy area and gigantic shade trees. Multipurpose rooms to rent. 646-5665.

▲ **Fisherman's Flats Park**, San Vito Street. 1.5 acres. Grassy area and a well-maintained sandy play area with benches for parents, BBQ, play equip.

▲ **Deer Flats Park**, on Deer Forest Road. 1 acre. Fenced in playground, small basketball court, quiet reading area, picnic area.

▲ **Neighborhood Tot-Lot**, 132 Spray Ave. in Del Monte Beach. Play equipment, benches, fabulous bay views.

Monterey County Parks Nearby

▲ **Jack's Peak County Park**, 2.5 miles east of Monterey on Jack's Peak Drive south of Highway 68. 755-4899. Entry fee: Fri-Sun $3/car, Mon-Thurs $2/car. Call Monterey County Parks Administration Office for free entrance days: 888/588-CAMP, 755-4899. 1068 ft. summit, highest peak on the Peninsula. 525 acres of wildflower meadows and pine and oak forests. Grasslands, hiking and equestrian trails. Dogs on leash. The Skyline Self-Guided Nature Trail offers a view of Carmel Bay and Point Lobos. Picnic areas with barbecues. Trails include: Skyline and Rhus Trail Loop, 2.8 miles, easy; Coffeeberry Lower Ridge Loop, 2.5 miles, easy; Madrone Trail Loop, 2.3 miles, moderate.

▲ **Laguna Seca**, off Highway 68, 8 miles east of Monterey. $5 day/car use fee. 185 campsites with hookups, showers, restrooms. Fishing, rifle range, hiking trails, nature preserve. Monterey County Parks, 755-4899.

World Class Laguna Seca Raceway

Laguna Seca is the site of a world class race track with special events throughout the year: The Sea Otter Classic, Cherry's Jubilee and more. Write to the Sports Car Racing Assn. of the Monterey Peninsula (SCRAMP) for event information and how you can volunteer to be involved (all proceeds to local charities): P.O. Box SCRAMP, Monterey, CA 93942. 648-5111. See Calendar of Events for all dates. Photo: S. Philip Nishikawa.

▲ **Presidio of Monterey**, site of the original Spanish Royal Presidential fortress in 1770, today home of the Defense Language Institute. 26 acres. Enter on Artillery St. from Pacific St. Turn right on Cpl. Ewing Rd. to see the Bouchard Monument, El Castillo site, and site of the first California Mass performed by Father Serra. Turn left to see the Sloat Monument, Indian Village, and Serra Monument. Site of an Ohlone Indian Village and burial ground. More Indian artifacts at the P.G. Museum of Natural History. Free walking tour map at the Public Affairs Office in Rasmussen Hall weekdays. 242-5104. http://dli-www.army.mil.

▲ **Soldier Field**, at the Presidio. 9.5 acres multi-use sports field with 3 baseball diamonds, shared with the Military. Programming info: 646-3969.

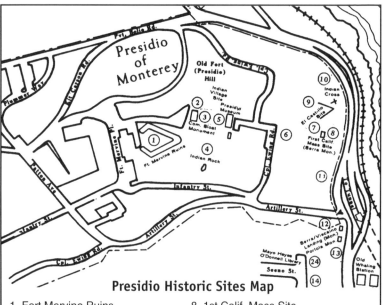

Presidio Historic Sites Map

1. Fort Mervine Ruins
2. Commodore Sloat Monument
3. Indian Village Site (entire hill)
4. Indian Ceremonial Rock
5. Presidio Museum (closed)
6. Bouchard Monument
7. El Castillo Site
8. 1st Calif. Mass Site
9. Alexio Niño Cross
10. Indian Cross (c.500 B.C.)
11. Bedrock Mortar
12. Serra/Viscaino Landing Monument
13. Portola Monument
14. F. Doud House

Left, Sloat Monument
Center, History markers
Right, Father Serra

Walks & Hikes

▲ **The Recreation Trail** along the coastline from Seaside to Pacific Grove follows the old railroad tracks and offers a wide avenue for walkers, bikers, rollerblades and strollers. Start at **Roberts Lake** in Seaside where there is ample parking and follow the path through a grove of Eucalyptus trees, past Del Monte beach, to Fisherman's Wharf where you can rest under the shade trees of **Peace Park**, visit the historic **Custom House**, and the shops of the Wharf. Downtown Monterey is just steps away. Follow the Trail again to the **Coast Guard Pier** and watch the seals and sea lions play. Next you'll pass through **Cannery Row** with all of its restaurants, sites and amenities. At the end of Cannery Row, you'll see the world famous **Monterey Bay Aquarium**, built on the site of Hovden's Cannery. Continue on the path past **The American Tin Cannery Outlet Stores**, **Hopkins Marine Station**, and follow the coastline to **Lovers Point** in Pacific Grove. Approx. 6 miles.

▲ Take a fun morning walk to the **Coast Guard Pier** to see the harbor seals, or to either of the Wharves to watch fishermen unload their catch and the markets open for business. Fabulous places to catch the sunrise.

Parks and Recreation Departments

▲ **Monterey Youth Center**, 777 Pearl St. Mon-Thurs 9am-9pm, Fri 9am-5pm, Sat 1-5pm. Closed Sunday. Call or visit today for a free catalog of activities. 646-3873.

▲ **Monterey City Parks & Recreation Departments**, Main office, 546 Dutra St. has many special events and programs and on-going activities for the entire family, such as: arts, crafts, cooking, dance, exercise, gymnastics, music, aquatics, aerobics, field sports. Pick up an Activities Guide at Dutra St., in the old Vasquez Adobe behind Colton Hall; 9am-4pm, 646-3866. Other centers: Archer Park Center, 542 Archer St., 646-3870; Monterey Senior Center, 280 Dickman Ave., 646-3878; Hilltop Park Center, 871 Jessie St., 646-3975; Casanova Oak Knoll Park Center, 735 Ramona Ave, 646-5665. For Monterey and other city residents.

Fitness & Sports

▲ **Workout station** at El Estero Park. There are three exercise stations in the World Trail around Lake El Estero. Enjoy your workout surrounded by the beauty of the trees and lake, while Canadian geese, American coots and other sea fowl witness your effort. Not recommended for young children.

▲ **Workout trail** at Monterey Peninsula College. Wells Fargo Game Field Walking Course. Park on Glenwood Circle and enter the campus through a gate by the National Guard Armory and football field. Equipment is old but usable for a good workout among the oak trees, with a beautiful view of the bay.

▲ **Bocce Ball.** There are three bocce ball courts at Custom House Plaza with free access to play this very old Italian game. The game is gaining in popularity and more courts are scheduled to be built soon.

Health Spas

● **Monterey Plaza Hotel & Spa.** European style spa atop the hotel. Hotel guests & conference and meeting attendees. 400 Cannery Row. 646-1700.

● **Spa on the Plaza** at the Doubletree Hotel. Yoga, fitness club, facials, massage and more. 201 Alvarado St. 647-9000.

● **The Body Suite.** Facials, massage, waxing, hair, hand, foot and body care. Heritage Harbor, 99 Pacific St. Suite 100E. 375-4375.

● **Hanz On.** Waxing, massage, nail, hair and skin care, and more. 176 Sargent Court. 372-4616.

More Fitness & Exercise

➤ **Monterey Tennis Center**, 401 Pearl Street downtown. 9am-10pm. 6 Lighted tennis courts, pro shop. Reservation or lesson info: 646-3881.

➤ **Monterey Sports Center**, 3.2 acre site at Washington & Franklin. Pool, gym, weights, aerobic, tot activity, sun deck, snack bar. 646-3700.

➤ **NFL Gatorade Punt, Pass & Kick** contest for boys and girls ages 8-15, usually in October. Free entry. Call 646-3969 for details.

➤ **Bicycle Rodeos** are held by the Monterey Police Department at several local schools. Safety inspection, presentations and a written and skills test, plus free gifts and prizes. Call Officer Michael Sargent at 646-3808 for dates.

➤ **"Rideshare Week"** , October, hosted by the Association of Monterey Bay Area Governments (AMBAG). Participants pledge to carpool, vanpool, take a bus, walk or telecommute at least one day, and are eligible to win prizes. Call 422-POOL, 429-POOL OR 637-POOL. www.rideshareweek.com.

Monterey Audubon Society Trips

The Society meets 2nd Thursdays, Sept–May, 7pm at the P.G. Museum of Natural History. Public is invited. Outings, call Robert Horn, 372-4608. Dates shown here are for the year 2000; most trips are repeated at approximately the same time each year. 831-645-6617.

January 23	Land Birds of South County. Chris Tenney, 753-1656.
February 5 & 6	Morro Bay & vicinity. Rick Fournier, 633-0572.
February 19	Los Banos Wildlife Area. Vitally Volmensky & Paul Eastman, 375-3906.
March 4	Beginner's Field Trip: Crespi Pond, near Asilomar, Pacific Grove, 9am. Robert Horn, 372-4608.
March 19	Monterey Peninsula coastline habitats. Brian Weed 373-2019. 8am at Wharf#2 base.
April 8	Pinnacles National Monument. 8:30am in the park. 7:30am Del Monte Center at Cinema #70. Vitaly Volmensky, 375-3906.
April 22	Point Lobos. Robert Horn, 372-4608.
May 6	Bird songs of upper Carmel Valley. Jim Booker, 624-1202.
May 13	California condors at Ventana Wilderness Sanctuary. Reservation only. Robert Horn, 372-4608.
May 20	Elkhorn Slough, Moss Landing. Rick fournier, 633-0572.
June 4	Pt. Lobos, meet at the park entrance 9am. Brian Weed, 373-2019.
June 10	Annual meeting. Point Lobos. Craig Hohenberger, 659-7249.
June 23-25	Birding the Great Basis, Nevada. Chris Tenney, 753-1656.
July 8	Inland Birds of South County. Tim Amaral, 663-4712.

More Hiking & Biking Fun

➤ **Monterey Bay Hash House Harriers** have noncompetitive 4-5 mile cross country fun runs at various locations in the Monterey Bay area every other Sunday at 1pm. Call Tim Thomas at 728-2117, 335-4FUN.

➤ **Bicycle Rentals:** Adventures-by-the-Sea, 201 Alvarado Mall near the Maritime Museum, 648-7235. Group sales 648-7236, fax 372-4103, www.adventuresbythesea.com. Offers some free pickup and delivery. They also rent kayaks and in-line skates.

➤ Bikes ride free on **Monterey-Salinas Buses**, 899-2555, 424-7695, www.mst.org. May is CleanAir Month–watch papers for bike activities.

➤ **Naturalist-led Hikes.** Ventana Wilderness, Carmel River Valley, State Parks of Big Sur, Monterey and Big Sur Coast. $10 per adult, $5 per child (no charge for children in backpacks or 2nd children). To make reservations, call 375-9831. www.mbay.net/~gat.

Favorite Monterey & Cannery Row Eateries

• Abalonetti's	Italian	57 Fisherman's Wharf	373-1851
• Billy Quon's	New American	1 Harris Court	647-0390
• Blue Fin Café	American	685 Cannery Row	375-7000
• Bubba Gump	Seafood	720 Cannery Row	373-1884
• Cafe Fina	Seafood	Fisherman's Wharf	372-5200
• Cafe Abrego	Californian	565 Abrego	375-3750
• Chart House	American	444 Cannery Row	372-3362
• Chong's	Chinese	485 Tyler St	373-5153
• Cibo	Italian	301 Alvarado St	649-8151
• Del Monte Express	American	2329 No Fremont	655-1941
• Domenico's	Italian	50 Fisherman's Wharf	372-3655
• El Palomar	Mexican	724 Abrego	372-1032
• Ferrante's	Italian	350 Calle Principal	647-4020
• Fish Hopper	Seafood	700 Cannery Row	372-8543
• Fresh Cream	French	99 Pacific Street	375-9798
• Gianni's Pizza	Italian	725 Lighthouse	649-1500
• Great Wall	Chinese	724 Abrego	372-3637
• Hula's	New American	622 Lighthouse	655-4852
• India's Clay Oven	Indian	150 Del Monte Ave	373-2529
• LALLApalooza	American	474 Alvarado	645-9036
• Lighthouse Bistro	New American	401 Lighthouse	649-0320
• Mandarin House	Chinese	2031 N. Fremont	375-9551
• Margie's Diner	American	320 Fremont	642-0148
• Monterey's Fish House		2114 Del Monte Ave	373-4647
• Monterey Joe's	Italian	2149 N. Fremont	655-3355
• Montrio Bistro	American	414 Calle Principal	648-8880
• Papa Chano's	Mexican	462 Alvarado	464-9587
• Paradiso	Mediterranean	654 Cannery Row	375-4155
• Rosine's	American	434 Alvarado	375-1400
• Sandbar & Grill	Seafood	Wharf No. 2	373-2818
• Sardine Factory	Seafood	701 Wave St	373-3775
• Sea Harvest	Seafood	598 Foam	646-0546
• Siamese Bay	Thai	131 Webster	373-1550
• Stokes Adobe	European	500 Hartnell St	373-1110
• Sunrise Grocery	Asian	400 Pearl St	372-2524
• Tarpy's	American	2999 Monterey-Salinas Hwy	655-2999
• Thai Cafe	Thai	731 Munras Ave	655-9797
• Turtle Bay Taqueria	Mexican	431 Tyler	333-1500
• Whaling Station	American	763 Wave St	373-3778

Accommodations in Monterey & Cannery Row

		(831)	Rates From:
• Bay Park Hotel	1425 Munras Avenue	649-1020	$80
• Bayside Inn	2055 North Fremont Street	372-8071	$40
• Best Western	825 Abrego	373-5345	$70
• Casa Munras	700 Munras Avenue	375-2411	$90
• Casa Verde Inn	2113 North Fremont Street	375-5407	$45
• Colton Inn	707 Pacific Street	649-6500	$90
• Comfort Inn	1262 Munras Avenue	372-8088	$50
• Cypress Gardens	1150 Munras Avenue	373-2761	$75
• Days Inn	1288 Munras Avenue	375-2168	$48
• Del Monte Beach	1110 Del Monte Avenue	649-4410	call
• DoubleTree Hotel	2 Portola Plaza	649-4511	$139
• El Adobe Inn	936 Munras Avenue	372-5409	$49
• Holiday Inn Express	443 Wave Street	372-1800	$99
• Hotel Pacific	300 Pacific Street	373-5700	$159
• Hyatt Regency	1 Golf Course Drive	394-1234	call
• Jabberwock	598 Laine Street	888-428-7253	call
• Merritt House Inn	386 Pacific Street	646-9686	call
• Monterey Bay Inn	242 Cannery Row	373-6242	$179
• Monterey Bay Lodge	55 Camino Aquajito	372-8057	$49
• Monterey Hotel	406 Alvarado STreet	375-3184	$129
• Monterey Marriott	350 Calle Principal	649-4234	$139
• Monterey Plaza Hotel	400 Cannery Row	646-1700	$185
• Montero Lodge	1240 Munras Avenue	375-6002	$36
• Munras Lodge	1010 Munras Avenue	646-9696	$49
• Old Monterey Inn	500 Martin Street	375-8284	call
• Otter Inn	571 Wave Street	375-2299	$99
• Quality Inn	200 Foam Street	649-8580	$109
• Padre Oaks	1278 Munras Avenue	373-3741	$39
• Ramada Limited	1182 Cass Street	375-2679	$59
• San Carlos Inn	850 Abrego	649-6332	$65
• Sand Dollar Inn	755 Abrego	372-7551	$65
• Scottish Fairway	2075 No. Fremont	373-5551	$35
• Spindrift Inn	652 Cannery Row	646-8900	$179
• Steinbeck Lodge	1300 Munras Avenue	373-3203	$49
• Super 8 Motel	2050 North Fremont St	373-3081	$42
• Vagabond Motel	2120 North Fremont St	372-6066	$35
• Victorian Inn	487 Foam Street	373-8000	$99
• Way Station	1200 Olmsted Road	372-2945	$79
• West Wind Lodge	1046 Munras Avenue	373-1337	$70

New Monterey & Cannery Row

Steinbeck Plaza

San Carlos Beach

The Fish Hopper

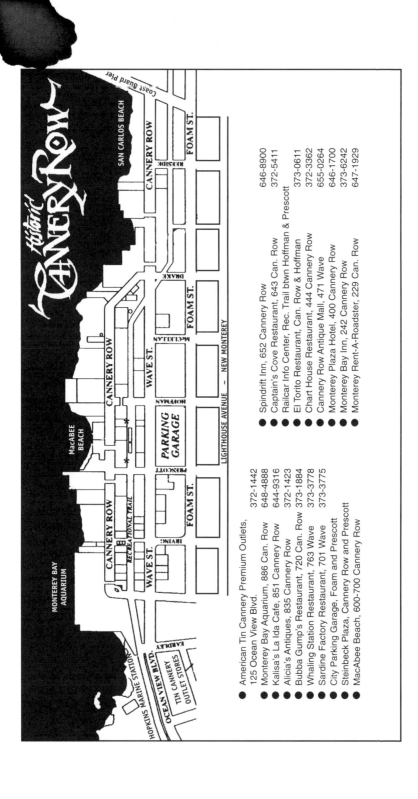

Historic Cannery Row
Walking Tour of Shops & Attractions

Cannery Row, originally called Old Ocean View Avenue, and often referred to as "America's Most Famous Street," was made famous by local author John Steinbeck in his book of the same name. He depicted the hardworking inhabitants – the Spanish, Chinese, Portuguese, Italians, Japanese and Scandinavians – who were the whalers, fishermen, and cannery workers. There were 21 canneries operating during the heydey years of 1921-1946.

Start your walking tour at the east end of Cannery Row near San Carlos Beach, at the entrance to the Breakwater Cove Marina and Coast Guard Pier. There is plenty of parking in this area.

The large concrete structure at 225, now home to **Adventures-by-the-Sea** and other shops, was the **Aeneas Packing Company**, built in 1945. It was one of the last canneries to be built.

Where to "Spot" Sea Otters

Municipal & Fisherman's Wharf, Coast Guard Breakwater, Cannery Row, Lovers Pt, Otter Pt, Pt Piños, Pt Joe, Bird Rock, Cypress Pt, Pescadero Pt, Carmel Pt, Pt Lobos.

The **Friends of the Sea Otter**, Retail and Educational Center, 381 Cannery Row Suite Q, is open daily, 10am-8pm, (9pm summer). Pick up free map for best places to spot otters, and educational material. 642-9037, www.seaotters.org.

At Drake and Wave Streets, look for the Jessie Cursault bronze memorial by the recreation path to **Edward F. 'Doc' Ricketts**, Steinbeck's friend and inspiration for several major characters in his books. Ricketts was a revolu-

tionary in marine biology and made tremendous contributions to modernizing the science. He was killed on this spot by the evening Del Monte Express train on May 8th, 1948. Daily an unknown admirer puts fresh flowers in Ed's outstretched hand. Birthday celebration, May 13. Call for information, 656-0967 or 644-9316.

At 425, you see the **Tevis Estate Carriage Houses**, part of an estate on 1000 feet of coastal frontage built in 1902. Major cannery figures Ben Senderman (owner, Carmel Canning Co.), Knute Hovden (owner, Hovden Food Products Corp.), and Frank Crispo (revitalization), also lived in these homes. Now home to a great antique store.

Encore Espresso, with home-made goodies and al fresco seating on the Recreation Trail, across from Doc Ricketts memorial, invites you to bring in your *Your Personal Guide* and receive one free coffee refill of the coffee of the day with any purchase. Open daily, 6:30am-5pm. 655-3001.

At 471 Wave, the **Cannery Row Antique Mall**, once Carmel Canning Co. Warehouse, is listed on the National Register of Historic Places. Open Mon-Sat 10am-6pm, Sun 10am-5pm. 21,000 sq.ft. Venture to the second floor lounge to view free changing displays of people's collections. Toy trains, 40s and 50s fashions, antique fishing tackle, toys from yesteryear, and James Bond are examples of past displays. Call Claudia to find out what's on display next, 655-0264. Free appraisal clinic for antiques and collectables 1st Wed, 11-3. Free off-street parking. antiques@redshift.com.

The pillars at 508 are all that remain of Cannery Row's first rudimentary canning shed opened on Ocean View Avenue in 1902 and sold in 1908 to become the Pacific Fish Company. Take the kids to the Carousel next door!

Edgewater Packing Company, 640 Wave St., is near the Recreation Trail and 600 Cannery Row. 649-1899. There's a good bicycle map on the side of this building; souvenirs; carousel. Adjacent is an information center in the Heritage Railroad car, a 1917 R.P.O. (rail post office car) from New York Central Railroad. It rests on some of the last rails used by the Southern Pacific Railroad to transport Cannery Row products to the world. Talk with Herb Behrens, volunteer, and pick up free maps and brochures. 373-1902.

645 Cannery Row, Beachside Sports, specializing in kayak tours, 647-0148. Restaurants, shops and offices now inhabit the old Marina Apartments at 651, which were built by the Wu family in 1929.

MacAbee Beach, at **Steinbeck Plaza**, Cannery Row and Prescott, was a lively whaling site for the Portuguese whalers in the 1870s and 1880s. Today there are many free events in the plaza and live music on weekends. The beach access affords views of the bay and steps to the water, favorite kayaking and diving spot; many benches to sit and relax. Follow the walkway next to the Spindrift Inn, open dawn to dusk, no fee.

Adjacent to the plaza, at 711, sits a replica of the **Monterey Canning Company** building, which was a major canning enterprise owned by George Harper and A.M. Allen. Today it's home to businesses and restaurants.

685 Cannery Row: Check out: **Boyz Toyz**, a unique and fun shop for boyz and girlz of all ages. 333-1060. boyztoyz@juno.com. **Riley Golf**, Free swing analysis and advice on how to play better and enjoy the game more. 373-8855. www.rileygolf.com.

700 Cannery Row: **Spirit of Monterey Wax Museum**. California history is reenacted in life-like prominent characters. A self-guided tour covers 400 years of history in about 20 minutes: scenes from John Steinbeck novels, dioramas of Kit Carson, Native Americans, friars and conquistadors. Open daily, 9am-9pm. Children 6 and under free; free to all costumed children, ages 10 and under, on Halloween. 375-3770. **Let it Bead**. #CC 2nd Floor. Open 10am-6pm, Tues at noon, closed Wed. 373-BEAD. www.letitbead.com.

A Taste of Monterey is upstairs over the water at 700 Cannery Row. Features over 30 local wineries, Monterey theme gift center, winery maps and tour information. The visitors' center has a panoramic view of the entire bay from Monterey to Santa Cruz, with entertaining and educational exhibits. Relax at one of their window tables, enjoy a glass of Monterey County wine; sample local produce plates and appetizers. 11-6 daily. 646-5446.

At 720, **Bubba Gump's Restaurant** occupies a rebuilt reduction plant which turned sardines into fertilizer and fishmeal. *"Forrest Gump"* greets and charms visitors on the bench, with his box of chocolates, in front of the restaurant, Saturday, 1-6pm. Gift shop of movie paraphernalia. Open 11am-10pm daily. 373-1884.

The two walls of murals on either side of Cannery Row depict scenes from its heydey. At **Bruce Ariss Way** and Cannery Row, peek into the preserved cannery workers' shacks which are furnished in 1930s style. Here again is the recreation trail which runs from Seaside to Pacific Grove, through the Row - a good venue for walking, bicycling or skating.

Jack's Trading Company at 799 is the site of Flora Woods' Lone Star Cafe and house of ill repute. John Steinbeck renamed it The Bear Flag Restaurant, owned by 'Dora Flood,' in his novel, *Cannery Row*.

The brown board building at 800 was Doc Rickett's **Pacific Biological Laboratories**, known as 'Doc's Lab' in *Cannery Row*. The Lab is occasionally opened to the public by the Cannery Row Foundation. Call 649-6690.

The Sea Pride Canning Company built in 1917, at 807, is now the Cannery Row Trading Company. **Old Cannery Row Fudge Company** gives <u>free fudge</u> samples made the old-fashioned way. Mail order available. 373-6672.

Wing Chong Market, 835, was built in 1918 by Won Yee, who became 'Lee Chong' in Steinbeck's *Cannery Row*. **Alicia's Antiques** houses the Steinbeck Remembrance Room of memorabilia, in the rear of the building, which is <u>open free</u> to the public. 372-1423.

Kalisa's, next door at 851, was originally a boarding house built in 1929, and re-named the 'La Ida Cafe' in Chapter 7 of *Cannery Row*. Kalisa Moore has run the little cafe since the 1960s. Steinbeck's Birthday Celebration Feb. 27. Call for other events, 656-0967, 644-9316.

More Things to See & Do on Cannery Row

➤ Held the second Thursday of each month at The Monterey Bay Aquarium Education Center by the Cannery Row Foundation. Forums present all the facts on aquarium exhibits, research, conservation efforts, education programs and membership–along with a cyber-tour of the bay, from the tidepools to the depths of a vast underwater canyon. Call 375-4982 or 372-8512.

➤ The **Monterey Hostel Society** should have opened their new hostel at Hawthorne Street and Prescott Avenue in late 1999. Part of the American Youth Hostels' Central California Council. Call Melissa Newlin at 899-3046 for details on the hostel and volunteering.

➤ **Otter-Mobile Tours and Charters:** <u>Free with mention of Your Personal Guide</u>: One Monterey Bay Aquarium ticket for every two paying people on the Monterey Peninsula tour which includes, in detail, Monterey, Pacific Grove, Pebble Beach and Carmel. Highly recommended tour with historic and current narrative. 9am-5pm. Paula DiCarlo, 649-4523, fax 333-0832.

➤ **Cannery Row Walking Tours:** Guided historic and literary tours. 373-5727.

"Forrest Gump"

Steve Weber appears as Forrest Gump Saturday afternoons at the Bubba Gump Shrimp Co. on Cannery Row. For information about a Forrest Gump appearance at your next event, call 408-241-6162.

The Monterey Bay Aquarium

At 886, the end of Cannery Row, the world famous **Monterey Bay Aquarium**, formerly the site of Hovden Food Products Corp., is the most visited aquarium in the U.S.

● Open 10am-6pm daily; closed Christmas. (9:30am-6pm during summer and holiday periods).

● There are more than 100 galleries and exhibits to see and touch the sea life of Monterey Bay, including sea turtles, fish and shrimp and video and hands-on displays.

● The three-story Kelp Forest exhibit, a dynamic, living kelp forest community has feeding shows by divers daily at 11:30 and 4.

● "Sea Otters along the Rocky Coast," is a nose-to-nose encounter with California sea otters swimming in a 55,000 gallon, naturalistic exhibit; three feeding shows daily at 10:30, 1:30 and 3:30.

● The Outer Bay has the largest window in the world. It's 54' long, 15' tall and 13" thick. See large yellowfin and bluefin tuna, bonito, barracuda, sea turtles and a giant ocean sunfish in the million-gallon tank.

● Current exhibits include "Mysteries of the Deep," the world's first major exhibit of living deep sea creatures; and "Splash Zone," a children's museum inside an aquarium with colorful, hands-on live-animal experiences and interactive learning. Features nearly 50 species from South African blackfooted penguins to leafy sea dragons, colorful corals and tropical sharks. For exhibit info, call Ken Peterson, 648-4922.

● The Aquarium offers several <u>free educational events, free admission to residents once a year, and volunteer opportunities. Discount admission rates for seniors, youth and groups.</u> For more information, call 648-4800. Automated information 648-4888; education 648-4850; volunteer office 648-4867; tickets 800-756-3737.

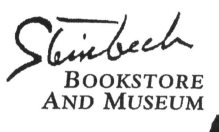

Art Galleries, Museums & Bookstores

● **Thomas Kinkade Archives**, 550 Wave St., 10-5 daily. 657-1554; 400 Cannery Row, Mon-Sat, 10-8, Sun, 10-5, 657-2350; 685 Cannery Row, 10-8 daily, 657-2365.

● **Crystal Fox**, 400 Cannery Row. Mon-Sat, 10-8, Sun 10-5, 655-3905.

● **Robert Lyn Nelson Studios**, 660 Cannery Row#105. 9-9 daily, 655-8500.

● **Ansel Adams Gallery**, 685 Cannery Row. Daily 10-6. Works by Ansel Adams and other fine art photographers, crafts, creative gifts, and Native American crafts and jewelry. 375-7215.

● **Sculptures by the Sea**, 685 Cannery Row. Mark Hopkins bronzes, Boehm, Armani and Lladro porcelain, and Swarovski crystal. 11-7 daily, 649-5250.

● **The Artist Colony**, second floor at 700 Cannery Row:

Frank Sunseri Sculpture. Welded-metal, stone and cast bronze sculptures by Frank Sunseri, since 1976 on the Row. 372-6345.

Enchanted Angels. #RR. Store of, by and for angels. Channeling lessons, Wed & Sun, 7pm. $10 first two times, then free. Doris, 655-8408.

● **MY Museum**, Monterey County Youth Museum, admission only $2 per person on Tuesday in August at 601 Wave St, Suite 100. Open free on special occasions. Mon-Sat 10-5, Sun 12-5. 649-6444.

● **A Book Search by McWilliams & Chee,** Old and Rare Books, 471 Wave. email: abooksearch@redshift.com. www.abooksearch.com. 656-9264.

● **Monterey Cypress Stained Glass,** 400 Foam St. Original designs. Open Mon-Sat, 10am-5:30pm. Sundays by appointment. 373-1989.

● **John Steinbeck Bookstore & Museum**, 551 Foam St. Free admission 10-6pm daily. Visit the past of Steinbeck and learn about the myths and legends of Cannery Row. Walking and lecture tours. Movies, memorabilia, gifts, first editions, new and used books. Closed some Sundays. 646-9117.

● **Books and Things**, 224 Lighthouse. Large and varied stock of old, used, out-of-print and rare titles. Mon-Sat, 11am-6pm, 655-8784.

● **Basset Books**, 626 Lighthouse. Large, varied selection of old, aged, and out-of-print books. Cafe, Sun-Fri, 10am-6pm., Sat, 10am-10pm, 655-3433.

● **Old Capitol Book Co.**, 639-A Lighthouse. Large and varied stock of old, used, out-of-print & rare titles. Mon-Sat, 10am-6pm, 375-2665.

● **Cross Roads International Bible Bookstore**, 699 Lighthouse. 10am-7pm daily. 372-3860, fax 372-4042.

● **Lighthouse Books**, 801 Lighthouse. Specializing in Steinbeck, photography, modern first editions. Wed-Mon, 10:30am-6:30pm. 372-0653.

Nature & Activities
Cannery Row Parks & Beaches

▲ **San Carlos Beach**, at the entrance to Cannery Row at the foot of Reeside Avenue and the Coast Guard pier. Site of one of Cannery Row's famous sardine canneries: the San Carlos Canning Co. Swimming, world-renowned scuba diving, picnic tables, grassy areas, restrooms. Check out the bronze starfish and seashells on the rocks. Open dawn to dusk. 646-3860.

▲ **MacAbee Beach**, narrow entry next to the Spindrift Inn, 652 Cannery Row. Popular with scuba divers. Open dawn to dusk. Grassy area, benches, restrooms. Kayaking takes you out on the water to enjoy the many marine birds and mammals: sea otters, seals, sea lions, brown pelican.

▲ **Ed Ricketts' Underwater Park**, extends from the breakwater to Hopkins Marine Station in Pacific Grove, near the Monterey Bay Aquarium.

New Monterey Parks

▲ **Cypress Park**, corner of Cypress Street and Hoffman Avenue. Full-size tennis court, grassy area and benches. Rocky area.

▲ **Scholze Park**, Dickman and Lighthouse avenues. Grassy areas, big trees, picnic tables. Location of Senior Center.

▲ **Archer Park Center and Hoffman Park**, on Archer Street between Hoffman and McClellan avenues. Clean play area and spacious, tree-lined barbecue area and multi-purpose rooms. Nice view of Monterey Bay.

▲ **Hilltop Park and Hilltop Park Center**, 871 Jessie Street. 2.8 acres with barbecue/picnic, lawn, play equipment, playground, basketball, baseball, tennis. Open dawn to dusk. 646-3975.

▲ **Oak-Newton Park**, between Oak and Newton streets. Quiet and well-equipped for children. Large grassy area, picnic areas, shade trees, basketball court. Clean rest rooms. A pedestrian gate on the eastern end connects the park to the Presidio.

Dive, Surf and Bike Free Offers

➤ **Bamboo Dive Shop,** 614 Lighthouse. Free air on Fridays. Mon-Fri 9-6. Sat-Sun 7-6. 372-1685.

➤ **On the Beach Surf Shop**, 693 Lighthouse, 646-9283. Free wax and stickers with any purchase.

➤ Free air and same day repairs at **Joselyn's Bicycles**, 398 E. Franklin, 649-8520.

Calendar of Events

Year 2000 dates shown. Updates at www.montereycountyguide.com.
Please call in advance to verify as information is subject to change.

February 27   **STEINBECK'S BIRTHDAY PARTY**   **FREE**
Cannery Row Birthday Party commemorating the famed author and Salinas' native son, John Steinbeck. 372-8512.

March 7   **MARDI GRAS**   **FREE**
"Fat Tuesday" with live broadcasts from New Wave radio stations and a "Doo Dah" parade. Entertainment throughout the evening. 649-6600.

May 14   **ED RICKETTS BIRTHDAY**   **$$**
Special birthday celebrations for Ed Ricketts. Call for more info 649-6690.

May 20   **RACE NIGHT ON THE ROW**   **FREE**
Row closed to traffic for the official Laguna Seca NASCAR Winston cars.

June   **MY MUSEUM BIRTHDAY CELEBRATION**   **FREE**
A fun place for kids with a creation center, magnetic center, giant loom, build a house plus lots and lots of other things to do. 601 Wave between Hoffman and Prescott. 3rd floor, 10am-5pm, closed Wed. 649-6444.

June 11   **THE GREAT CANNERY ROW REUNION**   **$$**
Reunion of cannery workers, dinner and entertainment. Info: 649-6690.

July 8   **WORLD SUPERBIKE RACE NITE**   **FREE**
6-10pm Saturday to honor Laguna Seca's McGraw Insurance U.S. World Superbike championship races. Cannery Row will be closed between Hoffman and David avenue; open to motorcycles for cruising, parking, exhibits. Live music, stunt shows, riders and racers. Volunteer with the Cannery Row Company to help out with this event if you like bikes. 372-2259.

August 19   **HISTORIC AUTOMOBILE RACES**   **FREE**
Vintage car displays and evening musical entertainment to welcome racers. 372-2259.

Sept 9   **HONDA GRAND PRIX ON CANNERY ROW**   **FREE**
AMA National Superbike Championships. Street closure, cycle displays, autograph sessions and musical entertainment on Cannery Row in celebration of Laguna Seca's motorcycle championships. 373-2259.

Sept 22   **CHERRY'S JUBILEE**   **FREE**
Restored hotrod and other classic car owners get together to celebrate with parties, dancing, food and souvenir booths. More than 800 restored classic cars cruise Monterey and settle on Cannery Row for a "Show and Shine" Friday from 5-10pm as cars parade and are judged for "People's Choice Awards" at Steinbeck Plaza, complete with a live band. 759-1836.

October 14   **VISA SPORTS CAR CHALLENGE**   **FREE**
Official Laguna Seca "Race Night on the Row." Call for info, 372-8512.

October 31   HALLOWEEN ACTIVITIES ON THE ROW   FREE
"Trick or treat" the merchants on Cannery Row (4-7pm) for free candy, balloons, coffee and hot chocolate, free face painting, free carousel rides for children under 10 and in costume at the **Edgewater Packing Company**, free admission to the **Spirit of Monterey Wax Museum**, free or discounted meals for every two children with one adult ordering from the regular menu, at participating restaurants. 649-6690. **The American Tin Cannery** holds its "Safe & Sane Trick or Treat" from 3-5pm at 45 store locations.

November 24   CHRISTMAS TREE LIGHTING CEREMONY   FREE
6pm. "Snow on the Row". Tons of real snow will decorate Steinbeck Plaza for the annual Cannery Row Christmas tree lighting. Music and caroling with the arrival of Santa Claus. Free pictures of kids with Santa. 649-6690.

December   FREE PARKING ON THE ROW   FREE
The Monterey Police Department will not enforce metered parking in Cannery Row on Sundays in December. Info: 372-2259.

Row Rats Wanted
Cannery Row's corps of volunteers, the "Row Rats," are seeking additional volunteers for public projects and events on the Row. Hard work, camaraderie and special perks from Cannery Row businesses and restaurants for jobs such as marshalls, vehicle control, communications, traffic barricade monitors. New "Row Rat" volunteers can call 648-8132 for more info.

Public Art at San Carlos Beach

Entertainment

Cannery Row

◆ **Schooners**, Fri-Sat, live music 9pm, <u>no cover</u>, validated valet parking. Monterey Plaza Hotel, 400 Cannery Row. 646-BOAT, www.montereyplaza.com.

◆ **Planet Gemini**, 625 Cannery Row, comedy club, 373-1449. Cover.

◆ **Bulwacker's**, 653 Cannery Row. Music Fri-Sat 9pm. 373-1353. <u>No cover</u>.

◆ **Blue Fin Cafe & Billiards**, 685 Cannery Row, Steinbeck Plaza, 3rd floor. Live music and dancing Fri-Sat 9pm. Wed jazz, Thurs DJ dancing. 375-7000, www.bluefin-billiards.com.

◆ **Fish Hopper Restaurant**, 700 Cannery Row. Tues-Fri, Happy Hour, 4-6:30, <u>complimentary</u> tropical hors d'oeuvres, live music. 372-8543.

◆ **Sly McFly's Refueling Station**, 700 Cannery Row. The hottest Swing, Blues & Jazz Club in Monterey. Music 7 nights a week. <u>No cover</u>. 649-8050.

KNRY–The Voice of the Central Coast

Outrageous, real, authentic talk radio with an attitude.

KNRYam 1240 Live from Cannery Row since 1935
651 Cannery Row Ste 1, 831-373-1234.

INTERGALACTIC RADIO, 9pm every Sunday.
Monterey Bay favorite since 1996.

CENTRAL COAST SHOW, with Susie Harrison and Karen Verga, longest running radio program on the Coast, Fridays at noon.

HOST YOUR OWN RADIO PROGRAM, call today.

CB MAXWELL

New Monterey

◆ **STARZzzz**, 214 Lighthouse Ave. New tenant in After Dark. Karaoke, Open Mic, pool leagues, DJ & live music, dancing. $3. Call for times, 375-3056.

◆ **Gianni's Pizza**, 725 Lighthouse Ave. <u>Dinner music</u>, Saturday, 6-8pm, and the best pizza in town anytime. 649-1500.

◆ Horon Turkish Fold Ensemble offers <u>free dance classes</u> from different provinces of Turkey every Thurs from 7-9pm at the **Monterey Senior Center**, Lighthouse and Dickman avenues. 646-1916.

◆ **Dream Theater**, 301 Prescott. Tues, all seats $2.50; come early! <u>Free refill on large popcorn & soda</u>. 372-1494. www.movie-tickets.com.

◆ **Hoffman Playhouse**, 320 Hoffman Ave. Call for info, 649-0259.

Pacific Grove

Lighthouse Keepers

Lovers Point

Victorian Houses

Pacific Grove, winter haven to thousands of Monarch butterflies, is a year 'round paradise for visitors and residents, with lots of free and fun things to see and do. Visit Victorian homes and gardens; browse the shops, museums, and art galleries; enjoy the parks and beaches. Ocean View Boulevard around the point of the Monterey Peninsula takes you past some of the most beautiful scenery in the world, including sea birds and sea mammals, Pt. Piños Lighthouse, and Asilomar Conference Center and State Beach.

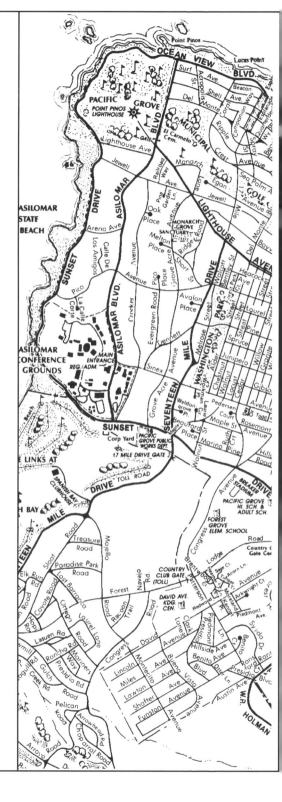

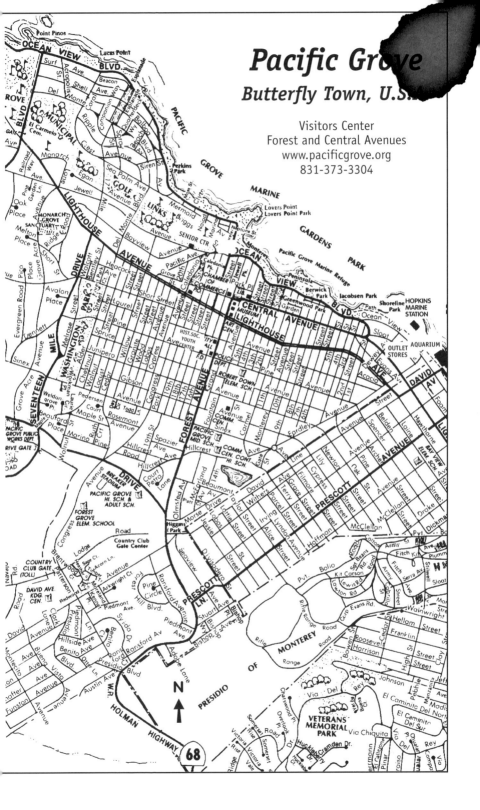

Historic Downtown Walking Tour

Get oriented with a leisurely stroll through this historic seaside village. The town had its beginning in 1875 as a summer Methodist camp, where several hundred people assembled to worship amidst rough tents. The first camp meeting of the Pacific Coast branch of the Chautauqua Literary and Scientific Circle was held here in June 1879. Fashioned after the Methodist Sunday school teachers' training camp established in 1874 at Lake Chautauqua, N.Y., this location was part of a nationwide educational/cultural network. In 1889, the resort was incorporated, becoming the City of Pacific Grove. The following is adapted from an historic walking tour prepared by local resident and historian Esther Trosow. You may take her complete tour from the Visitors Center, 10am, every Saturday.

Begin your walking tour at the **Chamber of Commerce and Visitors Center** building on the corner of Central and Forest Avenues. Here you'll find a lodging referral system, brochures, maps, postcards, and other helpful information. If you're staying in P.G., October Mrs. Myretta Steiner House, built in 1892 for A.J. Steiner (who owned a grocery store at Lighthouse and Forest in the 1880s and 90s), this house displays both Queen Anne and Stick details. The smaller house, originally detached, may have been a storage shed or servants' quarters. 122-124 – Paris Kilburn

House – Built in 1889, this unusual boat-like house features an eclectic array of detail work. 116 – "Bathhouse" Smith House – This 2-story barn-like house was built around 1910, and originally stood at Lovers Point. It features a gambrel roof, shed dormers, and a variety of paned windows.

At the foot of Fountain is: SEVEN GABLES, 555 Ocean View. Built in 1886. First owner Jane Page came from Salem, MA, and named her home after Hawthorne's novel. Mrs. Page and later owner Lucy Chase were civic leaders involved with the Museum of Natural History. It has

tures in the entrance and back garden. Free admission to the museum, Tues-Sun, 10am-5pm. Free lecture every 2nd Wed. at 7:15pm. Call ___ events and how you can volunteer to help, 648-3116.

┌───┐
| **Museum of Natural History 2000 Exhibits** |
| Jan 8–June 18   Whales 2000: Larry Foster |
| Jan 14–Jan 30   Whalefest 2000 Exhibits & Events |
| April 14-16   39th Annual Wildflower Show |
| July 1–Sept 24   MIRA–Exploring the Universe from Monterey |
| Oct 7–Jan 2001   Under Antarctic Ice Premier Photograph Exhibit |
└───┘

Continue on Central; turn left at Fountain: 100 BLOCK OF FOUNTAIN AVENUE. Below Central. An early residential street in the Retreat, this block retains many of its original structures. 138 & 138^1/$_2$, Mrs. Myretta Steiner House, built in 1892 for A.J. Steiner (who owned a grocery store at Lighthouse and Forest in the 1880s and 90s), this house displays both Queen Anne and Stick details. The smaller house, originally detached, may have been a storage shed or servants' quarters. 122-124 – Paris Kilburn House – Built in 1889, this unusual boat-like house features an eclectic array of detail work. 116 – "Bathhouse" Smith House – This 2-story barn-like house was built around 1910, and originally stood at Lovers Point. It features a gambrel roof, shed dormers, and a variety of paned windows.

At the foot of Fountain is: SEVEN GABLES, 555 Ocean View. Built in 1886. First owner Jane Page came from Salem, MA, and named her home after Hawthorne's novel. Mrs. Page and later owner Lucy Chase were civic leaders involved with the Museum of Natural History. It has recently been remodeled.

Next door is: GRAND VIEW INN, 105 Grand Ave. Once called "Roserox," this house was built in 1910 for Dr. Julia B. Platt, a pioneer neurobiologist and the town's first woman mayor. Now an elegant inn, the house boasts a commanding view of Lovers Point.

On Ocean View, walk one block to 15th, turn right: MRS. L.H. CODDINGTON'S HOUSE, 109 15th Street. Built in 1888, this is a pretty example of early P.G. camp meeting style. The facade's decorative frieze is especially pleasing. The cottage's careful restoration earned a Heritage House Award.

Continue up to Central, turn left, go one block to: ST. MARY'S BY-THE-SEA, 12th & Central. P.G.'s first formal church, cop-

...ied in 1857 from a Gothic church in Bath, England. Cyrus McCormick (the ...'s nephew) donated two Tiffany windows in memory of his wife, whom he married here in 1889. Sunday Eucharist is at 8am and 10am. You'll find bargains in their thrift store, Mon-Wed-Fri-Sat, 1-4pm. Watch for their Antique Show in July. The chapel is open free to visitors, 12:30-2pm, Mon-Wed-Fri. 373-4441.

Walk up 12th to Lighthouse, turn right to Fountain: STOREFRONTS, 541-553 Lighthouse. These detailed pre-1900 storefronts include 549 and 551 built in 1888; the Grove's first pharmacy, operated by pharmacist/photographer C.K. Tuttle, and 553 (originally a tobacco store).

Continue along Lighthouse to Forest: BRATTY REAL ESTATE, 574 Lighthouse. Built in 1904 by Watsonville architect W.H. Weeks, this was originally the Bank of Pacific Grove. It features simulated stone block siding, and is the only example of Romanesque revival style on the Peninsula. Free rental services, Mon-Fri 9-5, Sat 10-4, Sun 11-2.

Turn left at Forest, go one block to Laurel, CITY HALL, 300 Forest Ave. This structure originally served as both police and fire station. The tower housed hoses and the old fire bell (now in front of the fire station at 580 Pine). Plans are underway to make this building the cornerstone of a new Civic Center that would encompass the entire block and provide needed facilities to serve the Council and the community.

Turn right on Laurel and go to 17th: KETCHUM'S BARN, Laurel and 17th. Built in 1891 by H.C. Ketchum, animals were kept on the ground floor and hay and other provisions stored in the loft. This square board and batten barn is now the home of the P.G. Heritage Society. Free and open on Saturdays, 1-4pm.

Across 17th and Laurel is: OLD 17TH STREET. Above Lighthouse. Most of the cottages on this block were built in the 1880s; a few were built around 1900. Most of these cottages have been converted for commercial uses, yet the street retains its charming flavor.

Follow Laurel to 18th, turn right to Lighthouse: GOSBY HOUSE, 643 Lighthouse. In 1888, J.S. Gosbey, owner of P.G.'s first shoe store, opened his home to summer boarders. To house more guests, he added to the Queen

Anne building several times, resulting in the inn's irregular plan

Next door is: HART MANSION, 649 Lighthouse. This Queen Anne structure has not changed significantly since it was built in 1894 by Dr. Andrew J. Hart. The first floor was used for his medical practice, and the 2nd and 3rd floors for his residence, now a popular restaurant.

Continue 1 block on Lighthouse to 16th: WINSTON HOTEL, 16th and Lighthouse. Built in 1904 by B.C. Winston, a showman who brought buffalo and trained sea lions to P.G. The hotel boasted rooms on the 2nd and 3rd floors and a restaurant and shops on the ground floor.

Turn left down 16th: ELMARIE H. DYKE OPEN SPACE, 16th below Lighthouse. Dedicated to the woman affectionately dubbed "Mrs. Pacific Grove." Educator, civic leader and radio personality, her efforts ensured that P.G. remained (until 1969) the last dry town in California.

Next door, at the corner of Central is: CHAUTAUQUA HALL, 16th and Central. Since 1881, this has been a vital part of the community, serving as storage space for the Retreat's tents, church, school, gym, youth center, and meeting place. Last Chautagua was August 1926. In 1970, it became California Landmark #839.

Across Central is: CENTRELLA HOTEL, 612 Central. Built in 1889 to house Chautauqua-goers, the building originally faced 17th St. 1892 saw the addition of the square corner towers and porch. Completely restored.

Continue down 16th: 100 BLOCK OF 16TH ST. Below Central. Several tiny tent cottages line this street. 152 & 154 – Mrs. Eliza Beighle Houses, built in 1901 and 1892. 137 – Mrs. Caroline Thorton House. This Carpenter Gothic cottage was built in 1883. Its lower level has horizontal siding, while the upper portion has vertical siding. 122 – J. Kirk House. This Heritage House Award winner was built in 1891. It features decorative shingles in the gables; the segmented windows still have the original colored-glass panels. 118 – P.B. Chandler House was built almost entirely of redwood by the Pacific Improvement Co. in 1890. It features balloon framing, which is said to be very earthquake resistant.

Turn right on Ocean View, turn right on Forest. 100 BLOCK OF FOREST AVENUE. Below Central. An important residential street in the early Retreat grounds, it is lined with a variety of Victorian-era styles. 112 – W.H. Stephens House was built in 1892, and is quite elaborate, featuring stained-glass windows, gables, fish-scale shingles, and decorative bargeboard. In contrast, 119 – Mary Wilbur House is quite simple in style. Built in 1885, it features redwood siding and a gabled roof with sunbursts. 123 – Grove Hall was built in 1886 for Dr. Carrie Roe, one of the town's first physicians. She opened the house as a sanitarium, renting to and caring for invalids. 132 – Daffodil House – this gingerbread is a few years old, but replicates the era so well it was awarded a Heritage Design Award.

Other noteworthy sites beyond the range of a walking tour include:
Beacon House (circa 1907) 468 Pine Ave., Lacey House/Green Gables (1888) 104 5th St., Langford House (1884) 225 Central Ave., Trimmer Hill (1893) 230 6th St., Pacific Street houses, Palmer House (1887) 489 Lighthouse Ave., Pinehurst Manor (c.1890) 1030 Lighthouse Ave., Pomeroy House (1883) 106 7th St., Pryor House (1906) 429 Ocean View Blvd., Tennant House (1885) 312 Central Ave., Julia Morgan house (1917) at the triangle of 1st and 2nd streets.

Browsing The Pacific Grove Shops
The American Tin Cannery Premium Outlets

In this historic cannery building, at the 80-foot History Wall, you'll see pictures of Cannery Row's past. Take their self-guided historical exhibit and walking tour; look for signs throughout the center. There's also an information center with brochures, maps, and a free coupon book. ATM. Sun-Thurs, 10-6; Fri-Sat, 10-8. Across from the Aquarium at 125 Ocean View Blvd., 372-1442.

● **First Awakenings** Best breakfast in Monterey–gourmet food without the gourmet price; outstanding service. 372-1125.

● **Tin Cannery Cafe & Pizza** Old-fashioned brick oven pizza by the slice or to order, deli, sandwiches, espresso. Kid/family friendly. 375-4140.

● **Archie's American Diner** Outdoor dining right on the ocean. Kid/family friendly. Great burgers, sandwiches, shakes. 375-6939.

● **Adventure Comics & Sports** Pokemon merchandise, Star Wars, comic books, fantasy games. Great prices all year. 375-0553.

(831) 646-1922
mr Z
Fine Jewelry • Diamonds • Appraisals

(831) 646-8321
mrs Z's
Mineral Specimens & Fossils
Gemstone Jewelry & Appraisals

● **Mr. Z's,** fine jewelry, full service repair, custom design, diamonds, jewelry appraisals. 10% discount with this book. 646-1922.

● **Mrs. Z's Gems**, Worldwide exotic treasures, specimens, minerals, jewelry, gifts. 10% discount with this book. 646-8321.

● **Carter's Childrenswear** On-going 30%-70% discount storewide. Apparel, accessories, gifts, toys, full John Lennon line. 375-6498.

● **Maidenform** On-going sales, excellent prices, intimate apparel, accessories, sleepwear. !0% disc. on non-sale items with this book. 649-0626.

● **Nine West** offers 20% off all regular priced men & women's shoes. Take an additional 10% off all sale footwear with this book. 647-8779.

> **N I N E   W E S T**
> s h o e   s t u d i o
> American Tin Cannery
> 125 OceanView Blvd. #112
> 831-647-8779

● **Anne Klein Factory Stores** Missy and petite clothing available in sizes 0-16, full accessories including watches. 647-8804.

● **Eye Zoo** Sunglasses by Oakley, Arnette, Armani, Maui Jim and more. 10% discount with this book (some restrictions may apply). 657-0265.

● **Carole Little** Soft designer clothes at 40%-70% off retail. Sizes 2-24, petites and larger sizes included. 655-0160.

● **Totes** Be prepared in cold season: umbrellas, coats, knit accessories; in the warmer season, sunglasses and accessories. On-going sales. 655-3026.

● **Leather Loft** Discounted leather luggage by Carlo Ambaldi, Boulder Ridge. Traditional luggage by Skyway, Lexi Int'l, Riccardo Beverly Hills. 646-0416.

● **Samsonite** 35%-50% off comparably priced Samsonite and American Tourister Luggage. 10 year warranty. Accessories. 333-0809.

● **Van Heusen** Men and women's business and corporate casual apparel. Seasonal clearance sales well below dept. store prices. 373-7981.

● **Reebok & Rockport** Great prices year-round, frequently buy 1 get 2nd at half price. Mens, womens, kids. 644-0990.

● **L'eggs, Hanes, Bali** Excellent discounts year-round, intimate apparel, hosiery, knitwear, sleepwear. 372-6099. www.myfavoriteoutlet.com.

More Shops in the Area

Nob Hill Foods, Tillie Gort's Restaurant, The Clothing Store, Thai Bistro, Vivolo's Chowder House, and Patrick's Consignment Store invite you to stroll on Central Avenue, up two blocks from the outlet stores.

Waterfront Bus Service

WAVE, the Monterey-Salinas transit summer bus service, runs through Pacific Grove from the Tin Cannery Outlets, along the bay on Ocean View, up Pacific to Lighthouse, left on 17-Mile Drive, right on Sinex, right on Asilomar, back to Lighthouse, right to Forest, Forest back to Bayview. Ride all day for one low price. Bus comes at 1/2 hour intervals. (Subject to funding.)

Historic Downtown

Pacific Grove is known for its home furnishings and home and garden stores. There's free parking all over the city, with an extended hours parking lot

behind the theater on Lighthouse Ave. Park there to begin your walk at **The Grove Homescapes**, 472 Lighthouse, in the renovated old Grove Laundry building. Enjoy the sweeping staircase, local artworks, and natural fish pond, with colorful Koi and bass, in the garden. Pick up a newsletter with dates and times for <u>free events</u>. Try their <u>free testers</u> of exotic worldly perfumes and lotions. Daily 10am-6pm. 656-0864.

● **Hambrook's Auction House,** where auctioneers entertain you on auction day. If you want to bid on the merchandise, get a number at the service counter in the rear. You may pick up purchased items at the end of the auction, around 5pm. **2000 Auction Schedule:** Jan 7-8, 28-29; Feb 18-19; March 31-Apr 1; April 21-22; May 12-13; June 2-3, 23-24; July 14-15; August 4-5, 25-26; Sept 15-16; Oct 6-7, 27-28; Nov 17-18; Dec 8-9. Preview auction items, 12-8pm, Thursday before auction dates. 373-2101.

➤ Enjoy Old World Italian dining at its finest by a cozy fireplace or at any of the charming tables nestled into the "nooks and crannies" of this quaint Victorian, now home to **Pasta Mia Trattoria** at 481 Lighthouse Avenue.

Pasta Mia was voted Best Italian & Best Pasta Restaurant for the last 10 years. Antipasto, homemade pastas, Black Angus steaks, prime rib and veal. California and Italian wines and beer. Lunch buffet 11-1:30pm, dinner 5-10pm. Prices moderate, reservations appreciated. 375-7709.

● **Pier 1 Imports**, 490 Lighthouse Ave. Mon-Fri, 10am-9pm; Sat 10am-7pm; Sun 11am-7pm. Third largest sales store in California. 373-5959.

● **Central Avenue Pharmacy**, 133 15th St. Free bottle of Vitamin C with every purchase. Ask Dana Gordon, owner and compounding pharmacist, about his customized prescriptions, sold locally and nationally. 373-1225.

● **Chatterbaux Children's Shoppe**, 157 Fountain. Come see Mr. McGee, their petting rabbit. Mon-Fri, 10am-5pm; Sat 11am-3pm, 647-8701.

● **Pacific Grove Jewelers**, 311A Forest Ave., gives a free jewelry cleaning and checking of prongs. Tues-Fri, 10am-5pm; Sat 10am-4pm. 649-6258.

● **Mikoli Custom Tableware**, 581 Lighthouse. Impressive shop. Lots of Monterey and Pacific Grove logo souvenirs. 655-9736.

● **The Cubby Hole**, 580 Lighthouse. Eclectic collection of gifts, wall covered in bark pieces–must see it to believe it. 648-5344.

● **Alpha Stationers**, 221 Forest Ave., Mon-Fri 9-5:30, Sat 10-5, Sun 11-4. Cards, candy, stationery, and more. 372-4388, fax 372-7130.

● **Haider and Associates**, 591 Lighthouse Ave. Suite 2, offers a free stress management consultation. Call Paul for an appt., 641-9220.

● **Reincarnation Vintage Clothing**, 214 17th Street. 10% off any purchase when you mention this book. Mon-Sat 11-5:30. Clothing & Jewelry from the 1890s to 1950s.

● **The Holman Building**, across the street, is now an antique collective that will give hours of pleasant browsing and many historical perspectives. When Rensselaer Luther Holman constructed the building in 1924, as Holman's Department Store, it was the largest department store between Los Angeles and San Francisco. On the lower floor is the newly-opened **Harvest Natural Foods**, open daily 9am-7pm.657-2800.

➤ Interesting shops, many in Victorian homes, line both sides of Lighthouse all the way to Miss Trawick's Garden Shop near the Post Office. Side streets offer their own treasures; check out **Grove Market** on Forest for picnic supplies. 3 city directories on Lighthouse Ave. to guide you: on Forest, Park & Fountain.

Fairway Center, Forest Hill & Country Club Gate

Take David Ave. up the hill to another major shopping area where Highway 68 enters the city from the south and becomes Forest Ave.

■ **The Discovery Shop** is an upscale resale shop operated by the American Cancer Society, where you will find wonderful bargains and support a worthy cause. Special year 2000 sales: March 25, May 27, June 14, Aug 5, Oct 14. 182 Country Club Gate Shopping Center, 372-0866.

Art Galleries & Receptions

● **Pacific Grove Art Center**. Free admission, Wed-Sat, 12-5pm, Sun, 1-4pm. Four galleries in a variety of media; exhibits change frequently and free receptions are given for the new artists. Adults and children 7 and older can enroll in visual arts courses. Local artists have studios in the center. Each year the Center hosts a collection of art on the free Artists' Studio Tour and distributes tour maps. 568 Lighthouse, 375-2208.

Art Center 2000 Opening Night Receptions, Fridays 7-9pm

Jan. 14	Maria Park, Michelle Echenique, Joe Smolen, Craig Lovell
Feb. 18	Benny Alba, Kurt Jensen photos, Selleny jewelry
March 31	Don Anderson and A. Rheim, P.G. Art Center Tenant Show
May 12	Central Coast and pastels
	(Remainder undecided at press time.)

● **KAZU Arts Gallery**, 167 Central Avenue. Visual arts gallery combines contemporary work and events that verge on performance art. "Art After Lunch" radio interviews. Call for list of free events, shows, 375-7275.

● **KAZU Art by the Inch**, 167 Central Avenue. Purchase miniature artworks from a vending machine on the sidewalk outside the radio station offices. "Art is accessible, affordable, essential and inexhaustible." 646-2048.

● **The Grove Homescapes**, 472 Lighthouse Ave., featuring local paintings,

photography, sculpture and ceramics, will host an artist reception from 5-7pm on Feb 5, March 31, June 2, July 28, Sept 1, Nov 3. Store is open daily 10am-6pm. Free Sunday Salon Artist Seminar Series, 1-3pm, monthly. Call for those dates, 656-0864. Left, Anita Benson, resident artist at the Pacific Grove Art Center, and Thompson Lange, in front of a Homescapes' mural by Benson.

● **Stowitts Museum & Library**, 591 Lighthouse Ave., Wed-Sat, 1-5pm. Changing exhibitions. Free admission. 655-4488. www.stowitts.org.

● **The Quaint**, 623 Lighthouse Ave., Thurs-Sat 10:30-4:30, Sun 12-4:30. Artists: Bill Stone, Carol Guido, Charles Haas, Jane Bradford. 642-9136.

● **Artists Forum Gallery**, 223 Forest Ave. Mon-Sat, 11am-5pm. Arts and crafts, art nouveau, art deco and decorative and fine arts. 375-4278.

● **Back Porch Fabrics**, 157 Grand Ave. Mon-Sat, 10am-5pm; Sun 12-4pm. Local quilters exhibits, including wearable art; receptions. 375-4453.

● **Tessuit Zoo**, 171 Forest Ave. Artsy furniture and clothing. 648-1725.

- **Claypoole-Freese Gallery**, 216 Grand Ave. Fine art, framing, restoration, water gilding, and carving. 373-7179.

- **Hauk Fine Arts**, 206 Fountain Ave. Belle Yang, Gregory Kondos, Johnny Apodaca and other early California artists. Wed-Sat 11-5. 373-6007.

- **Sally Judd Griffin Senior Center**, 700 Jewell Ave. 8am-5pm, 375-4454.

- **Vest Pocket Gallery**, Forest Hill Manor, 551 Gibson. Daily 7:30am-7pm. Local artists, change monthly. Free "All Media Still Life Art Class, with Jane Flury, every Friday 1-3. Drop-ins welcome, open to all. 657-5200.

- **Spanish Bay Galleries**, 2108 Sunset Drive. Tues-Fri, 9am-5pm. Sat by appt. Skip Kadish bronze casting figure sculptures. 373-0554.

Public Art

"P.G. Historic Mural Project." The Irene Masteller Mural, 1998, by John Ton and volunteers, is beside the Recreation Trail at Berwick Park with scenes depicting the settling of the area. Phase II mural will be a Chinese laundry at 222 Grand Ave. If you have a wall downtown and would like a free turn-of-the-century mural on it, please call Irene, project advisor, at 375-6430.

Life at the Top, sea otter bronze, Berwick Park, Chrisopher Bell and Pacific Grove Rotary International, 1994.

Butterfly, Marble Granite, a gift of Hilda Van Sickle; Gordon Newell, sculptor, 1964, at Lovers Point.

Pictorial History of California in fresco by Bernard McDonagh & Richard Still, 1968, on an outside wall at Central & 15th.

"Once I saw two Victorian ladies rafting on Lake Majella that used to be down by Asilomar, before the Sand Plant ate all of the sand dunes." (Now Crespi Pond on Ocean View near Asilomar Ave.) May 1987 by the **Mural School**: Kate, Ramie, Sherry, Gerrica. On outside wall of the patio at Carrow's Restaurant, 300 David Ave.

> ➤ Check out the old cement bench on the upper Lighthouse Ave. meridian at 11th Street. Embossed with "GAR-Grand Old Republic, 1861-1866." The Grand Army of the Republic was a Civil War Veteran's organization.

John Steinbeck Homes in Pacific Grove

PHOTO: PAT HATHAWAY COLLECTION

<u>147 11th St.</u>, built by Steinbeck's father as a summer home for the family. Steinbeck lived here with his bride, Carol, from 1930-1941. After the failure of his second marriage he returned briefly in 1948 before he moved to New York City in 1949.

<u>425 Eardley Ave.</u>, purchased by Steinbeck in 1941.

<u>222 Central Ave.</u>, home of Steinbeck's maternal grandmother, Elizabeth Hamilton from 1915-1918.

<u>800 Asilomar Blvd.</u>, a cottage owned by Steinbeck's sister Esther and her husband from the 1930s to the 1950s, and now part of the Asilomar State Park.

Edward Rickett's Laboratory and Home

<u>165 Fountain Ave.</u> is the site of Rickett's first laboratory, opened in 1923. Dedicated by the City in 1994, Ricketts Row, between Lighthouse and Central avenues, goes from his lab on Fountain Ave. to 9th St., passing Steinbeck's home on 11th St.

<u>331 Lighthouse Ave.</u>, where Ed lived with his family in the 1920s.

Please do not disturb the occupants of these private homes. Thank you.

Pacific Grove Public Library
"The Ultimate Source of Intelligent Fun"

● **Pacific Grove Public Library,** at Central and Fountain avenues, was built with Carnegie funds in 1907-08. Hours: Mon-Thur 10am-9pm, Fri-Sat 10am-5pm, Sun 1-5pm. Library cards are free to residents of Monterey, Santa Cruz and San Benito counties who present proof of local address. The library is an intriguing and stimulating place to spend an afternoon or evening, with a helpful staff, comfortable chairs and desks. The newspaper/magazine rack provides something for everyone with nearly 280 titles. There is a wide range of literature in foreign languages: Spanish, French, German, Japanese, Russian, and Italian. Access the library catalog from your personal computer and modem: Dial 646-5680: 9600, none, 8, 1 dot, full duplex, emu VT100. 2-week check out items include: books, books on tapes, videos, CDs, cassettes, and art prints to hang on your wall. 648-3162.

◆ **2nd Pacific Grove Adult Spelling Bee**, sponsored by the library board, and organized by the Director, Bobbie Morrison, is March 17, 6:30-9:30pm, Asilomar Conference Grounds. Small fee. Adrienne Laurent, emcee.

> **Storytimes, Songs, and Crafts for Children**
>
> Preschool Storytime
> Wed 10:30am, ages 2-4
> Baby Storytime
> Thur 10:30am, ages 0-2
> After School Storytime
> Wed 3:30pm, ages 4-8
>
> Junior Friends of the Library
> ages 9 and up, Tuesdays (except summer months) at 3:30pm.
> Children's librarian
> Lisa Maddalena, 648-3160.

Bookstores

● **Bookmark.** This entire store is devoted to the performing arts. Tickets are available here for **Dance Kids** productions, a nonprofit children's theater and dance organization, which offers free tickets to all of its productions for groups dealing with at-risk children, seniors and physically-challenged adults. Reserve at 624-3729. 307 Forest Ave., 648-0508.

● **Bookworks.** Large selection of books and magazines, cafe with espresso, local art on the walls, restrooms. Writing clubs, music, special events. Tues-Sun, 9am-9pm. 667 Lighthouse. Call for info, 372-2242.

● **Learning Depot.** Bring your child in to explore the free play areas. Mon-Wed 10-5, Thurs-Sat 10-6. 168 Central Ave. 372-8697.

● **Book Warehouse** in American Tin Cannery, 125 Ocean View. 375-1840.

Calendar of Events

Year 2000 dates shown. Updates at www.montereycountyguide.com.
Please call in advance to verify as information is subject to change.

FEBRUARY

February 6   A TASTE OF PACIFIC GROVE $$
Local restaurants donate food and more than 12 vineyards provide the wine at an elegant setting at the Inn at Spanish Bay. $35 per person. Benefit for schools. Sponsored by P.G. Pride, 373-2891.

February 13   TOGETHER WITH LOVE   Spectators FREE
13th Annual 10K Run/5K Fitness Walk, Lovers Point to Asilomar Beach. 8am register, run/walk 9-10am. Benefits Rape Crisis Center, 373-3389.

APRIL

April 8-9   GOOD OLD DAYS   FREE

A downtown celebration of the late 1800s includes a crafts fair with over 225 exhibitors, parade, police officer's motorcycle competition and drill team. Pie eating, bubble gum blowing and other contests. Jaws of Life and Fire Departments' Muster-Hose Cart Race, Victorian Fashion Show, entertainment. 373-3304.

April 8-9   QUILT SHOW $$
Antique and contemporary works on display at the historic Chautauqua Hall on 16th St. at Central Ave. Co-sponsored by the Monterey Peninsula Quilters Guild and the Heritage Society of Pacific Grove. 372-2898.

April 14-16   WILDFLOWER SHOW   FREE
Museum of Natural History, Forest and Central avenues, 10am-5pm. Local enthusiasts gather from the wild and present over 500 varieties of local wildflowers for your viewing pleasure. Many local wildflowers are found in the museum's gardens. Shown at right is a very large jade sculpture in their back garden. Benches to rest on. 648-3116.

MAY

May 7 BRITISH CAR-MEET   FREE
8am - 5pm. Over 200 classic/vintage and racing British cars on display. Saturday's events include a tour of the Monterey Peninsula for car entrants. Entrants' fees benefit local Monterey Peninsula charities. Exhibits, vendors, food. 373-3304.

May 13 **THE HUMAN RACE** Spectators FREE
19th annual event, 8:30am, Lovers Point to Lake El Estero and back. 8K
Walkathon to benefit walker's charity of choice. Entrants, $25. 655-9234, 757-3206.

May 14, 28 **CONCERTS IN THE PARK** FREE
Jewell Park, Central and Forest avenues, 1-3pm. Bring a blanket and enjoy local
musicians in the gazebo, presented by Pacific Grove Arts Commission and Friends
of the Arts. Meredith, 647-1719.

May 29 **MEMORIAL DAY SERVICES** FREE
Tribute to veterans,11am Monday at the Pacific Grove cemetery with members
of American Legion Post #41. Public is invited. For more info, call 375-9015.

JUNE

June 4 **ANTIQUES & COLLECTIBLES STREET FAIRE** FREE
Inaugural event will feature 200 booths on Lighthouse Ave. between Park and
15th St. 8am-5pm. Free appraisals. Sponsored by the CofC and organized by
the Monterey Kiwanis Club to benefit charitable organizations. 641-0280.

JULY

July 4 **COMMEMORATION TO HONOR VETERANS** FREE
Jewell Park, Central and Forest avenues, at 11am. Following is a city barbecue
($5) with a variety of free activities for adults and children. 373-3304.

July 7-9 **ST. MARY'S ANTIQUES SHOW & SALE** $$
43rd annual at St. Mary's Episcopal Church, 12th & Central. $4 donation. Fri-Sat
10-4, Sun 12-5. Lunch served both days, 11:30-1:30. Snack bar. 373-4441.

July 25-29 **FEAST OF LANTERNS** FREE
In keeping with a tradition as old as the city of Pacific Grove, the community
celebrates with Feast of Salads Thurs.
11:30-2pm, Chautauqua Hall; Pet Parade Fri. (Mayor Koffman & pet, below),
2pm, Caledonia Park; Street Dancing, Fri., 6:30pm on Lighthouse near the
post office; BBQ and entertainment on Sat. Lovers Point (PG Chorus, below),
followed by the Feast of Lanterns Pageant (1999 Royal Court, opposite) and
fireworks at 8pm. 372-7625.

AUGUST

August 18   **CONCOURS AUTO RALLY**   Spectators FREE
Over 200 classic and sports cars line up on Lighthouse Avenue around 1pm, tour Pacific Grove, Carmel, Monterey and Pebble Beach. Barbecue ($20) and rally benefit Pacific Grove Youth Action, Inc., 372-6585.

SEPTEMBER

September 10, 24   **CONCERTS IN THE PARK**   FREE
Jewell Park, Central and Forest avenues, 1-3pm. Bring a blanket and enjoy local musicians in the gazebo, presented by Friends of the Arts. Meredith, 647-1719.

September 11   **TRIATHLON AT LOVERS POINT**   FREE+$$
Annual Olympic swim-bike-run event. Friday "Ride the Tri or Tri the Ride" 6pm. A family fun ride from Lovers Point to Asilomar and back. Saturday: free exposition with entertainment and activities. P.G. Pasta Party Friday at 5pm $4-$8. Sponsored by Tri-California, www.tricalifornia.com, 373-0678, fax 373-0679.

Sept/Oct   CONCERTS SUNDAYS   FREE
4pm, First United Methodist Church, Sunset and 17-Mile drives. Features a choral and instrumental music in the Chapel. Pacific Grove began as a Methodist retreat, and that tradition is reflected today in the large congregation of this church and its many community events and activities. For more information, call Mary, 372-5875.

OCTOBER

October   **WALK TO CURE DIABETES**   Spectators FREE
Sponsored by the Juvenile Diabetes Foundation. Two mile corporate and family walk to raise money to help find a cure for diabetes. Activities start at 8am, walk begins at 9am at Lovers Point. (800) WALK-JDF, 626-6254.

Oct/Mar   **MONARCH DAYS CELEBRATION**   FREE
Coinciding with the butterflies' stay in the city. P.G. businesses offer special promotions, packages of free gifts and discount vouchers. Free seminars and special exhibits at the Museum of Natural History. More than 30,000 visitors each year from all over the world inquire about the Monarch butterfly habitat, one of the world's last remaining. 373-3304.

October 7   **BUTTERFLY KIDS PARADE**   FREE
Children dress in costumes and march through downtown, followed by a Butterfly Bazaar at Robert Down School. Parade begins at Pine and Fountain avenues, Fountain to Lighthouse, down Lighthouse to 17th Street, back to Robert Down on Pine for games, food, arts and crafts. 646-6540, 373-3304.

October 8   **HISTORIC HOME TOUR** $$
A tour of prime and selected Victorian and historic homes, bed & breakfast inns, churches. Hostesses dressed in Victorian era provide a history of each location. Co-sponsored by the Chamber of Commerce, P.G. Art Center, and the Heritage Society. Volunteer opportunities, call 373-3304.

October 17   **COMMUNITY AUCTION** $$
Chautauqua Hall, 5-8pm. Annual fund-raiser for the Chamber of Commerce includes the best little hors d'oeurves contest, barbecue, live and silent auctions, live entertainment. Admission $15. 373-3304.

October 31 **HALLOWEEN ACTIVITIES** **FREE**

Free candies will be given out by The American Tin Cannery businesses to all children in costume, 3-5pm. Berwick Park neighbors put on a free pumpkin show every year, "Pacific Grove Pumpkins on the Path." Come by just to see or bring your own jack-o-lantern with a lit candle. Trick-or-treaters in costume may go to the P.G. Police Station, Pine and Forest avenues, to pick up their free glow necklaces at dusk.

NOVEMBER

November 4 **MARCHING BAND FESTIVAL** **FREE**

Approximately 30 bands from around California parade and perform downtown, starting at 11am on Pine Avenue. In the afternoon, at the P.G. High School Stadium, watch a field show and competition. 646-6595.

November 27 **TREE LIGHTING CEREMONY** **FREE**

Jewell Park, Central and Forest avenues, 5pm. Entertainment by local school bands, followed by caroling at the museum and a visit from Santa. 373-3304.

DECEMBER

December 5 **CHRISTMAS AT THE INNS** **$$**

Visit several bed and breakfast inns decorated in Victorian splendor for the holidays. A limited number of tickets are sold. Entertainment and refreshments served. Volunteer opportunities to dress up and greet the public, call 373-3304.

December 9 **STILLWELL'S SNOW IN THE PARK** **FREE**

Caledonia Park, on Central Ave. behind the post office, is transformed into a winter wonderland with snow and twinkling lights. There's a Santa's workshop and the Snow Queen, Frosty the Snowman, hayrides, carolling and more. Plenty of snow to play in! 373-3304.

December 15-31 **CANDY CANE LANE** **FREE**

The entire neighborhood puts up elaborate lawn and rooftop Christmas and Hannukah scenes. Drive in on Morse Drive or Beaumont, off Forest Avenue near David. Park and walk or join the nightly procession of cars.

December 16-17 **LIVING NATIVITY** **FREE**

Outdoor tableau of scenes from the story of the birth of Jesus Christ with angels, shepherds and live baby lambs. 7-9pm, pageant repeats every 15 minutes. First United Methodist Church, Sunset at 17 Mile Drive, 372-5875.

British Car Meet in May

Good Old Days in April

Entertainment

◆ **The Tinnery**, at Lovers Point, is open for breakfast, lunch and dinner. Entertainment in the Lounge, Wed-Fri-Sat nights. No cover. Happy Hour, Mon-Tues-Thurs-Fri. Free hors d'oeuvres during the Jazz Happy Hour, Wed 5-7pm. Ocean View and 17th, 646-1040.

◆ **Mariposa Grill**. Fri-Sat, free music with dinner, 5:30-9pm; Sunday music with breakfast-lunch, 10am-1pm. 1120 Lighthouse Ave., 642-9303.

◆ **Juice 'n' Java**. Fridays, 7:30-10:30pm. Free Open Mic night with host Rama P. Jama, all styles of performing arts, from comedy and poetry to music. Fireplace, sofa and chairs, local newspapers, sidewalk seating. Other entertainment, call for times, 599 Lighthouse Ave., 373-8652.

◆ **Caravali Coffees** Mon-Thurs Happy Hour 3-6; buy one espresso and get one free. Sun-Thurs 6:30-6, Fri-Sat 6:30-8. Gifts, coffee & tea. 655-5366.

◆ **Bookworks Bookstore**. Comfortable chairs, children's area, cafe with espresso, pastries and sandwiches, restrooms. Free live entertainment. 667 Lighthouse Ave. Call for more information, 372-2242.

◆ **Hootenanny**, bi-monthly at the P.G. Art Center. Free group sing-along (song books provided), blues to folk, rock and country, vintage sounds of 1920s to '50s and today's music. Bring snacks and beverages to share. Any contributions benefit the Center, 568 Lighthouse Ave., 375-2208.

◆ **Community Chorus** meets every Friday at 7pm, Sally Griffin Center, 700 Jewell Ave. Non-Pacific Grove residents also welcome. Come and sing! Call Scott Getline, 375-4897. Free.

◆ **Taize Services**, a free candlelight service for prayer and meditation draws on the music and style of worship in Taize, an ecumenical Christian community in France. Instruments accompany you in simple, chant-like prayerful song. There is also time for silent meditation and reflection. Infant care is provided (0 to 3 yrs.). 7:30pm, first Fridays at St. Angela's Catholic Church in the church hall, Lighthouse Ave. and 9th St., 373-3031.

◆ **Chautauqua Hall Ballroom Dancing**. All ages, 7-10pm, every Saturday, $5 includes refreshments. Dick Robins Quintet first and third Saturdays. Dance lessons $2 at 6:15pm. 16th at Central. 375-2903. Not free, but fun!

◆ **Lighthouse Cinema**. Regular admission $7.50; children, seniors (65+) and matinees before 6pm, $5. Free refill on large popcorn and drink. 525 Lighthouse Ave., 372-7300 (call 777-FILM x139).

Waterfront Recreation

Scenic Drive Around the Peninsula

Begin your scenic drive on Ocean View Blvd. at the **Monterey Bay Aquarium**. Follow the coastline beside the **Recreation Trail** to **Lovers Point**, where the trail ends. Continue around the point of the Peninsula, past Asilomar, to the P.G. gate into the **17-Mile Drive** at Pebble Beach. Along the way you may see harbor seals, sea otters, sea lions, whales (Dec-Mar), deer, squirrels, raccoons, and many kinds of birds. There are several turnouts with benches where you can park, watch the sunset, or explore the shore.

Walk, Run, Skate or Bicycle

▲ **The Recreation Trail** continues from the Highway 1 bicycle path at Castroville, north of Marina, through Seaside and Monterey, along old railroad tracks and the coastline of Pacific Grove to **Lovers Point Park**. Be aware that bicycles and skaters share the trail with walkers and runners. The trail is always open.

Parks and Attractions

▲ **Hopkins Marine Station**, at China Point, owned by Stanford University since 1891, has <u>free talks</u> on marine mammals and fisheries by the Ameri-

can Cetacean Society, Monterey Bay Chapter, which meets at 7:30pm, last Thursdays, for slide/lecture presentations on the grounds in the **Monterey Boatworks**. 130 Ocean View Blvd., (across from **The American Tin Cannery**). Call Allan Baldridge for info, 663-9488.

▲ **Jacobson Park**, Ocean View Blvd. and 7th St., a very small park with native plants, benches facing the Bay and rocky outcrops to climb.

▲ **Berwick Park**, Ocean View Blvd. and 10th St., one acre with a large lawn, a natural landscape with native vegetation, and spectacular bay views. Plenty of room for picnics and a game of frisbee. Dawn to dusk.

Explore the Tidepools

There are several turnouts along the shore where you can climb among the rocks and view the sea creatures in the tidepools. The Great Tidepool where "Doc" Ricketts collected specimens for his laboratory is located off Ocean View Blvd. at the foot of the Lighthouse. Unlawful to remove any marine life.

▲ **Lovers Point Park**, Ocean View Blvd. and 17th St., is a very popular spot that juts out into the bay with rocks to climb, barbecue/picnic facilities, large lawn area, sand volleyball court, sandy beaches, toddler's swimming pool, snack bar and restrooms. Fishing, surfing, swimming, diving. Site for weddings and city events including the Feast of Lanterns. Open dawn to dusk. Call 648-3130 to rent volleyball kits for $20.

▲ **Perkins Park** is the section of dramatically beautiful shoreline west of Lovers Point, where walking trails meander among the pink ice plant first planted by Hayes Perkins. Benches and stairways to the water.

▲ **Crespi Pond** on Ocean View near Asilomar Blvd. is a haven for sea birds of all kinds: gulls, mallards, coots, and an occasional heron. Parking, telephone, public restrooms.

■ **John Denver Memorial**, a commemorative plaque, 14″ by 14″, is set into a boulder at the car turnout on Ocean View between Acropolis Ave. and Asilomar Blvd, the closest on-shore spot to where his plane crashed Oct 12, 1997. Special events are planned each year; call for info,393-8346.

■ **Point Piños Lighthouse** (c. 1855) is the oldest functioning light station on the California coast. <u>Free admission</u>. Furnished Civil War-era kitchen, parlor and Victorian bedrooms. Fri-Sat, expert Bruce Handy, 1-4pm. Local theater actress, Roo Hornady, appears as Emily Fish, the socialite lighthouse keeper from 1893-1914, Sat-Sun, 1-4pm. 648-3116. *Park on Ocean View to watch the sunset, stay to enjoy the lighthouse light after dark.*

Other Open Lighthouses Near Monterey

Pigeon Point, 650-879-0633; Santa Cruz-Mark Abbott Memorial Lighthouse-Surfing Museum; Point Sur, 831-625-4419.

Free Lighthouse Depot Catalog

"The Most Complete Selection of Lighthouse Memorabilia Ever Assembled!" For catalog, call 800-758-1444. Order on-line at www.lighthousedepot.com.

GOOD PLACES TO SEE WHALES FROM SHORE

Pt. Piños, Cypress Pt., Pt. Lobos State Reserve, Garrapata State Park, Pt. Sur, Julia Pfeiffer Burns State Park

P.G. Municipal Golf Links, 77 Asilomar Avenue, 648-3175.

▲ **Asilomar State Park and Beach** at the end of Highway 68, on the border of P.G. and Pebble Beach. No entrance fee. Swimming, surfing, walking, kite flying, beautiful sunsets, fishing (license required), scuba diving, tidepools, picnics, boardwalk, native plants, wildlife viewing of harbor seals, sea lions, sea otters, cormorants, pelicans and other bird and marine species. Open dawn to dusk. Ocean danger, water subject to large waves. No lifeguard. Information center, 372-4076.

■ **Asilomar Conference Center**, 800 Asilomar Avenue, off Highway 68. No entrance fee. The early buildings were designed by Julia Morgan of Hearst Castle fame, from 1915 to 1928, as a YWCA retreat. This California State park welcomes visitors to enjoy the architecture, beaches and trails. Free Visitor's Guide, Julia Morgan Walking Tour booklet, and Dunes Walking Tour booklet in the gift shop which is open daily 7am-9pm. You may eat in the dining hall: breakfast, 7:30-9am, lunch 12-1pm, and dinner 6-

7pm. Latte, espresso and cappuccino are available in the lobby. Free campfire programs are held several Saturdays a month at dusk, with hot chocolate, hot cider and snacks. Lodging: 372-8016. Other information, 372-4076. www.asilomarcenter.com.

Julia Morgan Architecture at Asilomar

Stone Gate Pillars 1913	Engineer's Cottage (Outside Inn) 1913
Grace H. Dodge Chapel 1915	Mary Ann Crocker Dining Hall 1918
Stuck-Up Inn (Hilltop) 1918	Health Cottage (viewpoint) 1918
Visitor's Lodge (Lodge) 1918	Pirates' den (Tide Inn) 1923
Phoebe A. Hearst (Admin) 1923	Director's (Pinecrest) 1927
Scripps' Lodge Annex 1927	Merrill Hall 1928

In 1987, all were placed on the Registry of National Landmarks

Inner City Parks & Playgrounds

All city parks have free admission; some permits may be required for special uses; obtainable from the Recreation Dept., 515 Junipero St. 648-3130.

▲ **Jewell Park.** Lawn, big trees and native flowers, Victorian gazebo to sit or play in, benches with a bay view. Site of city Christmas tree, concerts and events. A good place to sit under the trees and relax while the kids play. One block up from the bay, at Central and Grand avenues, bordered by the Visitors Center, the museum and the library.

▲ **Elmarie Dyke Open Space** is located adjacent to Chautauqua Hall on Central Ave. Flowering plants, benches, tables and gazebo.

▲ **Caledonia Park** has lots of open space, slides, swings, jungle gym, picnic tables, tot's playing area, baseball field and basketball court. Restrooms. Open dawn to dusk. Caledonia St. and Central Ave., behind the post office.

▲ **George Washington Park**, a natural habitat with Monarch butterflies (Danaus plexippus), squirrels, deer and many species of birds. 20 acres, trails, play area, restrooms. $10 fee to use ballfield, barbecue/picnic area. Open dawn to dusk. Enter from corner of Spruce and Alder Streets.

▲ **Hayward Volunteer Park**, Crocker at Sinex.

▲ **Monarch Grove Sanctuary**, enter from Ridge Road just off Lighthouse. Oct-Mar, butterflies overwinter in the pine, cypress and eucalyptus trees.

▲ **Platt Park**, a triangle of grass and a few benches bounded by Morse and McFarland Streets and Platt Court, off David. Quiet. Elaborately decorated in December as part of a Candy Cane Lane Christmas tradition.

▲ **Earl "Topper" Arnett Park**, 3 acres with playground equipment. At Piedmont and Moreland Avenue, off David Avenue.

▲ **Higgins Park**, Highway 68 and David Avenue. Triangle park with benches, big trees and bay views.

```
┌─────────────────────────────────────────────────────────┐
│          The Eco-Corps of Pacific Grove                  │
│  • Celebrates Arbor Day with a work party to replant or repair a local park.  │
│  • Ongoing Washington Park restoration "Weed and Water" Party.  │
│  • Volunteers welcome to all outings, meetings and events. Call 375-2026.  │
└─────────────────────────────────────────────────────────┘
```

Lynn "Rip" Van Winkle Open Space

▲ Lynn "Rip" Van Winkle Open Space is but a remnant of a once dense Monterey pine forest that stretched for unbroken miles and may have totaled over 18,000 acres on the peninsula. The forest was inhabited by the Ohlone who found game, acorns, shelter, and water necessary for their survival. Today it is preserved in its natural condition as open space on the west side of Congress Ave. between Sunset and Forest Lodge Rd. The trees are protected and no buildings or improvements of any kind shall be erected. This park is dedicated in honor of Lynn Van Winkle. Open dawn to dusk, no fee. 659-4488.

Rocky Shores Open Space

The Ohlone people once gathered here to visit and harvest the finfish and shellfish, when great pines grew right down on the water's edge. Today, Rocky Shores is a part of Asilomar State Beach and has a new pedestrian trail and restored native habitat. What were once threatened with extinction but have been preserved for posterity are the incomparable sunsets, the solitude

of dawn walks, and the unobstructed public access. Dunes restoration in progress. Monterey Peninsula Regional Park District, 659-4488.

▲ **Open Space**s throughout Monterey County are dedicated to remain natural habitats without manmade structures. Call the Monterey Regional Park District to find out where the locations are for other Open Spaces. 659-4488.

Join a Walking Club

➤ Meet at the **Recreation Trail** behind the snack shop at Lovers Point, 2 pm Tues and Thur. All walking levels.

➤ The **Monterey Peninsula Walk Walk Walk Club**, Sat-Sun 8am, starting from the parking lot at the Senior Center, 700 Jewell Ave. near Lovers Point. All levels accommodated. Visitors welcome. Hansi, 626-6602.

Bicycle and Skate Info

➤ **Winning Wheels Bicycle**, 223 15th St. 375-4322. Free air, info, & maps.

➤ **In-Line Retrofit**, now on-line only at www.inline-retrofit.com.

➤ **P.G. Bike Rodeo**, licensing, DARE car, special activities. Call Officer Paul Gaske, 648-3147, for date and location.

Monarch Butterfly Habitats

From **The Friends of the Monarchs:** We recommend you visit the Museum of Natural History to view the short close-up video on the life cycle of the Monarch and to see the exhibits. You will then be able to appreciate what you see at the habitats. Butterflies begin clustering in the groves in early October, and reach their peak of thousands about the end of November, staying until March. Monarch Butterfly Docents begin service on the day of the Butterfly Parade and will help you at the Sanctuary between 9am and sunset, Sat-Sun, and between 12-3pm on weekdays. October through February. Special tours, call 375-0982 or 888/PG MONARCH.

The Friends of the Monarchs work to promote and protect the butterflies and their habitats, with meetings every 2nd Tuesday at 7pm at the P.G. Museum of Natural History. "Just imagine," says Ro Vaccaro, president of Friends of the Monarchs, "if someone promised you three hours a week when you could be away from all phones, breathe deeply the eucalyptus-scented P.G. air and stand quietly on ground so special it is called a sanctuary. Imagine sharing the glorious story of the monarchs' migration with gentle visitors who travel here to see the splendor of our trees draped with butterflies. We can promise you just that!" To volunteer as a butterfly docent, call Steve Bailey at the P.G. Museum of Natural History, 648-3118.

➤ Visit the **Butterfly Souvenir Shop**, to benefit Friends of the Monarchs, located in the beautiful **Wilkie's Inn**, 1038 Lighthouse Ave., 372-0982.

➤ **John Denver Memorial**, a bench in the Butterfly Grove, and a 6' Monterey cypress tree and plaque which reads "The legacy continues...John Denver...Still in our hearts." John Denver Monterey Bay Memorial Project.

Butterfly Kids

Dedication of the Butterfly Kids statue in bronze at the post office in 1997. At left, sculptor, Christopher Bell; the founder of the annual parade, Millie Gehringer; at the podium is Les Reed of the Pacific Grove Arts Commission, attended by local children in butterfly costumes.

Education & Recreation Centers

■ **Pacific Grove Adult Education Department** offers a variety of educational, physical and cultural activities for all ages and abilities, <u>some free</u>. 1025 Lighthouse Ave., Pacific Grove, 646-6580, www.pqusd.orq. Call Maria Nunez, Principal, at 646-6580, for more information.

▲ **Pacific Grove Recreation Department** offers many and varied <u>free programs</u> to visitors and residents. Quarterly Activity Guides are available at the P.G. Library. Picnic kits include softball bats, softballs, bases, volleyball net, frisbee, soccer ball, football, volleyball and horseshoes, available for a non-refundable fee of $20. Open 8-4:45 weekdays. 515 Junipero Ave., 648-3130. www.pacificgroverecreation.org.

■ **Sally Griffin Senior Center**, and **Meals on Wheels**, 700 Jewell Ave. Informational forums on various topics of interest to seniors, exercise workshops, parties, volunteer opportunities, AARP meetings and artist receptions are just some of the <u>free events</u>. Free blood pressure checks every Tues 10-11am; <u>free exercise classes</u> include hatha yoga at 9am and aerobics at 10am, Mon-Wed-Fri; flexibility and low-impact aerobics at 9am Tues/Thurs; movement group at  10am Tues, and Wed 4-5pm. Free Senior Poetry Readings every fourth Thursday at 3pm. 373-5602. Volunteers always welcome by Meals on Wheels to help deliver warm food to homebound persons on the peninsula. Call 375-4454 for more information on activities, and how you can help.

 ▲ **Pacific Grove Youth Center,** The Nodilo Building. Open, <u>no admission fee</u>, to P.G. students in grades 6 through 12, Mon-Thurs 2:30-6:30pm, Fri 2:30-10pm, Sat 1-5pm and 7-11pm. Special events include dances, concerts, karaoke, movie matinees, coffeehouse/Open Mic nights, tournaments and more. Job Teen Fair, March 25, 4-6pm. Refreshments. Street Dance, April 9, 7-9pm, Bank of America parking lot. Voice your opinions, concerns and ideas at the **Youth Advisory Committee** meetings every 2nd Wed at 7pm. Obtain a complete calendar of events at the Youth Center, 302 16th St., or the Recreation Center at 515 Junipero. 648-3134 or 648-3130.

The Energy Center Health Spa

Aromatherapy, Thai massage, yoga instruction, myofascial release, foot reflexology, acupressure and more. 667 Lighthouse Ave, Ste 201. 658-0173.

Favorite Pacific Grove Restaurants

• Allegro Gourmet Pizzeria	Italian	1184 Forest Ave	373-5656
• Archie's American Diner	American	125 Ocean View Blvd	375-6939
• Bay Cafe	American	589 Lighthouse Ave	375-4237
• Brazilian Café	South American	1180 Forest Ave	373-2272
• Cedar Deli	Middle Eastern	1219 Forest Ave	373-3993
• Chili Great Chili	Continental	620 Lighthouse Ave	646-0447
• China Garden	Chinese	100 Central Ave	646-9400
• Chopsticks	Japanese	209 Forest Ave	375-7997
• Crocodile Grill	Tropical cuisine	701 Lighthouse Ave	655-3311
• Fandango	Italian	223 17th St	372-3456
• Favaloro's	Italian	542 Lighthouse Ave	373-8523
• Fifi's Cafe	French	1188 Forest Ave	372-5235
• First Awakenings	American	125 Ocean View Blvd	372-1125
• Gernot's	European	649 Lighthouse Ave	646-1477
• Goodies Deli	American	518 Lighthouse Ave	655-3663
• Joe Rombi's	Californian/Italian	208 17th St	373-2416
• Juice & Java	American	599 Lighthouse Ave	373-8652
• Korean Ga Zan	Korean	2006 Sunset Drive	372-2526
• Lighthouse Café	American	602 Lighthouse Ave	372-7006
• Michael's Grill	Mexican	197 Ctry Club Ctr	647-8654
• Monarch Cafe	American	162 Fountain Ave	373-7911
• Ocean Sushi Deli	Asian	2701 David Ave	649-1320
• Old Bath House	European	620 Ocean View Blvd	375-5195
• Pasta Mia	Italian	481 Lighthouse Ave	375-7709
• Patisserie Bechler	French	1225 Forest Ave	375-0846
• Peppers	Mexican	170 Forest Ave	373-6892
• Red House Cafe	American	662 Lighthouse Ave	643-1060
• Rocky Coast Ice Cream		708 Lighthouse Ave	373-0587
• Round Table Pizza	Italian	1116 Forest Ave	373-1391
• Shnarley's Bronx Pizzeria	Italian	650 Lighthouse Ave	375-2002
• Takara Sushi	Japanese	218 17th St	655-2730
• Taste Café & Bistro	New American	1199 Forest Ave	655-0324
• Thai Bistro	Thai	159 Central Ave	372-8700
• The Fishwife	Seafood	1996 1/2 Sunset Drive	375-7107
• Tillie Gort's	Vegetarian	11 Central Ave	373-0335
• Tinnery	American	Lovers Point Park	646-1040
• Toasties Cafe	American	702 Lighthouse Ave	373-7543
• Victorian Corner	Italian	541 Lighthouse Ave	372-4641
• Vivolo's Chowder House	American	127 Central Ave	372-5414
• Yang's Happy Family	Chinese	1116A Forest Ave	648-9624

*Pacific Grove Preferred Accommodations**

Bed and Breakfast Inns

		(831)	(800)	Rates
• Centrella Hotel	612 Central	372-3372	233-3372	$129-239
• Gatehouse Inn	225 Central	649-8436	753-1881	$110-165
• Gosby House Inn	643 Lighthouse	375-1287	527-8828	$100-170
• Grand View Inn	557 Ocean View	372-4341		$155-275
• Green Gables Inn	104 5th Street	375-2095	722-1774	$110-240
• Inn at 17-Mile Dr.	213 17-Mile Drive	642-9514	526-5666	$135-240
• Martine Inn	255 Ocean View	373-3388	852-5588	$155-300
• Old St. Angela Inn	321 Central Ave	372-3246	748-6306	$110-195
• Pacific Grove Inn	581 Pine Street	375-2825	732-2825	$135-225
• Seven Gables Inn	555 Ocean View	372-4341		$155-350

Lodges–Inns–Motels

• Andril Fireplace	569 Asilomar	375-0994		$74-215
• Asilomar Conf. Ctr	800 Asilomar	372-8016		$70-92
• Beachcomber Inn	1996 Sunset	373-4769	634-4769	$100-125
• Bide-a-Wee Motel	221 Asilomar	372-2330		$79-139
• Butterfly Grove Inn	1073 Lighthouse	373-4921		$89-189
• Deer Haven	750 Crocker	373-4921		$89-189
• Days Inn	660 Dennett	373-8777	221-9323	$98-225
• Larchwood Inn	740 Crocker	373-1114	525-3373	$79-$179
• Lighthouse Lodge	1249 Lighthouse	655-2111	858-1249	$99-299
• Lovers Point Inn	625 Ocean View	373-4771		$99-295
• BW Monarch Resort	1111 Lighthouse	646-8885	232-4232	$80-200
• Olympia Mtr Lodge	1140 Lighthouse	373-2777		$54-150
• Pacific Gardens Inn	701 Asilomar	646-9414	262-1566	$110-175
• Pacific Grove Motel	1105 Lighthouse	372-3218	858-8997	$69-149
• Rosedale Inn	775 Asilomar	655-1000	822-5606	$125-215
• Seabreeze Motel	1100 Lighthouse	372-7775		$79-159
• Sunset Inn	133 Asilomar	375-3936		$69-199
• Terrace Oaks Inn	1095 Lighthouse	373-4382		$69-159
• The Wilkies Inn	1038 Lighthouse	372-5960		$95-125

Time-Share Rentals

• Pacific Grove Plaza	620 Lighthouse	373-0562		$170-210
• Pine Acres Lodge	1150 Jewell	732-6651		$125-185

**Courtesy of Pacific Grove Chamber of Commerce, Moe Ammar, President
Roomfinders: Vacation Ctr Resrv (800)466-6283/Resort II Me (800)757-5646/Mtry Pen
Resrv (888)655-3424. Vacation Properties: Mtry Bay Prop Mgt (831)655-7840*

Pebble Beach

The Lone Cypress

Golf Courses

The Restless Sea

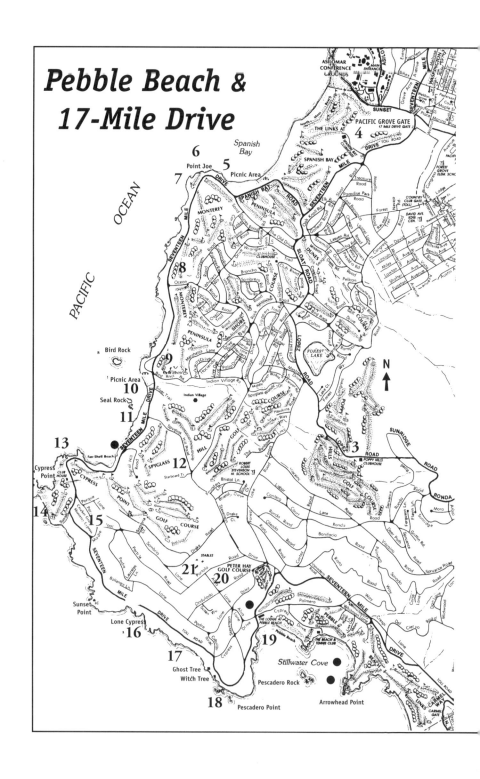

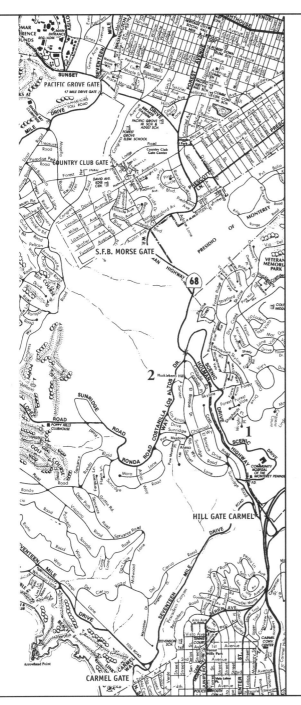

Pebble Beach, an upscale paradise for coastal living, offers many recreational, scenic, shopping and sightseeing opportunities ~ from surfing at Spanish Bay, bicycling one of the best courses in the world, picnicking next to the ocean, wildlife viewing, hiking trails, world-class shops and art galleries, events and entertainment.

The Scenic 17-Mile Drive

Originally called the "Circle of Enchantment," this scenic drive originated at the elegant Hotel Del Monte in Monterey, home to the Naval Post Graduate School, and was used to entice would-be investors to the area. Begin tour at any of the five gates, and although there is an entrance fee of $7 per car, it is reimbursed to resort guests. Dining at any of the restaurants –or shopping–will get the fee waived. The world-famous drive winds along the coastline, through scenic Del Monte Forest and past stately mansions and world-class golf courses. Open to the public daily during daylight hours. <u>Bicyclists, walkers and hikers enter free.</u> Information, 624-3881, 625-8553, 800/654-9300.

Here are 27 scenic points of interest, presented here in the order in which they appear once you've passed through the Highway 1 gate. Bicyclists must sign a waiver at the P.G. gate; no bicycle entry at Carmel gate.

1 Shepherd's Knoll Vista Point. There is a turnout here to view Monterey Bay and the San Gabilan Mountains.

2 Huckleberry Hill. Huckleberry Hill, one of the highest points in Del Monte Forest, offers hiking trails and spectacular views. Pick luscious huckleberries in the fall.

©Pebble Beach Company, reproduced by permission

3 Poppy Hills Golf Course, home of the Northern California Golf Association, with a clubhouse, pro shop, restaurant, and bar; open to visitors.

4 The Inn and Links at Spanish Bay. Site of Gaspar de Portolá's landing in 1769, it is now home to a 270-room luxury hotel and 18-hole golf course, restaurants, pro shop, and several fine shops. The Clubhouse Bar & Grill, an informal bar and grill featuring spectacular sunsets, also presents Scottish bagpipers playing each day at sunset for your enjoyment. This is an excellent place for breakfast and lunch. With al fresco dining on the ocean-view patio, and sea birds to accompany you, you can watch groups of golfers tee off with the beautiful Pacific behind them.

5 Spanish Bay. Have your picnic here and enjoy the fabulous ocean vista. Hikers can take a dirt path from the Pacific Grove gate, through the pines, past the golf course, to The Inn, then to a boardwalk to the beach. You can reach Sunset Drive on a path behind the parking lot.

6 The Restless Sea, just south of Moss Beach, accessible by boardwalk, bike or car. Underwater topography is responsible for the exciting colliding currents off this point. Stop and watch the waves crash from different directions.

7 Point Joe. Site of numerous shipwrecks of mariners looking for Monterey Bay, in the 1890s there was a small Chinese fishing village here. The point is supposedly named after a Chinese man named Joe who was the lone inhabitant at the turn of the century. Surfing for the experienced only.

©Pebble Beach Company, reproduced by permission

• **Coastal Bluff Walking Trail and Restoration.** Take a pleasant walk along the scenic trail on the coastal bluffs overlooking the rich tidepools. Extensive programs are in progress to reestablish the area's natural balance and encourage native plants and wildlife; stay on trails.

8 China Rock. China Rock was named in memory of the Chinese who settled in fishing villages here in the late 1800s and early 1900s.

9 Bird Rock Hunt Course. Prior to World War II, the 11th Cavalry used these grounds for riding and saber practice.

10 Bird Rock. Home to countless shoreline birds as well as offshore herds of sea lions and harbor seals. A one-mile, self-guided nature walk leads away from the beach here, through the dunes and into the forest, looping through Indian Village.

11 Seal Rock Picnic Area. A good place to picnic and watch the birds and the waves. Restrooms.

12 Spyglass Hill Golf Course and Pro Shop. Open to the public, Spyglass Hill is ranked one of the top 40 courses in the U.S. Legend has it that while writing *Treasure Island*, Robert Louis Stevenson was inspired by the view from his favorite hill. In honor of this literary heritage, the course and each of its 18 holes were named from Stevenson's classic.

• **The Spyglass Grill.** The Grill is a great spot for a snack or lunch while claiming a bird's-eye view of the 9th green of Spyglass Hill Golf Course.

13 Fanshell Overlook. Fanshell Beach boasts pure white sand. Harbor seals return here to bear their young every spring.

14 Cypress Point Lookout. This lookout offers the finest view of the Pacific coastline on the drive. Excellent whale-watching, Dec-Mar.

• **Cypress Point Club.** Opened for play in 1928, Cypress Point Club is ranked among the top 10 golf courses in the U.S. A private club, it is reserved for members' use only.

15 Crocker Grove. 13 acres of native pines and cypress in a protected reserve. Crocker Grove and Pt. Lobos are the only places where the Monterey Cypress grows wild, and the oldest and largest Monterey Cypress is here.

©Pebble Beach Company, reproduced by permission

16 The Lone Cypress. One of California's most familiar landmarks, access is restricted to protect the roots of this famous tree, which is also the symbol of the Pebble Beach Company. A favorite place to stop, enjoy the scenery and have your picture taken.

17 Ghost Tree. With a trunk bleached white by wind and sea spray, the Ghost Tree is one of the more fanciful examples of the Monterey Cypress.

18 Pescadero Point. Pescadero Point marks the northern tip of Carmel Bay and Stillwater Cove. The film *Rebecca* was made here.

19 The Lodge at Pebble Beach. The Lodge is one of the world's best known resorts. Built in 1919, it offers travelers superb accommodations, with 161 guest rooms and suites presenting sweeping views of the ocean and the famed 18th green of Pebble Beach Golf Links. New spa scheduled to open in January 2000. 624-3811. Enjoy a variety of dining options: The Tap Room - Casual pub with a collection of golf memorabilia. Club XIX - Fine dining offering award-winning French cuisine.The Gallery - Breakfast and lunch in an informal atmosphere. Stillwater Bar & Grill - Overlooking the 18th hole; a comfortable seafood grill. The Pebble Beach Market - Gourmet deli and market featuring fine wines, cheeses, meats, and fruits, with picnic tables conveniently close on a nearby lawn.

• **The Pebble Beach Shops.** Only a few steps from The Lodge at Pebble Beach, the Pebble Beach shops offer the finest in goods and services.

• Considered by many to be the world's premier golf course, **Pebble Beach Golf Links** entices golfers and spectators alike with emerald fairways buttressed by the rugged Pacific coast. Opened in 1919, Pebble Beach has been a favored site of the U.S. Open and PGA Championship.

20 Peter Hay Golf Course. A 9-hole, par-3 course, Peter Hay is open to the public. Greens fees, $15 adult, ages 13-17 $5, 12 and under free. Inquire at the Pebble Beach pro shop for golf club rentals. 625-8518.

• **Stillwater Cove** is recognized for its rich and undisturbed marine life, and is a haven for visitors and diving enthusiasts. Enter through the Beach & Tennis Club parking lot. Call ahead to reserve parking space: 625-8507. No parking between 11am-2pm. Restrooms.

21 The Pebble Beach Equestrian Center and Collins Polo Field are the sites of many major West Coast equestrian events, free to spectators.

17-Mile Drive by Bicycle

The 17-Mile Drive in Pebble Beach, through the Del Monte Forest, may be considered one of the top one hundred places to ride a bike in America. Enter at the Pacific Grove gate on Sunset Drive near Spanish Bay and Asilomar. Fill out the Rules and Regulations form on the sidewalk, receive a free map of bike trails, and <u>enter the Del Monte Forest free</u>. The bicycle path follows the 17-Mile Drive and begins with .9 miles of unimproved bike route, followed by a coastal loop of 4.4 miles, turning around at Bird Rock for the return to Spanish Bay. Further on, the Spyglass Hill Loop of 1.7 miles is very steep; turn around at Stevenson Drive or it's .8 miles to the Forest Lake Road just past the Lodge. After that, there is no bike lane on the 17-Mile Drive into Carmel. It's a 1.8 mile narrow road with heavy traffic to the Carmel exit which has no bike entry.

Hiking in the Del Monte Forest

<u>Free nature walks</u> 10am-2pm Thurs and Sat. RSVP at least 45 min in advance at The Inn at Spanish Bay. 649-7493. Self-guided tours: pick up a

free pamphlet with bridle trail directions at the Equestrian Center or in the Del Monte Lodge. There are color-coded bridle trails from 3 to 9 miles in length; the Firebreak Trail (coded yellow) leads through the **Morse Botanical Reserve**. Another pleasant and easy one-mile walk begins 1.1 miles south on Congress from the intersection of Con-

©Pebble Beach Company, reproduced by permission

gress and Forest Lodge Rd., where you may park off the road. Follow the trail to a fire road, turn left and then left again onto fire road #2. Walk down to Congress Ave., about .2 miles from where you started. You will see Monterey pines, oaks, ferns and wildflowers.

Pebble Beach Golf Courses

▲ **Peter Hay Golf Course**, 17-Mile Dr. at Stevenson Dr. $10 adult, $5 ages 13-17, <u>under 12 free</u>. A beautiful nine-hole, par 3, 819 yard course. Call 625-1555 for information about <u>free lessons for resident children</u> ages 7-17. <u>Free golf</u> at Peter Hay during the P.B. Equestrian Classics. 625-8518.

▲ **Poppy Hills**, home of the Northern California Golf Association, 3200 Lopez Road, 625-1513.

▲ **The Links at Spanish Bay**, 2700 17-Mile Drive, 624-3811, 647-7495.

▲ **Spyglass Hill**, Spyglass Hill & Stevenson Dr., 622-1300, 800-654-9300.

▲ **Pebble Beach Golf Links**, 17-Mile Drive, 625-8518, 800-654-9300.

Calendar of Events

Year 2000 dates shown. Updates at www.montereycountyguide.com.
Please call in advance to verify as information is subject to change.

Jan 31-Feb 6 AT&T PEBBLE BEACH NATIONAL PRO-AM $$
Spyglass Hill, Pebble Beach and Poppy Hill golf Courses. 800/541-9091, 649-1533. 72-hole PGA Tour Championship Tournament with a $4 million purse, the largest ever to attract top-flight tallent.. Tickets range from daily tickets ($20-$30), Season badge and grandstand badge ($95-$110). Under 12 free with paid adult. Teen ticket for entire week is $10. There's a long waiting list for volunteers, but the Pebble Beach Company is always looking for temporary help, apply at The Pebble Beach Company Employment Office, 2790 17 Mile Drive (next to Pacific Grove gate). Job Hotline 649-7694, fax 649-7696. www.attpbgolf.com.

March 29 & April 2 SPRING HORSE SHOW FREE
Pebble Beach Equestrian Center, Alva Rd. and Portola Ln. Free horse-jumping competition. Pony rides (book ahead $20, under 6 free), food and horse items for sale. Gate fee only. 8am-5pm. 624-2756.

April 1 HARBOR SEAL PANELS FREE
Local schoolchildren paint large murals which are put in place at Cypress Point to entertain visitors and to protect the pupping harbor seals from curious onlookers. Sponsored by The SPCA and the Pebble Beach Company. 625-8402.

May 27-28 MEMORIAL DAY REGATTA $$
Contact The Beach & Tennis Club, 625-8507.

June 4 KERNES MEMORIAL BENEFIT HORSE SHOW Spectators FREE
8am-5pm at the Equestrian Center. Hunter-jumper show. Rider entries support the Kernes Memorial Pool in Monterey for people with disabilities. 372-1240.

June 10-18 U.S. OPEN $$
100th Anniversary at Pebble Beach Golf Links. 625-8518.

July YOUTH CONCERTS FREE
Young musicians ages 12-23 at California Summer Music workshops through July at Robert Louis Stevenson School. Concerts, master classes open to the public free of charge. For dates, call 626-5300.

July 17-21 CA STATE AMATEUR GOLF CHAMPIONSHIP $$
Bayonet-Blackhorse, Seaside, this year. Back here in 2001. Roger Val, 625-4653.

July 25-30, Aug 1-6 EQUESTRIAN CLASSICS FREE
Pebble Beach Equestrian Center, corner of Alva Road and Portola Lane. 624-2756. 8am-5pm each day. Hunter and jumper events, a petting zoo and food booths, free ice cream sundaes on Thursday afternoons both weeks at ringside. Pebble Beach gate fee only. Special events include: The $10,000 Pebble Beach Jumper Derby Brunch, benefiting the YWCA of Monterey. Tickets 649-0834. SPCA of Monterey County Auxiliary Cocktail Party and Benefit Luncheon. Tickets 373-2631 ext. 224. Family Fun Day benefitting Chartwell School. "Annual Horse Show Dog Show" with prizes. Peter Hay Welcome Golf, free for kids.

August 14-18 NCGA AMATEUR GOLF CHAMPIONSHIP $$
Spyglass Hill Golf Course. Contact Roger Val, 625-4653.

August 16-20 BLACKHAWK COLLECTION OF CLASSIC CARS FREE
Traveling showcase of rare, vintage, classic and one-of-a-kind automobiles featuring over 60 of the world's premier examples for sale. Pebble Beach gate fee only applies. Wed-Sun, 10am-8pm. Peter Hay Golf Course. 925/736-3444.

August 20　　　**CONCOURS D'ELEGANCE**　　　FREE+$$
50th Anniversary. Prestigious event to view more than 100 classic automobiles at The Lodge. Tickets: United Way 372-8026, fax 372-4945. Info, 659-0663, 375-1747. www.pebble-beach-concours.com. On August 18, a 50-mile tour of the antique cars drives from Pebble Beach through Pacific Grove and Monterey, out on Hwy 68 to Laureles Grade, and to the Holman Ranch for lunch before returning via Carmel Valley Road and downtown Carmel. The tour provides a great chance for many more people to see the magnificent cars free. 624-3811.

September 2-3　　　**LABOR DAY REGATTA**　　　FREE to spectators
Contact The Beach & Tennis Club, 625-8507.

September 13-17　　**STRIDES & TIDES HORSE SHOW**　　　FREE
Contact Tim Postel, 624-2756.

November 8-12　　　**EQUESTRIAN CHAMPIONSHIPS**　　　FREE
Contact Tim Postel, 624-2756.

November 14-19　　　**CALLAWAY GOLF, PRO-AM**　　　$$
Del Monte Golf Course, Pebble Beach Golf Links and Spyglass Hill. Call 625-8575.

Entertainment

◆ **Lobby Lounge**, next to Roy's Restaurant at the Inn at Spanish Bay. Happy Hour, Mon-Fri, 4-7pm. No cover, free valet parking. 647-7423.

◆ **Tap Room**, dance, Fri-Sat, 10pm-1am, no cover, The Lodge. 625-8535.

◆ **Terrace Lounge**, live music, 7-10+pm, The Lodge, no cover. 624-3811.

◆ **Spanish Bay Clubhouse**, from the patio, bagpiper plays at sunset.

Art Galleries

● **Richard MacDonald Galleries**, 17-Mile Drive, at the Lodge. Sculpture by MacDonald; also the only ongoing show of MacDonald's original drawings, paintings, lithographs, and serigraphs. Sun-Thurs 10-6, Fri-Sat 10-9. 648-7356. May 2000 dedication of golf sculpture. www.richardmacdonald.com.

● **Coast Gallery**, 17-Mile Drive, at the Lodge. Unique collection featuring wildlife bronze sculptures of Loet Vanderveen, paintings by Van Megert, prints of Henry Miller, eagle sculpture of Dennis Lee. Daily 10-6. 624-2002.

● **Pebble Beach Post Office**, at The Lodge. Exhibits works by local artists.

Classy Transportation for Rent

➤ If you get the urge to drive or own a classic automobile yourself, call **Auto Gallery**, 624-3438, fax 624-3033, for rent to drive, chauffeured tours, special events and sales. Dolores & 5th in Carmel.

Salinas

Steinbeck House

Creekbridge Park

Salinas Farm Show

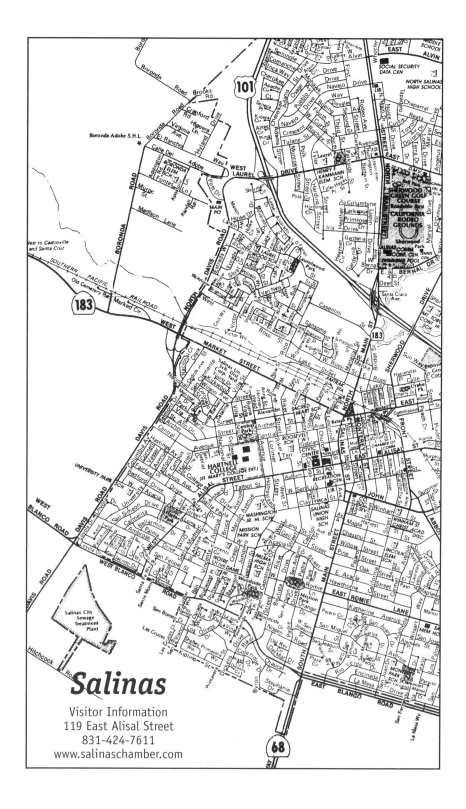

Salinas

Visitor Information
119 East Alisal Street
831-424-7611
www.salinaschamber.com

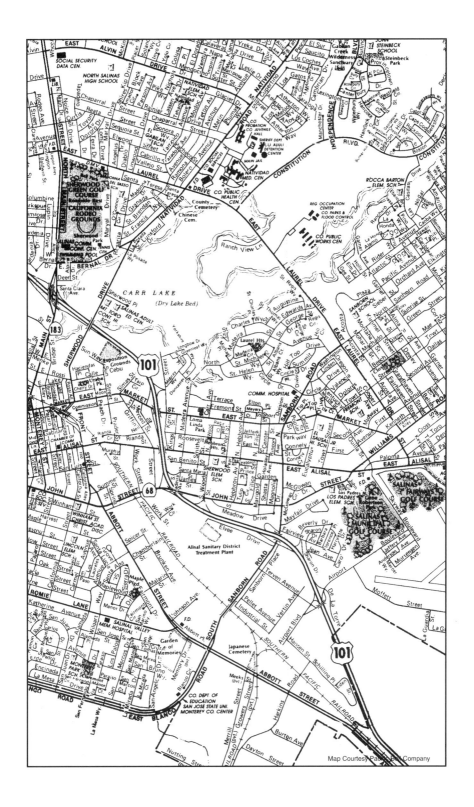

Map Courtesy Pacific Bell Company

Interesting Places to Visit

■ **National Steinbeck Center**, One Main Street, near Market Street. Tele 796-3833, fax 796-3828, www.steinbeck.org. A new, multimedia experience of literature, history and art. Located in the heart of historic Oldtown

Salinas. 10am-5pm daily. <u>Occasional free days</u>. Adults $7, Seniors (over 62) and students with ID $6, Children 11-17 $4, <u>free to members and children 10 and under</u>. Closed Thanksgiving, Christmas and New Years Day. Museum and archives celebrate the life and work of Nobel & Pulitzer Prize-winning author John Steinbeck (1902-1968) with seven themed galleries and changing art and cultural exhibits. Special programs, classes and children's events are scheduled throughout the year. Gift shop and cafe. Oldtown walking tour with paid admission on Wed. The Same Page book group reads Steinbeck stories 5pm Thurs. 775-4729. Birthday celebration last week in February. To volunteer: 775-4729.

■ **The Steinbeck House**, John Steinbeck's birthplace and boyhood home, 132 Central Ave. This Victorian is now a restaurant featuring local produce, wines and beers. Photos and memorabilia of the Steinbeck family are on display. Dining 11:30-2pm, Mon-Sat. Gift shop Mon-Fri, 11am-3pm, Sat 11am-2:30pm. Profits to local charities. 424-2735.

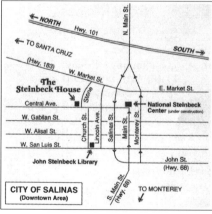

■ **Harvey-Baker House**, previously at 238 E. Romie Lane, may be moved in early 2000 to the transportation center off Market Street, near the National Steinbeck Center. The fully-restored house, 1868 home of Salinas' first mayor, Isaac Harvey, is now a public museum with period furniture and decor. <u>Free admission</u>, open Sundays, 1-4pm. Info: please call 424-7155.

■ **Boronda History Center**, 333 Boronda Road at Calle Del Adobe. Mon-Fri 9am-3pm. Tours 10&2 by appointment; Archival Vault by appointment only. The José Eusebio Boronda Adobe, built in 1844, and the Lagunita school-house, built in 1848, are the highlights of this history center. 757-8085.

■ **Center for Medieval Studies**, Fritz Auto Clinic, 276 E. Market. Call Tom for a free tour of the Armory, a coal forge using anvils to make helmets and armor, 8am-5pm, Mon-Fri. Join the Center for $35 a year and receive a newsletter, access to the forge equipment, and an open invitation to spend weekends brushing up on your jousting. 443-6451.

Shopping & Farmers Markets

● **Northridge Shopping Mall**, 796 Northridge. 449-7591. Largest mall in town. Free 'a la carte' shuttle service from your car to mall entrances and back to your car. Mon-Sat 10-9, Sun 11-7. 449-7591.

● **Northridge Mall Certified Farmers Market**, 8am-noon on Sundays, N. Main St. at Boronda Road. Under colored umbrellas on Main St. 728-5060.

● **Oldtown Salinas**, Main Street. Lots of unique and interesting shops. For information, call Paula at 758-0725.

● **Oldtown Salinas Farmers Market**, Apr-Sept, 3-7pm, Wed, weather per-mitting, 200 block Main Street. Live entertainment, produce, fish, flowers, baked goods, crafts. Free parking. 758-0725.

● **Productos Mexicanos**, including foods, spices, piñatas. You'll think you're in Mexico when you visit the Indoor Swap Mall. 626 E. Alisal. 759-8560.

● **The Chocolate Dipper**, 1126 S. Main St. Mon-Thurs 10-6, Fri 10-8, Sat 10-6. Extended hours Dec-April. 754-1931.

● **The Farm**, March 1-Thanksgiving, Mon-Sat 10-6. Tours $5. Organic pro-duce stand featuring fresh fruits and vegetables as well as specialty food products and ag-related souvenirs. Off Spreckels exit on Hwy 68 west of Salinas where the John Cerney murals are. Cut your own flowers and pick your own berries, beans, tomatoes and squash. Free tractor rides on Sat. Free petting zoo with sheep, bunnies, ducks, chickens and goat. 455-2575.

Driver Fernando Garcia and guests

"One Voice" Monterey County Murals Project

The goal of the "One Voice" Murals Project is to enhance awareness of local cultural identities for Monterey County youths and their communities and is part of a greater, federally funded Summer Youth Employment Training Program. Locations for those in Salinas pictured above, starting at the top, Walgreen's, 575 Madeira Ave.; Steinbeck Center, One Main St.; 26 W. Market St. Call 758-738 for addresses of other murals in Carmel, Castroville, Gonzales, Greenfield, Marina, Monterey, Pájaro, Salinas, Sand City, Seaside and Soledad.

Wild Things, Animal Rentals Inc.

➤ Enjoy a 1 hour tour of an Exotic/Wild Animal facility dedicated to providing professionally trained animals to film, television, live productions, education, and more. Learn how they are trained for film work and what they are like to house and maintain. VISION QUEST RANCH, 400 River Rd. Tours at 1pm. Adults $7, 14 and under $5 . 455-1901. www.wildthingsinc.com.

Kids Learn How to Fly

➤ **Experimental Aircraft Assn** offers a free seminar at the Salinas Municipal Airport, also <u>free rides for kids</u>. Carl, 455-2089; Jack, 422-8035.

Art Galleries

● **Artistic Hangups**, 257 John St. Mon-Fri, 10am-5:30, Sat 10-5. Local art, Western and local event posters, fine art reproductions, gifts. <u>Free coffee</u>, seating area. www.artistichangups.com. 757-4703.

● **Theodore's Art Gallery**, 210 Main St. Tues-Fri, 10am-4pm. Limited & open editions, seriographs, originals, gifts, custom embroidery. 422-6861.

● **Salinas Valley Art Gallery**, 218 Main St. Tues-Sun, 10am-5pm, Mon 11am-3pm. Co-op of 37 local artists since 1969; all media. 422-4162.

● **Peninsula Arts & Crafts**, 225 Main St. Mon-Fri, 9am-5:30pm. Lithographs, Eng Tay, fine art, fine art supplies. 758-2741.

● **Hartnell College Seminar Gallery**, 155 Homestead Ave. Mon-Fri, 10am-1pm and 6pm-8pm. Student art. 758-9126.

● **Salinas Courthouse**, 240 Church St. Works by local artists.

● **Zeph's One Stop:** Local photographer showing. Wine Shop tastings Thurs 5:30-7, $10; Java & Juice, Portobello Deli, 1366 S. Main St. 757-3947.

Public Art

● **Hat in Three Stages of Landing,"** sculpture by Claes Oldenberg in Sherwood Park behind the Salinas Fairgrounds Auditorium at 900 Main St.

● **Salinas Murals** adorn several buildings along East Alisal and East Market streets, providing insight into local history and Latino culture while gracing the buildings with beautiful works of art. See the John Steinbeck mural opposite the National Steinbeck Center with images of his literary works. An eagle clutching Mexican and American flags in its talons is on the Club Metropolis at East Lake and Soledad. On Carr Avenue and 600 block of East Market see farmworkers and agriculture. East Market at Pearl Street: Spanish expeditions, mission life and dustbowl migration to California. Call Jesse Armenta for a complete list of murals: 831-758-7387.

Interesting Architecture in Salinas

- McDougall Building, 1898, 5 E. Gabilan, architect Wm. Weeks
- Glikbarg Building, 1907, 6 W. Gabilan, designed by W.E. Greene
- Old Salinas Post Office, 12 W. Gabilan
- Monterey Bank Bldg, 1907, 201 Main St., architect Wm. Weeks
- Bank of America, 1907, Main & Gabilan. Mediterranean Revival Style
- Franci Home, 1904, 62 Capitol, architect Wm. Weeks
- Sheriff Nesbitt's Home, 1882, 66 Capitol St.
- Sargent House, 1896, 154 Central, architect Wm. Weeks
- Gilfillan Home, 153 Central
- Glen Graves Home, 1910, 147 Central Ave. American 4-Square Style
- Krough Home, 1894, 146 Central Ave. Queen Anne style
- Mayer House, 1890, 134 Central Ave. Next door to Steinbecks
- Railroad Depot, Station Ave. Murals inside by Don Kingman, WPA project
- Menke Home, 1800s, 325 N. Main St.
- Lagunita School, 1897, 975 San Juan Grade Rd.
- Sam Black House, 1900, 418 Pajaro, architect Wm. Weeks
- Peter Iverson House, 1894, 226 Pajaro St. Built entirely of redwood
- Silacci Home, 124 W. San Luis
- R.L. Porter House, 1868, 116 E. San Luis
- Hinrick Home, 338 Church St. Six Gable Home
- Dr. Murphy House, 402 Cayuga St. Delivered John & Mary Steinbeck
- St. Paul's Episcopal Church Rectory, 418 Cayuga
- Salinas High School, 1920, 726 S. Main St.
- Buddhist Temple, 1929, 14 California St. Oldest temple bell is U.S.
- Salinas Confucius Church, 1937, 1 California St.
- Austin House, 1886 or 1896, 40 Central Ave. Victorian
- Empire House, 1870 or 1880, 119 Cayuga St. French 2nd Empire style
- Rossi Building, 113 Cayuga St. Italian Renaissance structure
- Sacred Heart Catholic Church, 14 Stone St.

Personal Tour Guide
➤ Historic downtown walking and step-on bus tours by **Carol Robles**. Learn past and present importance of Monterey's county seat. Also Steinbeck and Valley tours. Professional narrated tours. Fees vary, call 751-3666.

Calendar of Events

Year 2000 dates shown. Updates at www.montereycountyguide.com.
Please call in advance to verify as information is subject to change.

JANUARY

Ongoing   UNITY CELEBRATION PRAISE CONCERT   FREE
Every two or three months. Free food and clothing. 7pm at Washington Middle School, 560 Iverson St., with Christian music by local singers and musicians. Admission is free, but guests are asked to bring a canned food donation for the needy. Art Garcia, 449-8758.

January 25   MONTEREY SYMPHONY $$
Sherwood Hall, Roberto Minczuk, conductor. Ginastera, Barber, Copland. Tickets 624-8511.

FEBRUARY

February 22   MONTEREY SYMPHONY $$
Sherwood Hall, Vladimir Spivakov, conductor and violinist. Mozart and Tchaikovsky. Tickets 624-8511.

February 27   STEINBECK BIRTHDAY CELEBRATION $$
Free tours of Steinbeck House, www.infopoint.com/mry/orgs/steinbeck, 424-2735. The National Steinbeck Center speakers and luncheon highlight this annual celebration. Call 796-3833 for more information.

MARCH

March-Sept   "GRAFFITI NIGHTS AT ROY'S DRIVE-IN"   FREE
Bi-weekly meets at Roy's Drive-In. All makes and models cars, raffles, '50s & '60s music. Presented by the Salinas Valley Street Rodder's Assn. 305 N. Main Street, 449-2525.

March 21   MONTEREY SYMPHONY $$
Sherwood Hall, Alexander Anissimov, conductor. John O'Conor, piano. Glinka, Shostakovich and Brahms. Tickets 624-8511.

APRIL

April 8   CULINARY CLASSIC $$
Salinas Community Center on North Main by the Entre Nous Society to raise money for Shelter-Outreach Plus. Cooking demos, vendor booths, specialty food & wines. 484-2291.

April 18   MONTEREY SYMPHONY $$
Sherwood Hall, Jean Louis Steuerman, conductor and pianist. Haydn, Mozart and Beethoven. Tickets 624-8511.

April 22   EARTH DAY/ARBOR DAY '99   FREE
Natividad Creek Park. Food, displays, sports demos. 758-7152.

MAY

May   **FESTIVAL OF THE ARTS**   **FREE**
Older Americans Month with senior activities at Firehouse Recreation Center, 1330 E. Alisal St. Dancing, bread making, magic. Call for calendar, 758-7900.

May 2   **SALINAS FARM SHOW**   **FREE**
3rd Annual all-day demos of the latest farming and ag techniques and equip-

ment. Seminars, barbecue lunch, rodeo contest and more. Proceeds benefit the Gonzales Young Farmers Ag Scholarship Fund. Approximately 1000 growers and over 150 exhibitors. Wednesday, 8:30am-4pm, Salinas Sports Complex/ California Rodeo grounds. Show information: Kevin Hall, 559/248-0924.

May 18-21   **SALINAS VALLEY FAIR**   **$$**
King City Fairgrounds: livestock, 4-H exhibits, food contests, horticulture showing, carnival and more. An old-fashioned good time. 385-3243.

May 23   **MONTEREY SYMPHONY**   **$$**
Sherwood Hall, Federico Cortese, conductor, Symphony Chorus. Bellini, Cherubini and Saint-Saëns. Tickets 624-8511.

JUNE

June 3-4   **KENNEL CLUB AGILITY TRIAL**   **FREE**
Del Monte Kennel Club presents an opportunity for the public to see many different breeds of dogs perform over very complex and entertaining obstacle course. A great spectator sport! 8am-5pm. Toro Park. Parking, $6 per car. 333-9032.

June 10-11   **SALINAS VALLEY SALAD DAYS**   **$$**
From the "Salad Bowl of the World," a two day food, music, arts and wine festival at Sherwood Park in the Salinas Sports Complex. 5Krun Sat, Hispanic dancers, 75 arts and crafts. Greek, Oriental, Mediterranean, Mexican and American salads. 3 entertainment stages and the "Salinas Salad Sprint." Salinas Sports Complex/Sherwood Park. 10am-6pm. $8 adults. 372-6400.

June 26   **NATIONAL STEINBECK CENTER**   **FREE**
2nd Anniversary - Open free to all Monterey County residents 10-5. 775-4720.

JULY

July   **EL DÍA DE LA FAMILIA**   **FREE**
Annual concert at Salinas Sports Complex, 1034 N. Main St. 771-9950.

July   **SALINAS OBON FESTIVAL**   **FREE**
Buddhist Temple of Salinas, 14 California Street. Noon-9pm Sunday. Sponsored by the Buddhist Temple of Salinas, featuring Japanese food and drink, martial arts and flower-arranging demonstrations, tea ceremony, taiko drumming, Japanese dancing, children's games, raffle. Culminates with the Obon dance at 7pm; continuous free shuttle service from Salinas City Parking Lot No. 4 on Monterey Street, between Gabilan and Market. 424-4105.

July 4   CHILI COOK-OFF & FIREWORKS EXTRAVAGANZA $$
Dancing, horseshoe tournament, kids' corral, food, fireworks at 9. At the Salinas Rodeo Grounds, 1034 N. Main Street, 12-9pm. $6 adults, under age 12 $3. 775-3100 or 800-771-8807.

July 15-18   CALIFORNIA RODEO   FREE+$$
Wed, 7pm, free Kiddie Kapers parade in Oldtown Salinas, featuring children in Western togs, with their pets, decorated bicycles and neighborhood floats. Free horse parades to the Rodeo grounds proceed down Main Street beginning at 12:15pm Saturday and Sunday. Other rodeo-related events include a barbecue at the Yellow Hat Area, Cowboy Poetry at the Rodeo Arena, dances at the Salinas Community Center, and Big Week Carnival at Expo Park at 101 Market St. Tickets $10-$17. 757-2951, 800/771-8807, 775-3100.

AUGUST

August   SALINAS AIRPORT OPEN HOUSE   FREE
The Salinas Owners and Pilots Association, the Women's Monterey Bay 99's and the Salinas Chapter of Experimental Aircraft Association invite you to experience the thrill of flying and small aircraft. Older and home built aircraft. Cars of the same vintage. Tour air traffic control tower and maintenance shops. 30 Mortensen Avenue.

August   CHILDREN'S SUMMER MASQUERADE   FREE
Games, crafts, food, magic. Nativad Creek Park, 1395 Nogal Dr. Call 758-7900.

August 3-6   STEINBECK FESTIVAL XIX   FREE+$$
The Steinbeck Center presents Steinbeck Festival XIX. Walking and bus tours, speakers, films, panels, theater. Call for more info, 796-3833.

August 20   TORTILLA FESTIVAL   FREE
Tortilla King & Queen. Foods to roll in tortillas, beverage booths. Music, games, contests for all ages. Sponsored by Salinas Valley League of United Latin American Citizens, Mrs. Maya 758-6947, Juan 754-2849. 11am-7pm at Monterey County Sheriff's Posse Grounds, Old Natividad Road, Salinas. Parking $3.

SEPTEMBER

Sept   STREET RODDERS NOSTALGIA RUN TO OLDTOWN   FREE
Four block street rod display, daily motorcade through Oldtown, over 50 awards each day at 3pm; additional four blocks with swap-meet booths, kiddie carnival, food booths, entertainment stage with music of the 1950s, '60s and '70s. Car registration begins at 8am Sat-Sun, activities until 4pm. 200-300 blocks South Main St., 449-9334, 758-0725.

Sept   COMMUNITY CARE DAY   FREE
United Way of Salinas Valley hosts an annual Community Care Day of painting projects, small construction, clean-ups, landscaping, office work. Have breakfast, get a free t-shirt and win one of 150 raffle prizes. United Way at 424-7644.

Sept 10   "EL GRITO FIESTA"   FREE
11th Annual. Two stages for entertainment, booths. Noon-6pm, East Alisal Street between No. Maderaand Filice streets. Sponsored by the Hispanic Chamber of Commerce of Monterey. Vendor opportunities: Jessika Juarez at 757-1251.

Sept 16-17   FOX 35 KIDFEST   FREE
Free admission & live entertainment, fun zone, fun jump, face painting, clowns, song & dance. Sat 10-4, Sun 11-4. Northridge Mall. 422-3500.

Sept 29-Oct 1   CALIFORNIA INTERNATIONAL AIRSHOW $$

Friday will be Fireworks and Pyrotech-
nic Extravaganza featuring air acts,
ground acts, breathtaking fireworks
and the Wall of Fire. Sat-Sun will fea-
ture air acts, ground acts, military fly-
bys and demos, warbirds plus military
and civilian displays. Features Cana-
dian Snowbirds military jet team and
more celebrities. Show also includes
monster trucks, pyrotechnic extrava-
ganza. At the Salinas Airport. Children
under 6 free. Tickets $6-$16; private
boxes available, $160-$400. 754-
1983. Ticket information: 888/845-
SHOW. www.ca-airshow.com.

OCTOBER

October   BIKE RODEO AND SAFETY FAIR   FREE
Bring bike and helmet. Prizes, free bicycle, registration and some helmets. Emer-
gency vehicles on display. Face painting, refreshments, door prizes. Call for more
information, 758-7906.

October   AUTUMN FESTIVAL   FREE
Quilt show, art show, bake sale. Student works on show and for sale. At Salinas
Adult School, 20 Sherwood Place. End of month. 753-4268.

October   PUMPKIN CARVING CONTEST   FREE
Free, preregistration required, one adult with one child, bring carving kit. Prizes,
refreshments. Sponsored by Salinas Recreation Dept. and California Culinary
Academy. 1-3pm at Hebbron Heights, 683 Fremont St., Salinas. 758-7900.

October 2   FALL FEST   FREE
Church of the Good Shepherd, 301 Corral de Tierra Road, will hold its Fall Fest
beginning at 10am. Games, pony rides, music, crafts fair with children's activi-
ties. 10K run, 5K family walk and barbecue. Kim, 484-2153.

October 28   A HALLOWEEN SPOOKTACULAR   FREE+$$
The weekend before Halloween at the Firehouse Recreation Center, 1330 E.
Alisal Street. $4 per person includes 1 visit to each carnival game, a treat bag, a
tour through the haunted hallway and entry in the costume contest. Sponsored
by the City of Salinas Recreation Dept. 758-7948, 758-7223. Drop by during the
month for the October Fun Program which features a Pumpkin Face Contest,
Pumpkins Krispies and Pumpkin People. 758-7900.

October 31   TRICK OR TREAT   FREE
For costumed youngsters at stores and businesses in Oldtown. 758-0725.

NOVEMBER

November 1   HALLOWEEN CANDY TRADE   FREE
Drop by the Children's Miracle Network Dental Center at 631 E Alvin Dr., Suite
E1, so your kids can trade Halloween candy for bags of fun items and healthy
treats from 9am-1pm. Call 443-5801.

November   **EL DIA DE LOS MUERTOS**   **FREE**
Celebrated by the Steinbeck Center with a children's procession from the 200 block of Main Street to the Steinbeck Museum, where admission will be free to county residents, 10am-5pm. 796-3833. www.steinbeck.org

November 10-17   CHRISTIAN FILM FESTIVAL   FREE
Fourth annual Central Coast Christian Film Festival at the Northridge Cinema, 350 Northridge Shopping Center. Information: 424-7020.

November 25   THANKSGIVING DINNERS   FREE
Dinner will be served at Dorothy's Kitchen, 30 Soledad St. 757-3838. Dinner will be served by the Salvation Army, 424-0588. Volunteers and donations welcome.

DECEMBER

December   STREETS OF BETHLEHAM   FREE
First week. First Baptist Church on corner of San Vincente & Blanco presents live nativity pageant with live animals and costumes. Call 422-9872 for details.

December   LAS POSADAS   FREE
Nativity procession. Midmonth. Alisal merchants. Call Micky Ito or Carlos Ramos, 373-6767.

December   KWANZAA $$
African-American holiday celebrations at Hartnell College. 755-6860.

Entertainment
Music and Dancing

◆ **Dakota's Corral**, 808 N. Main St. No cover unless noted. Country music and dancing. DJs and local bands, pool tournament on Mondays. Full bar and late night food. 424-8661.

◆ **The Endzone**, 1081 S. Main St. No cover. Sports bar, pool and darts. Live music on the weekends. 422-9031.

◆ **Book Worm Cabaret**, 342 Main St. Live music at 6pm. 753-2099.

◆ **King's Den**, 22 W. Alisal. Karaoke Thursdays, no cover. 422-1116.

◆ **Spados**, 66 W. Alisal. Fridays, Happy Hour 5:30-7:30pm, vocal jazz, pop-jazz and R&B. No cover. 424-4139.

◆ **The Penny Farthing Tavern**, live music every Fri-Sat. No cover. 9 E. San Luis St., Oldtown Salinas. 424-5652.

◆ **Chapala Restaurant**, 438 Salinas St. Happy Hour 4-7pm, Mon-Fri. 757-4959.

◆ **Club Metropolis**, 115 Lake St. Latin music Thurs-Sun. 757-8302.

◆ **Introduction to Vocal & Guitar.** Accompaniment with Caminos del Arte sessions at Bread Box Recreation Center, 745 N. Sanborn Road. Call for times. Free, everyone welcome. Preregistration: 758-7908, 594-9407.

◆ **Ballroom Dancing**, Active Senior Center, Pajaro & Harvest. Music by the Joe Ingram Group. $5 includes refreshments. Every Tues 7-10pm. 424-5066.

◆ **All-City Band** No charge to play but must have own instrument. Call Jeannie Echenique, 753-5740 days, 476-1322 evenings.

◆ **Hartnell College Community Band** gives free concerts. Call for dates and times, 755-6905, 755-6906.

Movies and Theater

◆ **Gay Movie Night** 7-9pm, second/fourth Tuesday at Monterey County AIDS project office, 12 E. Gabilan; open to all ages in the gay, lesbian, bi and transgendered community. Free, refreshments. 772-8202..

◆ **Adele O'Grady Theater**, formerly Fox Theater, a Main Street landmark, is to be a cultural film and performing arts venue early in 2000.

◆ **Century Park Cinema**, 10 E. Market at Simas, 753-1055. Fox California, 243 N. Main at Boronda Road, 449-9101.

◆ **Salinas Concert Assn.** Free concerts at Main Stage of the Performing Arts Center at Hartnell College, West Alisal St. and Homestead Ave. Call for dates and times of all concerts. 754-6829.

◆ **ARIEL Theatrical**, 182 San Benancio Road. 484-2228 or 759-1530.

◆ **The Western Stage**, 156 Homestead Avenue. 755-6818 or 375-2111.

Bookstores, Coffeehouses, Libraries

● **Corpus Christi Book Store**, 47 San Miguel Avenue. 422-6609.

● **Educational Stuff Inc**, 908 1/2 S. Main Street. 422-5044.

● **Books-by-Mail**, 26 Central Ave. Mon-Fri 9-1. 800-322-6884.

◆ **B.Dalton Booksellers**, Northridge Shopping Center. 449-7245.

◆ **Book Worm**, 342 Main St. Live music at 6pm. 753-2099.

◆ **Books Then & Now**, 956 Park Row. 753-0658.

◆ **Family Book Center**, 144 E. Laurel Dr. 759-2665.

◆ **Mr. Ed's Comics**, 17593 Vierra Canyon Rd. 663-4022.

● **Cesar Chavez Library**, 615 Williams Rd. 758-7345. Hours Mon-Wed, 10am-9pm, Thurs-Sat, 10am-6pm. Homework Center Mon-Thurs, 2-5pm. Volunteers needed. Reading garden, ages 6-11, Tues 10am; Adventure Seekers, ages 6-11, Tues 4pm; Preschool storytime, Thurs 10am; Cuentos Para la Familia, all ages, Thurs 4pm. Kids–submit your poems in April for display.

● **El Gabilan Library**, 1400 North Main. 758-7302. Hours Mon-Wed, 10am-9pm, Thu-Sat, 10am-6pm. Call for program information: Thumbkin stories for kids ages $2^1/2$-4, 10:15am, Rookie Readers $3^1/2$-6, Thurs 10am.

● **John Steinbeck Library**, 350 Lincoln Avenue, 758-7311. Mon-Wed, 10am-9pm, Thu-Sat, 10am-6pm. Preschool stories ages $3^1/2$-6, Tues 10am; Salina's Night (meet 'library snake'), first Tuesday, all ages; Thumbkins, ages $2^1/2$-4, Wed 10am; Grandparents and Books, kids of all ages practice listening and reading skills with a library grandparent, Mon & Wed 3-5pm. On-going book sale by Friends of the Salinas Public Library - 15% off retail.

● **Toy Lending Library**, 344 Salinas Street, Ste. 201, across from the John Steinbeck Library. To May 5 from 1-5pm. Call Margaret Sirtak, 753-4977.

● **Hartnell College** hosts free events, lectures, concerts. 156 Homestead Ave. Seniors learn free at Hartnell College. For more information or a complete schedule of classes, contact program coordinator Glenna Teti in the college's office of instruction, 755-6721, or 759-6086, 755-6912.

● **Cherry Bean Coffee House**, 332 Main St. 424-1989

● **Ground Zero** Coffee Shop in Rite-Aid Center, 1134 S. Main St. 757-5282.

● **Number One Java Drive**, Blanco Rd at So. Main St. 753-2326.

● **The Gift Peddler** offers free coffee and samples of gourmet foods. 105-100 E. Alisal St. Tues-Sat 9:30-3:30. 758-5006.

Restaurants

● **Bumble Bean Cafe & Expresso**, 8059 San Miguel Canyon, 663-1625.

● **Bagel Cafe & Bakery**, American, 1257 N. Davis Road, 757-9933.

● **Chapala Restaurant**, Mexican, 438 Salinas Street, 757-4959.

● **China Garden Chinese**, Chinese, 1333 N. Main Street, 449-6868.

● **First Awakenings**, American, 171 Main Street, 784-1125.

● **Fish House Salinas Valley**, Seafood, 172 Main Street, 775-0175.

● **Fridays**, American, 1816 N. Main Street, 444-8443.

● **Mi Tierra Restaurant**, Mexican, 18 E. Gabilan, 422-4631.

● **Jake's Cactus Cafe**, Mexican, 107 Kern, 422-5297.

● **The Motherload**, American, 711 S. Main Street, 758-5623.

● **Olive Garden**, Italian, 1580 N. Main Street, 449-6158.

● **Pajaro Street Grill**, California, 435 Pajaro Street, 754-3738.

● **Sea Harvest Restaurant**, Seafood, 1136 S. Main Street, 422-2016.

● **Yangtse Taste of Thai**, Thai, 328 Main Street, 754-2223.

Accommodations

● **Comfort Inn**, 144 Kern Street, 758-8850. $75+

● **Continental Motel**, 1165 N. Main Street, 424-1459. $40+

● **Days Inn**, 1226 De La Torre, 759-9900. $59+

● **Econolodge**, 180 S. Sanborn Road, 422-5111. $42+

● **Holiday Inn Express**, 131 John Street, 757-1020. $72+

● **Rodeo Inn**, 808 N. Main Street, 424-8661. $59+

● **Royal Hotel**, 201 Market Way, 424-8281. Call

● **Super 8 Motel**, 1030 Fairview Avenue, 422-6486. $42+

● **Vagabond Inn**, 131 Kern Street, 758-4693. $66+

Parks and Recreation

▲ **Central Community Park**, corner of Homestead and Central avenues, behind Hartnell College. 8 acres. Large park with big trees, exercise course, tennis courts, playground with a full-size locomotive, small recreation center with games and crafts, barbecues and picnic tables. Parks Dept. 758-7945.

▲ **Claremont Manor Park**, San Fernando Dr. and San Miguel Ave. 5 acres. Ballfield, picnic area, playground, tennis, restrooms.

▲ **Closter Community Park**, Towt St. and Dewey Ave. 7 acres. Ballfield, basketball, horseshoes, picnics, playground, tennis, restrooms.

▲ **El Dorado Park**, El Dorado Dr. near Alvin. 20 acres. Ballfield, basketball, community building, picnic area, playground, restrooms.

▲ **Hartnell Park**, West Acacia and Alisal streets. Grassy areas, trees, basketball court, playground, restrooms and water fountains.

▲ **Rodeo-Sherwood Recreation Area**, 940 N. Main St. near Bernal Dr. 100 acres. Ballfield, community building, horseshoe pits, picnic area, playground, swimming, tennis, volleyball, restrooms.

▲ **Toro County Park**, three miles west of Salinas, 11.7 miles east of Monterey, 27742 Portola Drive off Highway 68. 4882 acres. Mon-Fri, $3/car, Sat-Sun, $5/car. Hiking and equestrian trails, views, mountain biking trails, grasslands and wooded hillsides, ballfields, volleyball courts, horseshoe pits, picnic facilities and playgrounds. Interpretive Trail with signs in Braille, English & Spanish. 8am-5pm. Camp for youth groups. Dall 755-4899.

▲ **Skateboard Park**, on Las Casitas Drive in the **Natividad Creek Park** near Creekbridge. New skateboard course of 1500 square feet and a BMX track. Daily, 7am-dusk. Safety equipment required: helmets, knee & elbow pads. **Twin Peaks Golf Course set to open here in April, 2000.

Activities

▲ **Card Collecting Star Cards & Collectibles**, 1241 South Main St. Pokémon tournaments every Saturday, 2-5:30pm. 757-8234, for more information.

▲ **Toys Galore, Inc.**, 921 So. Main Street, 424-3488, has free play days on 2nd Saturdays, reservations recommended. Always take something home free! Paper Stick Horse, Pipe Cleaner Bug, Color A Picture Frame.

▲ **Drop in and Play.** Free Parent/Child Activity class for children 5 and under, Tues-Wed 3-5pm. The Parent Center, Salinas Adult School, 20 Sherwood Pl. Call Karen Estes or Carole Singley at 753-4273. Parent must stay.

▲ **Kid's Cafe** operated by the Salvation Army for ages 7-16 at 180 Williams Road. Karate lessons, swimming, computers, reading, library, athletic programs, Cub Scouts, Sunbeams, Girlguards, art and other classes. Recreation room with board games, ping-pong, pool, video games, homework help; hot nutritious dinner at 5pm. Everything is free, volunteers and donations needed, call Chuck Rowe, 424-0568.

Recreation Centers

Salinas Parks and Recreation Centers. Administration: 758-7945.

▲ **Sherwood Center**, 758-7218, teen lounge, Mon-Thurs, 6:30-8:45pm; Tues and Thurs 3-4:45pm, ages 12-18. Pool tournaments every Tues 6:30-8:45pm, 12-18. Ping-pong tournaments Thurs 6:30-8:45pm, ages 12-18, paddles provided.

▲ **Firehouse Recreation**, 758-7900, 758-7354, 758-7220, drop in program, Mon-Fri 3-5pm. Holiday, vacation hours, 12-4pm Evening hours, 5:30-9pm. 1330 E. Alisal St. Trips, brown bag program, social times, walking, square dancing, and more. Free Chair & Dance Movement classes, 10-11am, Tues. Gentle program designed with seniors in mind.

▲ **El Dorado Community Park**, 758-7223, 758-7305, 758-6220. Volleyball Tues-Thurs 3:30-4:30pm, 12 and up.

▲ **Central Community Park**, 758-7305, 758-7223, 758-7220.

▲ **Breadbox Recreation Center**, 758-7905, 758-7304, 758-7220.

▲ **Hebbron Heights Service Center**, 758-7905, 758-7304, 758-7220, Kids Bingo every Thurs 3:30-4:30pm, 6 yrs and up, small prizes will be awarded.

Creekbridge Community Park
1793 Declaration Street

Friday movies 3-5:30, free with popcorn and punch.

▲ **Lincoln Street Recreation Center**, 320 Lincoln. Many free activities and programs. Pick up a free guide. 758-7326 or 758-7413.

▲ **Closter Community Park**, 758-7905, 758-7304, 758-7220, variety of free programs. After school Mon-Fri, 3-5:30pm during school year, Holiday/vacation hours noon to 4pm. Ping-pong tournaments every 1st Thursday, 3:30-5:20, ages 8 and up. Teen lounge, Tues & Thurs, 3-4:45pm, vacation hours Mon-Thurs, 1-4:45pm, evening hours 6:30-8:45pm. 758-7352.

Walking at Toro Park

➤ **Fifty-Plus Fitness Association** walks at Toro Park. Call Gloria for details. 422-9937. **Walk and Run** meets on first Saturdays at 7:45am at the Toro Park entrance near Salinas off Hwy. 68. Leaves at 8am. For more information call Gloria Drake at 422-9937 or (650) 323-6160.

You Can Adopt-a-Park

➤ **Salinas Adopt-a-Park** is a program by which businesses, civic organizations, groups and individuals can aid in supplementing park maintenance by working 2-3 hours, once a month, pulling weeds, cleaning, and planting. Call 758-7382 to adopt a park.

Salinas Commuter Club

➤ **Commit to using an** alternative to driving alone in your commute to work (bicycling, walking, public transportation, telecommuting, etc.) 424-7611.

South Monterey County

Historic Churches

The Hearst Hacienda

Rural Life Museum

Spreckels

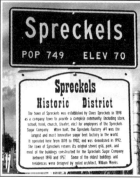

March 11-12   GEM & ROCK SHOW   FREE
Gems and rock displays. Children's activities, rock bags, rock wheel of fortune, food booths. 10-6 Sat, 10-5 Sun at Spreckels Memorial Bldg., corner of 5th and Llano. 422-0530.

July 4 FOURTH OF JULY   FREE+$$
10K Run and Special Olympics 10K run, One-Mile Run for children (free), at Spreckels Park, Third and Llano. Children's Parade register, 10:30am, Memorial Bldg. Entertainment, crafts, children's games at 1pm. Firemen's Muster on Llano Avenue, 1-4pm. Benefit for Volunteer Fire Co. 455-8548, 455-2211.

● **Buena Vista Free Public Library**, in the Middle School, 18250 Tara Drive, off River Road. Tues-Sat. Preschool storytime. 455-9699.

Gonzales

Visitor Information, 147 Fourth St., 831-675-9019.

■ **Community Presbyterian Church**, built in 1883, has been placed on the National Register of Historic Places. 301 4th Street.

● **Library**, 851 Fifth St. Tues/Thurs 12-8, Wed 10-6, Fri/Sat 10-5. Family night, storytimes, Homework Center; call for times. 675-2209.

▲ **Senior Center**, 675-9057.

▲ **Central Park**, 5th and Center Streets, 3 acres. Basketball, picnic area, playground, sand volleyball court, restrooms. 659-2809.

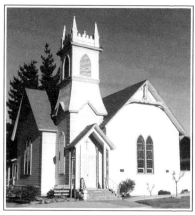

▲ **Centennial Park**, Elko St. & Centennial Dr. (June-Aug). Baseball, picnics.

▲ **Meyer Park**, 5th & Center St., soccer field, tot-lot, basketball, picnics.

San Ardo

● **MoCo Free Library**, 62350 College St. Wed-Fri 11-5. 627-2503.

● **South County Bookmobile**, call for schedule, 385-3677.

Soledad

City Hall, 248 Main, 831-678-3963. Visitor Information, 678-2278.

June 25, 2000   **MISSION BBQ FIESTA**   **FREE+$$**
Mass at 10:30am, barbecue at 12:00. Call Grace at the Mission, 678-3197.

July 4   **OLD-FASHIONED FOURTH OF JULY**   **FREE**
Celebration & fireworks begins at 9am in Gallardo and Little League parks, Metz Road and Andalucia Drive. Games, old-timers' softball, music, food. Fireworks at 8:45pm. Call Raquel, 678-3963 ext. 116.

October 1   **MISSION GRAPE STOMP**   **FREE**
Help stomp the grapes to make wine! Call Grace at the Mission, 678-3197.

December 2   **CHRISTMAS PARADE**   **FREE**
Down Front Street, starts at 5pm after the merchants light up the stores. Food and craft booths will open at noon and entertainment will begin at 1:30.

Places to Visit in Soledad

● **Soledad Library**, 179 Main St. Homework Center Tues and Thurs, 2:30-5:30pm. Volunteers needed. Mon/Wed 10-8, Tues/Thurs 10-6, Fri 10-5, Sat 12-6. 678-2430.

■ **Soledad Correctional Training Facility.** Hobby Store with leather goods, jewelry, etc.; reasonable prices. Open to public Sun-Mon, 8am-3pm, Thurs-Fri, 11am-5pm. Off Hwy 101 between Soledad and Gonzales. 678-3951.

■ **Mission Nuestra Senora de la Soledad**, originally built in 1791, the 13th of 21 California missions. The current building is a smaller chapel built in 1828 and restored in 1954. Free and open to the public. Gift shop, museum and gardens are open daily except Tuesday. Grounds: 8am-4pm. Museum/Chapel 9am-4pm. Gift Shop 10am-4pm. The original adobe ruins can be seen in the rear of the quadrangle. Continued restoration and maintenance of Soledad Mission is made possible by donations and money earned at two major fund-raisers, first Sunday in June Barbecue and first Sunday in October Fall Fiesta. Your donations are appreciated: Mission Soledad Restoration Committee, 36641 Fort Romie Road, Soledad 93960. 678-2586.

▲ **Pinnacles National Monument**, the east side of the park is south of Hollister, 5 miles off Calif. 25. The west side can be reached from Soledad off U.S. 101 via Hwy 146. There is NO direct road connection between the east and west sides. Distinctive geological features with caves to explore and an abundance of wildflowers in the spring. Bring flashlights for the caves. Fabulous scenic hiking trails. Rock climbing formations provide nesting habitat for several hawk and falcon species and should not be attempted during the nesting season, January 15 to July 1. Trailhead climber information boards give specific guidelines on climbing. Base camp with restrooms and picnic tables is free; there is a fee to enter the hiking area. Very hot in the summer. Private campgound on East side with swimming, pool and store, RVs, tents, trailers. Camping on West side in tents only. Call East side: 389-4485. West side: 389-4526.

▲ **Paraiso Hot Springs Resort**. Paraiso Springs Road. Fee. A private resort with small rental cottages, camp, trailer and picnic sites. Indoor and outdoor hot pools with temperatures from 70° to 100°. Snack bar, recreation room with ping-pong, books, magazines. Originally used by the padres at the mission to heal the sick or afflicted. From an elevation of 1400 feet, the Salinas Valley, the Pinnacles and the Gabilan Mountain Range views are superb. Open 10am-6pm, May through October. 10am-4:45pm, November-April. $25/person. 678-2882.

Greenfield

Visitor Information, 831-674-3222.

● **Monterey County Free Library**, Ninth Street and Palm Avenue, 674-2614. Family storytime Sat 11am. Preschool storytime 2nd and 4th Wed 1:15pm. Call for regular hours. ▲ **Jay Hicks Park** is adjacent to the library, offering a place to sit outside, read a book, and enjoy the sunshine. Downtown Greenfield is a pleasant stroll away.

Downtown Greenfield

▲ **Oak Park**, located three miles east of town on Elm Avenue, named for its impressive stand of oak trees. Picnic tables, barbecue area, tennis courts, horseshoe pits, community swimming pool open in summer months. View of the Pinnacles.

▲ **Patriot Park**, on 13th Street, between Oak and Elm. 20 acres. 2 baseball/softball fields, soccer field, skateboard ramp, amphitheater and Children's Services Center. Other neighborhood parks: Vintage Estates, Woodridge, Meadows and Primavera subdivisions; playgrounds, basketball, volleyball.

▲ **Arroyo Seco Recreation Area** Take Greenfield turnoff from King City, turn left on Elm Street (G-16), follow Elm until it ends at Arroyo Seco Road. Turn left on Arroyo Seco Road–15 miles to the Recreation Area. Camp, fish, swim, canoe, access to the Ventana Wilderness. Lake Abbott, Millers Lodge and cafe. 674-5726.

■ **Elm Avenue Bridge**, built in 1915-16 and designated by Monterey County Supervisors as having historical significance; reflects distinctive characteristics of the era; construction methods are significant in engineering history. Spans the Arroyo Seco River and connects Arroyo Seco Road and Greenfield. 268 feet long.

▲ **Ventana Wilderness**, also known as "A Window to the Wild." Contains 167,323 acres straddling the Santa Lucia Mountains and located entirely within Monterey County and the Los Padres National Forest. There are approximately 197 miles of trails. Pine Ridge trail is the most popular and most heavily traversed. Other trailheads include: Carmel River, China Camp, Arroyo Seco, Memorial Park, Bottcher's Gap, Cone Peak, Kirk Creek and Partington Ridge. Topographical Ventana Wilderness Maps and Los Padres National Forest recreation maps are available for $3 each at the Forest Service Office at 406 S. Mildred Street in King City.

King City

Visitor Information, 203 Broadway, 831-385-3814.

April   **JUNIOR RODEO** $$
King City Riding Club at the Fairgrounds. 385-3814.

May 18-21, 2000   **SALINAS VALLEY FAIR**   FREE+$$
Livestock, 4-H exhibits, food contests, carnival, horticulture showing. King City Fairgrounds, 625 Division Street. 385-3243.

September 16-17, 2000   **SALSA FEST** $$
Salinas Valley Fairgrounds. Salsa recipe contest. Country Western entertainment, carnival, crafts. 386-3281.

Places to Visit in King City

▲ **San Lorenzo County Park**, 1160 Broadway off Hwy 101, 384-8020. Fee. 380 acres. **Monterey County Agricultural and Rural Life Museum:** Antique farm equipment and mining, farming and local history displays. A working blacksmith shop, a century-old farmhouse and a one-room schoolhouse. Exhibits: tack shop, country store and antique printing press, cook wagon, railroad caboose and the old King City train depot. The main exhibit barn and the outdoor displays are open daily, 10am-4pm, year-round. The other buildings are open weekends, April-October, call for hours. Free guided tours of the historic buildings. Park has horseshoe pits, picnic and barbecue areas, playgrounds, walking trails, campground, water activities in the Salinas River. Spreading oak trees and eucalyptus groves. 385-5964. Celebrates the 4th of July with a Valley Heritage Day – a 4-day camping rally; call 800-588-2267. Tourist information center in Museum barn, 10am-4pm daily.

▲ **Leo Meyer Senior Center**, 385-4562. **Recreation Center**, 212 S. Vanderhurst Ave., 385-3575.

▲ **Public Golf Course**, on Golf Drive behind the Fairgrounds on Division Street. 9 hole course, clubhouse, pro-shop. Public welcome. 385-4546.

● **Monterey County Free Library**, 402 Broadway, 385-3677. Tues-Thurs 11-8, Wed 10-8, Fri-Sat 10-4.

▲ **King City Park** & Recreation Center, Division and San Lorenzo Ave. 17 acres. Ballfield, community building, horseshoe pits, multi-use field, playground, swimming, tennis, racquetball courts, lap and wading pools, dive tank, water slide, restrooms. 385-3575, 385-0102. Pool $2, open 1-4pm..

■ **Town Square** new development downtown with restaurants, shops, a tourism center with wine tasting, beer tasting and farmer's market.

San Lucas

● **Monterey County Free Library**, 54692 Teresa, 382-4382. Tues-Wed 12-5, Thurs 8-11, 12-5.

■ **San Lucas Bridge**, built in 1915 and designated by Monterey County Supervisors as having historical significance; reflects distinctive characteristics of the era; the construction methods are significant in engineering history. Spans the Salinas River and connects the community of San Lucas with Jolon Road. 870 feet long.

Bradley

● **MoCo Free Library** Dixie St. Call for hours. 805-472-9407.

■ **Nacimiento Lake Drive Bridge,** built in 1921 and designated by Monterey County Supervisors as having historical significance; reflects distinctive characteristics of the era; the construction methods are significant in engineering history. Spans the San Antonio River and connects the Bradley-Jolon Road and the town of Bradley to the Lake San Antonio area. 292 feet long. May be demolished in 2000.

▲ **Lake San Antonio Recreation Area**, 85 miles south of Salinas on Highway 101. Turn on Jolon Road. Picnic areas, fishing, swimming, boat launches, convenience store. 755-4899. Eagle Watch tours, Jan-Mar, 888/588-2267.

▲ **Lake Nacimiento Resort**, Highway 101 south of Salinas to Lake Nacimiento Drive. Campsites, general store, marina, boat ramps, hiking trails, fishing. 805-238-3256.

Parkfield

● **MoCo Free Library** 70643 Parkfield-Coalinga Rd. 805-463-2347. Call for hours. Earthquake maps: wrgis.wr.usgs.gov/open-file/of97-30.

▲ **Cholame Road Bridge**, built in 1932 and designated by Monterey County Supervisors as having historical significance and reflects distinctive characteristics of the era and construction methods significant in engineering history. Spans Little Cholame Creek on the county road that connects Parkfield with State Hwy. 46 east of Paso Robles in San Luis Obispo County. 135 feet long.

■ **Parkfield-Coalinga Road Bridge**, built in 1932 and designated by Monterey County as having historical significance. Spans Little Cholame Creek, connects Parkfield with Coalinga in Fresno County. 118 feet long.

■ **Parkfield Inn and Cafe, V-6Ranch**, shown at right, "Old West" working ranch with guest houses. Ranch-style bed and breakfast inn. 20,000 acres to roam. Horse camping, weddings, fishing, swimming, cycling, 805-463-2323.

Jolon/Ft. Hunter Liggett

■ **The Hacienda** was the Ranch House for William Randolph Hearst, newspaper magnate of Hearst Castle fame. Now open to the public as a lodge, restaurant and lounge. Near to Mission San Antonio. From Hwy 101 just north of King City, take Jolon Rd. southwest 17.5 miles to Mission Rd., go west 5 miles into Hunter Liggett and Del Ventura Rd. 831-386-2900, fax 831-386-2262. www.usawines.com/hacienda/

■ **Mission San Antonio**, founded by Fr. Junipero Serra in 1771, the third of the California Missions and still active as a parish church. Jolon Road to Mission Road. Annual Fiesta in June. $1 donation. Picnic grounds with tables under the shade trees to relax and enjoy the peace and quiet of the secluded area and the many varieties of roses in the garden. Mass Schedules: Daily at 7:30am, Sunday at 10am. Museum hours, 9am-6pm daily. Gift Shop hours: Sun 11:15-4:30pm, Mon-Sat 10am-4:30pm. 385-4478.

■ **Tidball Store & Dutton Hotel**, preserved ruins located on Jolon road off of G14. Tidball Store was placed on the National Register of Historic Places in 1976. Dutton Hotel, 1849-1929, was a stage coach stop on California's first highway, El Camino Real. National Register 1971.

Monterey Wine Country

Monterey Area Code is 831

Monterey County Vintners & Growers Association, 375-9400, fax 375-1116, www.montereywines.org.

Monterey County Wine Country Magazine, call 373-3720 for a free copy.

AgVenture Tours, custom winery tours, 643-WINE, fax 645-WINE.

Steinbeck Country Tours, 659-0333.

Rancho Cellars has introductory seminar and van tours of Chateau Julien, Talbott, Durney & Bernardus wineries. $52/person. Reservations, 659-4025.

USAWines.com - Buy Monterey County wines on-line

Club Taste - Delivers wine to your home. 646-5446.

CV Wine Tour & Tasting Seminar - Winery tours, 659-4025.

Burchellhouse.com - Buy homes with wine cellars

Important Wine Events

Dates shown for year 2000. Updates at www.montereycountyguide.com
Please call in advance to verify as information is subject to change.

February 23-27   MASTERS OF FOOD & WINE $$
At the Highlands Inn, various times. Exceptional gastronomic event with internationally famous chefs and winemakers. Lunches, dinners, winery tours, wine tastings. Call info, 620-1234.

March 30-Apr 2   MONTEREY WINE FESTIVAL   FREE+$$
Monterey Bay Aquarium & various locations. Tastings, lectures, dinners, seminars, wine display, parties, tours. Open house and complimentary tastings at participating wineries. Call for dates, places and times. www.Montereywine.com. 656-WINE.

April 29   STEINBECK WINE COUNTRY OPEN HOUSE   FREE
At Chalone, Cloninger, Jekel, Paraiso Springs, Scheid, Hahn, Smith & Hook.

August to November   WINE HARVESTING   FREE+$$
Observe grape harvest activities at these wineries: Chateau Julien, Monterey Vineyards, Chalone, Smith & Hook/Hahn Estates, Paraiso Springs and Cloniger. September & October most active time; call for dates and times.

August 12-13   WINEMAKERS' CELEBRATION   FREE+$$
Custom House Plaza, Monterey. Over 30 Monterey County wineries participate in this outdoor festival. Wine tasting, exhibits, silent auction, music, food. Free open house events at wine tasting rooms. 375-9400.

October 1   MISSION GRAPE STOMP   FREE
Mass at 10:30am, Chicken barbecue at 11:45 ($6), participants invited to stomp grapes to make wine at 1:30pm; wine auction after the stomp. At the Soledad Mission. Grace, 678-3197.

November 4   **6TH ANNUAL WINE TASTING EVENT**   **FREE**
Cornucopia Community Market, 11am-3pm. Outdoor courtyard music, entertainment, wines and food from local vendors. 26135 Carmel Rancho Blvd, just east of Highway 1 at CV Road. 625-0230.

November 10-12   **GREAT WINE ESCAPE WEEKEND**   **$$**
4th annual. Winery & vineyard tours, winery open houses, winemaker dinners, golf tournament and concert. Restaurant promotions & special hotel rates for the weekend. Monterey County Vintners & Growers Assn., 375-9400.

Wine Tasting & Vineyard Tours
Follow the numbers on the map opposite.

1. **Bargetto Winery** – Free wine tasting. Daily 10:30am-6pm. 700 Cannery Row, Monterey. Oldest Monterey tasting room, over 30 selections. 373-4053.

2. **A Taste Of Monterey** – $5 for 6 tastes, rebate with purchase. Daily 11am-6pm. 700 Cannery Row. Exhibits: corks, barrel-making, viticulture. 646-5446.

3. **Bottles N' Bins** – Retail store, deli. Sun-Thurs 10am-12am, Fri-Sat 10am-1am. 898 Lighthouse Ave., New Monterey. 375-5488.

4. **Savor Monterey Market** – Retail wines, local art work. Daily 11-7. 1280 Del Monte Ave. Monterey. 642-0708.

5. **Ventana Vineyards** – Free wine tasting. Daily 11am-5pm. 2999 Monterey-Salinas Highway, Monterey. 372-7415.

6. **Mediterranean Market** – Retail store, specialty food market since 1959. Daily 9am-6pm. Ocean Ave. and Mission, Carmel. 624-2022.

7. **Bountiful Basket** – Free wine tasting. Mon-Sat 10:30am-5:30pm, Sun 12-5pm. 153 Crossroads Blvd., Carmel. 625-4457, 800-930-0077.

8. **Rancho Cellars** – Wine tasting $10-$40. Mon-Sat 11am-7pm. Sun 12-5pm. Carmel Rancho Center in Carmel Rancho. 625-5646.

9. **Chateau Julien** – Free wine tasting Mon-Fri 8:30am-5pm. Sat-Sun 11am-5pm. Free tours of the vineyards, 10:30 & 2:30, 7 days. 8940 Carmel Valley Road, Carmel Valley. www.chateaujulien.com. 624-2600.

10. **Heller Estate/Durney Vineyards** – $3 tasting charge. Mon-Fri 11am-5pm, Sat-Sun 10am-5pm. 69 West Carmel Valley Road, Carmel Valley Village. 659-6220. 800-625-8466. Produces 100% certified organic wines.

11. **Talbott Vineyards** – Free glass with tasting price. Thurs-Sun, 11am-5pm. 53 W. Carmel Valley Rd. Mail order, gift shop. Emily, 659-3500.

12. **Georis Winery** – Minimum half bottle purchase. Thurs-Sat 12-4pm. Call for information about special events. 4 Pilot Road, CV Village. 659-1050.

13. **Bernardus** – Free white wine tasting, red $3. Daily 11am-5:30pm. 5 W. Carmel Valley Road, Carmel Valley Village. 659-1900.

14. **River Ranch Vineyard** – Tasting room in the White Oak Grill. 11:30am-4pm. 19 E. Carmel Valley Rd. 659-1525.

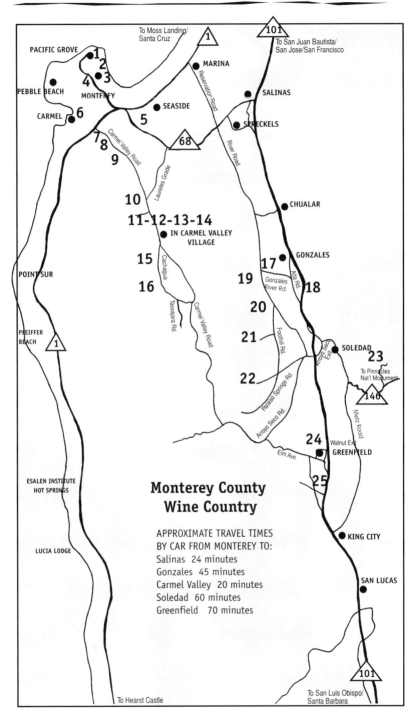

To Moss Landing/
Santa Cruz

1

101
To San Juan Bautista/
San Jose/San Francisco

PACIFIC GROVE

1
2
4 3

MARINA

Reservation Road

PEBBLE BEACH

MONTEREY

SALINAS

CARMEL

6

SEASIDE

SPRECKELS

5

68

River Road

Carmel Valley Road

7
8
9

Laureles Grade

CHUALAR

10

11-12-13-14

IN CARMEL VALLEY
VILLAGE

Cachagua

GONZALES

15

17

POINT SUR

16

19

Gonzales
River Rd.

Alta Rd.

18

Tassajara Rd.

Carmel Valley Road

20

PFEIFFER
BEACH

1

21

Foothill Rd.

Arroyo Seco Ext.

SOLEDAD

23

To Pinnacles
Nat'l Monument

146

22

Paraiso Springs Rd.

Metz Road

Arroyo Seco Rd.

24

Walnut Ext.

GREENFIELD

Elm Ave.

25

ESALEN INSTITUTE
HOT SPRINGS

Monterey County
Wine Country

APPROXIMATE TRAVEL TIMES
BY CAR FROM MONTEREY TO:
Salinas   24 minutes
Gonzales   45 minutes
Carmel Valley   20 minutes
Soledad   60 minutes
Greenfield   70 minutes

KING CITY

LUCIA LODGE

SAN LUCAS

101

To Hearst Castle

To San Luis Obispo/
Santa Barbara

15. **Galante Vineyards** – <u>Free wine tasting</u> by appointment, <u>free tours</u>, Sun-Fri 11am-3pm. 18181 Cachagua Rd., Carmel Valley. 1-800-GALANTE.

16. **Joullian Vineyard** – Mon-Thurs 11am-3pm. 20300 Cachagua Rd., Carmel Valley. 659-2800.

17. **Cloninger Cellars** – <u>Free wine tasting</u>. Mon-Thurs 11am-4pm, Fri-Sun 11am-5pm. Call for special winter hours.1645 River Road, Gonzales. 675-9463. www.usawines.com/Cloninger.

18. **Riverland Vineyards/Mystic Cliffs** – Grand Opening May 2000. Wed-Sun 11am-5pm. 850 S. Alta St. Gonzales. 675-8838.

19. **Morgan Winery** – To open in the fall of 2000. 1520 River Road. 751-7777.

20. **San Saba Vineyards** – To open in the fall of 2000. Where River Rd. and Foothill come together. 753-7222.

21. **J. Hahn Estates/Smith & Hook** – <u>Free wine tasting, free tours</u>. Daily 11am-4pm. 37700 Foothill Road, Soledad. Highway 101 exit Arroyo Seco, right on Fort Romie road, left on Colony, right on Foothill. www.hahnestates.com. 678-2132.

22. **Paraiso Springs Vineyards** – <u>Free wine tasting, tours</u>. Mon-Fri 12-4pm, Sat-Sun 11am-5pm. Special events. 38060 Paraiso Spgs Rd., Soledad. www.usawines.com/Paraiso. 678-0300.

23. **Chalone Vineyard** – <u>Free wine tasting, tours</u>. Picnic area. Sat-Sun 11:30am-5pm. By appt weekdays. Highway 146 at Stonewall Canyon Road, Soledad. www.chalonewinegroup.com. 678-1717.

24. **Jekel Vineyards** – <u>Free wine tasting</u>. Daily 11am-4pm. 40155 Walnut Ave., Greenfield. Highway 101 to Greenfield exit, then west on Walnut. www.usawines.com/Jekel. 674-5525.

25. **Scheid Vineyards** – <u>Free wine tasting</u>. Daily 11am-5pm (winter), 11am-6pm (summer). 1972 Hobson Ave. exit off Highway 101, 5 miles south of Greenfield. New hospitality room, tours available. www.scheidvineyards.com. 386-0316.

WINE
STEINBECK COUNTRY
TASTING

Stonewall Cyn Rd & Hwy 146 •
Soledad • Adjacent to west side of
The Pinnacles • Tasting Sat. &
Sun. 11:30am-5pm, by appt
weekdays, call (831) 678-1717 •
www.chalonewinegroup.com

CHALONE VINEYARD

1645 River Rd • Gonzales •
(831) 675-WINE (9463) •
Tasting Mon-Thurs 11am-4pm
& Fri-Sun 11am-5pm, call for
special winter hrs •
www.usawines.com/Cloninger

CLONINGER CELLARS

40155 Walnut Ave • Greenfield •
(831) 674-5525 • Tasting daily
11am-4pm • www.usawines.com/
Jekel

JEKEL VINEYARDS

38060 Paraiso Springs Rd •
Soledad • (831) 678-0300 •
Tasting Mon-Fri Noon-4pm &
Sat-Sun 11am-5pm •
www.usawines.com/Paraiso

PARAISO SPRINGS VINEYARDS

850 S. Alta St • Gonzales •
(831) 675-8838 • Tasting room
Grand Opening May 2000,
Wed-Sun, 11-5pm

RIVERLAND VINEYARDS/MYSTIC CLIFFS

1972 Hobson Ave • Greenfield
(look for the American Flag) •
(831) 386-0316 • Tasting
daily 11am-5pm, Summer hrs
(Memorial Day Wknd thru
Labor Day Wknd), 11am-6pm •
www.scheidvineyards.com

SCHEID VINEYARDS

37700 Foothill Rd • Soledad •
(831) 678-2132 • Tasting daily
11am-4pm •
www.hahnestates.com

HAHN ESTATES

37700 Foothill Rd • Soledad •
(831) 678-2132 • Tasting
daily 11am-4pm •
www.hahnestates.com

SMITH & HOOK

Complimentary wine tasting at each winery

2000 CALENDAR OF EVENTS
Saturday, April 29
Steinbeck Wine Country Spring Open House
Saturday, August 12
Monterey County Winemakers' Celebration
Saturday & Sunday, November 11 & 12
Monterey County Great Wine Escape

Seaside & Sand City

Del Rey Oaks, CSUMB, Ft. Ord

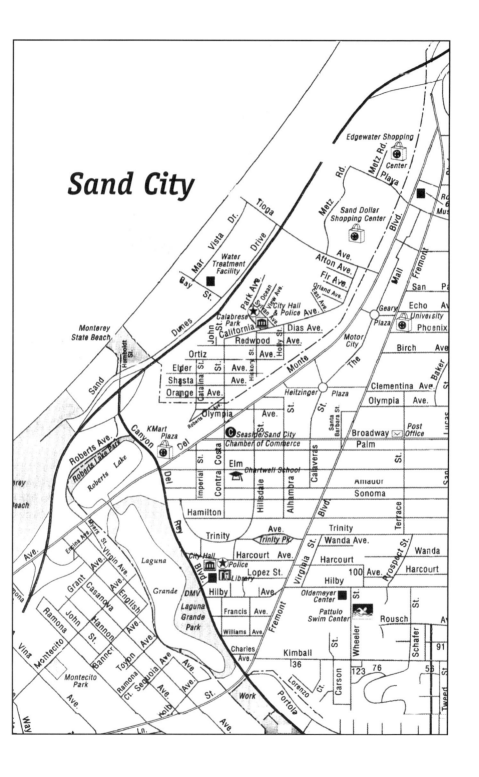

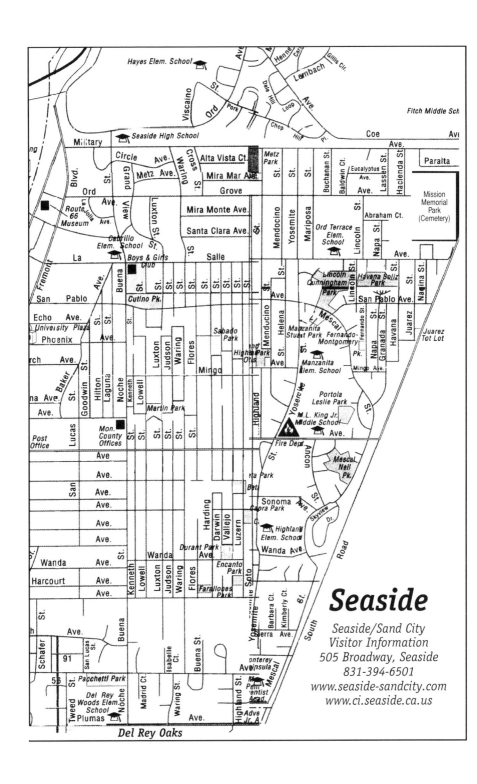

Seaside

Seaside/Sand City
Visitor Information
505 Broadway, Seaside
831-394-6501
www.seaside-sandcity.com
www.ci.seaside.ca.us

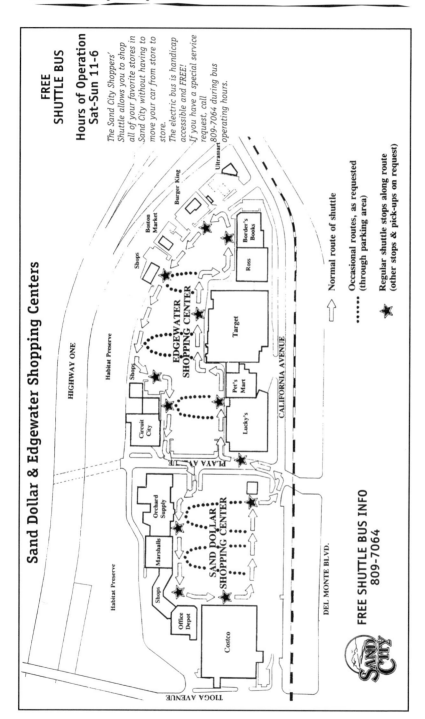

Sand Dollar & Edgewater Shopping Centers

FREE SHUTTLE BUS

Hours of Operation
Sat-Sun 11-6

The Sand City Shoppers' Shuttle allows you to shop all of your favorite stores in Sand City without having to move your car from store to store.
The electric bus is handicap accessible and FREE!
If you have a special service request, call 809-7064 during bus operating hours.

⟹ Normal route of shuttle

••••• Occasional routes, as requested (through parking area)

✦ Regular shuttle stops along route (other stops & pick-ups on request)

FREE SHUTTLE BUS INFO
809-7064

Browsing the Shops

● **Sand Dollar and Edgewater Shopping Centers**, see map at left for shops and free shoppers' shuttle bus service. Sand City, Hwy 1 and Fremont Blvd.

● **Big K-Mart Plaza**, on Canyon Del Rey and Highway 1, Seaside. K-Mart, Smart & Final, Staples, McDonald's Playplace.

● **Laguna Plaza Shopping Center**, Fremont Blvd., near Kimball, Seaside. The Breakfast Club, Radio Shack, Mail Boxes Etc., Hollywood Video.

● **University Plaza**, Fremont Blvd. and Echo Ave., Seaside. Olympia Beauty Supply, Gold's Gym, Beverly Fabric Store.

● **Motor City**, billed as the largest auto mall in the world, between Del Monte Ave. and Fremont Blvd., enter at Plaza or Echo Ave., Seaside.

● **Route 66 Museum**, 1933 Del Monte Blvd., has memorabilia and lots of classic cars on display. Stop in for a lot of free fun for the whole family. 393-9329. Appraisals: 1-888-393-9329. Buy-Sell-Trade.

● **Gil's Gourmet**. Try before you buy: free samples at the Wall of Flame and of other gourmet items–try the Chardonnay Garlic-Stuffed Olives and Simply Zinful Garlic Salsa, Mon-Fri 9am-6pm. 577 Ortiz Ave, Sand City. 394-3305.

The Chocolate Factory, 1291 Fremont, gives free tours and chocolate samples.Store hours: Mon-Fri, 9:30am-8:30pm, Sat 10am-8:30pm, Sun 12:30-5:30pm. 899-7963.

Free Wooden Cat

Show *Your Personal Guide* at Mary's Angels, 425 Elder Avenue, Sand City, and receive a free handcarved 50-year-old wooden cat with a purchase of $50 or more. Handcarved wood & cast stone for home & garden. Monday-Saturday 10am-5pm. 393-0345.

Dr. L.D. Roberts, Founder of Seaside

Dr. Roberts, a medical doctor, came to the Monterey Peninsula in 1887, bought his uncle's ranch and became the first subdivider in what he named the City of Seaside. He also founded the Seaside Post Office in 1890 and was postmaster there for 42 years. In 1892 he was elected to the Monterey School Board on which he served for 36 years. In 1908 he was elected to the Monterey County Board of Supervisors and served for 20 years, four of which were as chairman of the board. Dr. Roberts saw to it that the Presidio of Monterey reservation was enlarged and rebuilt in 1902. He pioneered the building of Hwy 1 between Monterey and Castroville. During his lifetime, Dr. Roberts saw a dream come true– the building of the $10,000,000 Carmel-San Simeon highway. He fought to have the highway built for 20 years and finally realized his dream when the road was opened June 27, 1937. He died in 1949 at the age of 88. Researched by Seaside Historical Commission for the Millennium 2000.

Genealogy Center

Monterey Family History Center, of the Church of Jesus Christ of Latter Day Saints, is <u>open free to the public</u> to conduct genealogy research; linked to World Center in Salt Lake City, Utah. This is great fun for all the family. Docents there will help you find information on your ancestors. Open Tues-Wed 9am-9pm, Fri-Sat 9am-5pm. 1024 Noche Buena, Seaside, 394-1124.

Helpful Genealogy Websites

www.myhistory.org - a toolbox of resources; www.cyndislist.com - links to 1,000 sites; www.rootsweb.com - discussion lists; www.genealogy.com; www.ancestry.com, www.myfamily.com, and www.familyhistory.com - do research and post information for others to find.

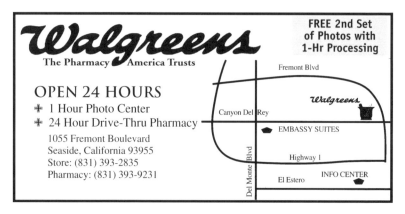

Art and Art Galleries

● **Three Spirits Arts Center**, 361 Orange Ave., Sand City, 393-2787.

● **Sand Dollar Art & Framing Center**, 824 Playa Ave., Seaside, 394-1618.

● **Seaside City Hall**, Seaside Arts Commission, changing exhibits of local artists. 440 Harcourt. 8am-5pm. Sponsors **Seaside Jazz Art Show** in August. Call for more information, 899-6336.

● **Borders**, 2080 California, Sand City. Art in Café Espresso. 899-6643.

● **Family Center for the Arts**, 530 Elm Ave., Seaside. Affiliated with the Salvation Army. Low cost classes in painting, piano keyboard, computers and martial arts. Anita Amos, 899-0525, 899-1335.

● **Oldemeyer Center**, changing exhibits of local art. 986 Hilby Ave. 899-6270. **Cowboy Week** in July is a cowboy venue and cowboy art reception. Children's Artfest lets kids get hands-on experience for $5; call 899-6273.

● **"The Past and Future of Art"**, mural by teenagers in the Employment Training Youth Program. On the wall of Artmax at 680 Broadway Ave. Seaside. Teens in the program are painting 8 other murals around the county.

Seaside Restaurants & Markets

● **Bangkok Grocery**, Thai, 1482 Fremont Blvd., 394-4161.

● **Café Beach**, Monterey Beach Hotel, 2600 Sand Dunes Dr., 394-3321.

● **El Migueleno**, Salvadorean, 1066 Broadway, 899-2199.

● **Ferdi's**, Cajun/American, 740 Broadway, 394-4609.

● **Fish Wife Seafood Cafe**, seafood, 789 Trinity Ave., 394-2027.

● **Ichi Ricki**, Japanese, 1603 Del Monte Blvd, 394-7733.

● **Indian-Filipino Market**, 1906 Fremont Blvd., 393-9175.

● **Magat Oriental Store**, 1760 Del Monte Blvd., 393-1383.

● **Nipa Hut**, Philippine cuisine, 1257 Fremont Blvd., 583-0722.

● **Puerto Nuevo Mariscos**, Mexican seafood, 580 Broadway, 583-0411.

● **Stammtisch**, German, 1204 Echo Ave, 899-3070.

Seaside Accommodations

● **Embassy Suites**, 1441 Canyon Del Rey, 831-393-1115. Call.

● **Gateway Lodge Motel**, 1909 Fremont Blvd, 394-6606. $30+.

● **Hampton Inn**, 1400 Del Monte Blvd., 394-5335. $99-149.

● **Howard Johnson**, 1893 Fremont Blvd, 394-8566. $35-75.

● **Magic Carpet Lodge**, 1875 Fremont Blvd., 899-4221. $49+.

● **Pacific Best Inn**, 1141 Fremont Blvd., 899-1881. $35-89.

● **SunBay at Monterey Bay**, 5200 Coe Ave., 800-285-3131. $129+.

Calendar of Events

Year 2000 dates shown. Updates at www.montereycountyguide.com.
Please call in advance to verify as information is subject to change.

JANUARY

January 17   MARTIN LUTHER KING JR. PARADE   FREE
11am march starts on Broadway and concludes at Oldemeyer Center, 966
Hilby St. Seaside. 1pm speakers. Elias Oxendine IV, 333-9106.

FEBRUARY

February all month   BLACK HISTORY MONTH   FREE
Art exhibition, cultural program and reception at City Hall, 440 Harcourt Ave.
Art Gallery hours are 8am-5pm, Mon-Fri. 899-6270.

APRIL

April 22   2 EASTER EGG HUNTS   FREE
In Del Rey Oaks Park, 11am, hosted by Monterey Peninsula Nisei Veterans
of Foreign Wars Post 1629. Call 372-0219. In Seaside, 11am at the Oldemeyer
Center, 986 Hilby St, sponsored by the Avenue of Flags, American Legion
591, VFW Seamont Poster 8679, and the City of Seaside. 899-6273.

April 29   YOUTH SUMMIT   FREE
6th Annual at Oldemeyer Center, Seaside. Open to middle and high school
students in the county. Sponsored by NAACP's Youth Council. 394-2869.

MAY

May 6   MAYFAIRE   FREE
Weave a flower wreath, grind wheat, maypole dancing. 10am-3pm. Laguna
Grande Park. Sponsored by Monterey Bay Charter School. Julie, 394-5888.

May 7   CINCO DE MAYO   FREE
Mariachi bands, folkloric dancing, games and food at Seaside City Hall, 11am-
5pm Games, arts and crafts, piñatas, children's activities. 899-6273.

JUNE

June   MONTEREY BONSAI CLUB EXHIBITION   FREE
11am-4pm. Numerous trees on display and for sale. Demonstrations of bonsai
techniques, door prizes. Buddhist Temple, 1155 Noche Buena. 649-5300.

June   INTERNATIONAL EXTRAVAGANZA   FREE
Entertainment, ethnic foods, arts & crafts. Laguna Grande Park at Canyon
Del Rey, Seaside. 11am-5:30pm. 899-6270.

June/October   HOT CARS/COOL NIGHTS   FREE
Every Friday. Rod and Classic Car Show, 5-8pm, West Broadway at Fremont.
Hosted by Gold Coast Rods, pre-'73 cars, awards, raffles, 50-50 raffle, music.
After the show, cruise with the winners to downtown Monterey and Cannery
Row. No registration fee. 394-4254.

JULY

July   **OBON FESTIVAL**   **FREE**
Entertainment, exhibits, Japanese food. 1155 Noche Buena St. Seaside. Bonsai demos, flower arrangement, taiko performance, raffle. 394-0119.

July 4   **SEASIDE PARADE OF CHAMPIONS**   **FREE**
At noon on Fremont Blvd. at Harcourt Ave., with main reviewing stand on West Broadway at Alhambra. Participants include Central California marching units, drill teams, bands, floats, horses, antique cars with numerous dignitaries. 899-6270, 899-6273.

July 9-Aug 13   **BLUES AND ART IN THE PARK**   **FREE**
Sundays, 1-4:30pm. Six free concerts of blues and art in the park on Sundays. Laguna Grande Park, Canyon Del Rey near Highway 1, across from Seaside Police Dept., 899-6270. No dogs, please.

July 13-16   **COWBOY CRAZY DAYS**   **FREE**
For senior citizens, at Oldemeyer Center, 986 Hilby Ave. Salinas Rodeo Week event. Police horses, line dancing, cowboy art exhibit, country-style dancing. Call for times. Seaside Cultural and Leisure Services, 899-6270.

AUGUST

August   **MONTEREY BAY RIB COOKOFF**   **FREE+$$**
Noon-6pm on the lawn at Seaside City Hall, across from Laguna Grande Park. Part of the nationally recognized California Cookoff Series attracts amateur barbecue enthusiasts from around the state. Live music, games, rides, arts & crafts, foods, beverages and the best ribs you ever wrapped your lips around! Seaside Chamber of Commerce, 394-6501, 899-6270.

August   **FALL FUN FEST**   **FREE**
Carnival, crafts, food, music, fireman's relay, pie eating contest, cake cutting for city's birthday. **Annual Diaper Derby**: Parents of children from crawling age to age 4 are encouraged to bring them to participate in the race on Canyon Del Rey in front of Seaside City Hall. Entry is free and prizes awarded to the fastest babies. Preregister: 899-6270 or on-site. **Annual Bed Races**: Teams push double beds that have been modified with wheels and extra-long push bars for the races. 899-6270.

August 5   **WALK FOR THE GOLD**   **Spectators FREE**
Gather at Sand City beach, 10am-2pm, with a team of 10 or more people; pledge $100 or more per person, for 5K walk followed by barbecue and live music. To benefit Special Olympics Monterey Bay Region. 373-1972

OCTOBER

October   **BIKE RODEO & SAFETY FAIR**   **FREE**
10am-2pm at Boys & Girls Club of the Monterey Peninsula, 1332 LaSalle Ave. Bring bicycle and helmet to participate. Police motorcycle and canine demonstrations, free bicycle inspections and licensing, free child fingerprinting and photos. Emergency services vehicles on display. Prizes. Appearance by McGruff the Crime Dog, Vince & Larry the Crash Test dummies, Buckle Bear, Spanky the Fire Dog. 759-6678.

NOVEMBER

November 23   **THANKSGIVING DINNERS**   **FREE**
Thanksgiving Dinner open to the public at American Legion Post 591, 1000 Playa Ave. $6 per person. 394-6604 for reservations.

DECEMBER

December   **DOLLS' TEA PARTY**   **FREE**
Tea party and refreshments by the Salvation Army. Holiday items for sale to benefit needy children and local programs. 1491 Contra Costa. 899-4911.

December 9   **SEASIDE HOLIDAY FANTASY FESTIVAL**   **FREE**
Real snow for the children! Parade of floats, cars, bands, drill teams, clowns and Santa Claus down Fremont Blvd. at Broadway to City Hall, 440 Harcourt St. where the city tree is lighted at 6:30pm in the Stephen E. Ross Park. Santa treats for the children, who are invited to bring handmade decorations for the community tree. 899-6273.

December 21-31   **HOLIDAY PLAYLAND & POSADA**   **FREE**
Holiday break activities for children ages 5-11, from 1-5:30pm. Call Oldemeyer Center for details, 899-6270. Posada at 440 Harcourt Ave. 899-6270.

December 25   **CHRISTMAS DINNER**   **FREE**
Noon to 4pm at Seaside Assembly of God Church, 1184 Hilby Ave. The church youth group and other volunteers will deliver dinners to shut-ins as well as public servants who have to work. Volunteers call 899-4198.

Entertainment

Movies & Music

◆ **Seaside MCAP** sponsors Gay Movie Night, 7-9pm, first and third Wednesdays at 780 Hamilton Ave. Free and open to all ages in the gay, lesbian, bi and transgendered community. Refreshments. 772-8202.

◆ **Embassy Suites**, jazz Fri 5:30-7:30. No cover. 1441 Canyon Del Rey Blvd, Seaside, 393-1115.

Books & Poetry

◆ **Seaside Library**, 550 Harcourt Ave. 899-2055. Hours: Mon 12-8, Tues-Thurs 10-8, Fri 12-6, Sat 10-6, Sun 1-5. Preschool Storytimes, ages 3-5, Thurs 10:30am. Homework Center, Tues-Thurs 3-6pm.

◆ **Borders' Bookstore**, 2080 California Ave, Sand Dollar Center. Local musicians, speakers, poets, writers, book groups. Call for your copy of their ree newsletter which gives all the times and dates. Store hours: Mon-Sat, 9am-11pm. Sun 9am-9pm. 899-6643.

◆ **Hayes Education Center.** Free classes, 200 Coe Ave., Seaside, 899-5033.

Parks and Recreation

▲ **Seaside State Beach**, Canyon Del Rey at Highway 1. Long, walkable stretches of sand and beautiful dunes. Fly a kite, walk the dog, take a sunset stroll, check out the native plant dune restoration project currently underway. Volunteer to assist by calling 659-4488.

▲ **Bicycle Trail**, by Roberts Lake, down Tioga Ave to Fort Ord, provides a continuous bicycle trail linking Pebble Beach and Castroville.

▲ **Cutino Park**, Noche Buena St. and La Salle Ave. 10^1/2 acres. Ballfield, basketball, picnic area, playground, tennis, restrooms. 899-6270.

▲ **Roberts Lake**, across Del Monte Blvd. from Laguna Grande Park, is a nesting place for a variety of sea birds: Canadian geese, mallards, American coot, seagulls, cormorants, and others. Model boat racing Sat-Sun afternoons. Named for the "Father of Seaside," Dr. John L. Roberts. 659-4488.

▲ **Monterey Bay Dunes Open Space** includes nearly half of Sand City's dunes to be restored and added to the Monterey Bay State Seashore as open space and endangered species habitat. Open dawn to dusk. Off Highway 1, north of Seaside State Beach. 659-4488.

➤ **Seaside Green Team and Neighborhood Improvement Program.** Free help to beautify your property. Volunteer to help! Call 899-6200.

➤ **Students for Parks.** Help out on Earth Day and Arbor Week in April. Volunteer to help anytime! Call 899-5562.

➤ **Borders Explorer Camp.** A free July-Aug activity for children of all ages–exploring art and wildlife. Come in to sign up or call 899-6643 for info.

Monterey Bay Dunes Open Space

The Monterey Bay dunes extend inland under most of Marina, Sand City, and Seaside. These ancient inland dunes exist as consolidated sandhills while the dunes on the shoreline are the progeny of a once receding ocean that is now reclaiming them as sea-level rises. The first Europeans found little use for the dunes and settled in the sheltered forested areas and uplands where the ground was suitable for building. Later, after WWII, sand mining became the most prevalent use for the dunes and several operations established themselves along the 12-mile stretch of dunes from Sand City to Marina. Landfill dumping and off-road use was another activity in the dunes. In the near future almost half of Sand City's dunes will be restored and added to the Monterey Bay State Seashore as open space and endangered species habitat. Monterey Peninsula Regional Park District, 659-4488.

Laguna Grande Community Park

Once a source of tules for Ohlone structures, boats and other uses, Laguna Grande was later a regular watering spot for Spanish military horses and civilian use. The lake is now two district lakes with the northern and smaller lake named after Dr. John Roberts, the "Father of Seaside." With generous Federal, State and Joint Powers Agency funding, the 34 acre park now offers trails, children's play areas, bicycling, picnic facilities, restrooms, lake restoration, and landscaping. Site of Russian Orthodox Church near picnic areas. Seaside Cultural & Leisure Services, 899-6270.

Del Rey Oaks

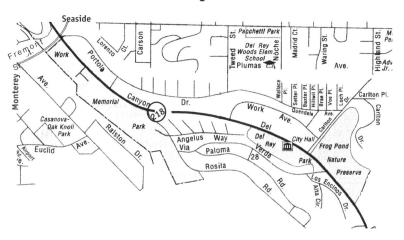

■ **Del Rey Oaks Golf Shop & Driving Range**, 899 Rosita Road. Al Braga–professional. Discount golf shop, night light, deli, golf schools, private lessons. Open 9am-9pm. 394-8660.

▲ **Frog Pond Natural Area**, Canyon Del Rey at the Via Verde intersection, Del Rey Oaks. 17 acre habitat for the rare Pacific Tree frog. Park and pick up guided walk brochure across the street at City Hall. The entrance is along the northbound shoulder of Highway 218. Dawn to dusk. 659-4488.

Recreation Centers

▲ **Seaside Recreation Department.** The City of Seaside sponsors games, sports activities, swimming, excursions and special events free for children ages 5-11. Register at Oldemeyer Center, 986 Hilby Ave. or Del Rey Woods School, 1281 Plumas Ave., 899-6270.

▲ **Oldemeyer Center.** Activities for seniors and others. 986 Hilby Ave., 899-6270. Sage Stompers Square Dance Club welcomes all square dancers Tuesdays at 7:30pm. For info call Bill Herrold at 647-9392. Scrabble players meet every Wed 6-9pm. No dues, all welcome; for info call 633-4649.

▲ **B.J. Dolan Youth and Education Center**, 1136 Wheeler St., Seaside. Mon-Thurs 3-8pm, Fri 3-9pm, Sun 1-9pm. Center offers educational, social and recreational opportunities to Seaside students in middle and high schools: job hunting assistance, volunteer opportunities, pool, air hockey, Nintendo, television and recording studio facilities. 899-6270, 899-6375.

▲ **Boys & Girls Club**, 1332 LaSalle Ave., Seaside. Programs for Youths ages 7-18. Annual fee is $3. Support for their activities is welcomed. 394-5171.

Rock Climbing • Martial Arts • Golf, Mini Golf • Spa

➤ **Sanctuary Rock Gym**. Indoor rock climbing, art gallery and proshop. Free indoor rock climbing orientation and tour. Mon-Fri 12-10pm, Sat 10am-10pm, Sun 10am-6pm. 1855a East Avenue, Sand City, 899-2595.

➤ **BodyWorx, Kickboxing and Martial Arts**. First class free! Kickboxing, Tang Soo Do karate, and kempo karate. 1173 Broadway Ave., 899-WORX.

➤ **Junior Golf Program**. Free to ages 7-17. Organized by Salvation Army, staffed by PGA professionals. Bi-weekly, 3-4:15pm. Call 899-4911 ext. 25.

➤ **Mini Golf Course**, a challenging nine holes, is open to the public Sat-Sun, 1-5pm. $1 for resident youth, $1.25 for non-resident youth, $2 for resident adults and $2.50 for non-resident adults. 1136 Wheeler Street, next to Pattulo Swim Center at 1148 Wheeler. 899-6272.

➤ **Water City Roller Hockey**, 2800 Second Ave, off Lightfighter Dr., CSUMB campus. Free Player Evaluation Clinics. Call for times: 384-0144.

➤ **Waterfall Spa**. Five hot pools with waterfalls, steam, sauna, beauty salon, massage center. 1201 LaSalle Ave, 393-1725.

California State University (CSUMB)

Ft. Ord, which lies between Seaside and Marina, is now home to California State University at Monterey Bay (CSUMB), which schedules many <u>free events</u>, call 582-3588. Earth Day Celebration, 582-3689.

◆ **Black Box Cabaret.** Spin Cycle techno show, Tues 8:30-11:30pm; Hip-Hop night, Weds 8-11pm; Open Mic, Thurs 8-11; <u>no cover</u>. Live bands, Fri 8-11pm, $3. Bldg #81, off 3rd St., near North-South Road. 582-3597.

◆ **Music Hall.** 6th Ave. near Colonel Durham St. <u>Free events</u>. Call for monthly calendar, 582-4085.

◆ **World Theater.** Building 28, 6th Ave. <u>Free events</u>. 394-0410.

◆ **Poetry Center.** 6th Ave. in the University Center. <u>Free events</u>. 582-3588.

◆ **Visual & Public Art.** 3rd St. btwn 5th & 6th aves. <u>Free events</u>. 582-3588.

◆ **Monterey Institute for Research in Astronomy.** <u>Free events</u>. 200 8th St. 883-1000 ext. 58. Laura Cohan, Director.

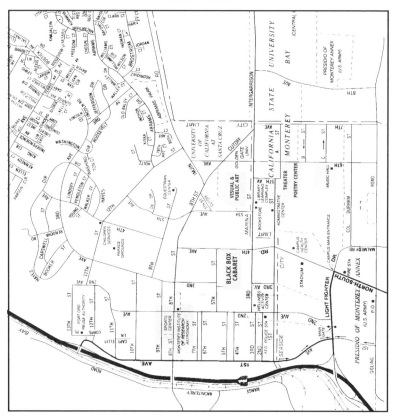

Fort Ord Public Lands

Fort Ord Public Lands, on the site of the former Army base, <u>with free entry</u>, are managed by the Bureau of Land Management (BLM) to protect 35 species of rare plants and animals and their native coastal habitats. More than 50 miles of roads and trails for hiking, bicycling and horseback riding. For information, or to participate in BLM Volunteer Programs, call 394-8314.

➤ **California Native Plant Society** wildland restoration volunteers needed for National Public Lands Day (www.npld.com) and beautification, trail brushing, assessment, weed eradication. Call Bruce Delgado at 394-8314.

➤ **Weed Warriors** destroy non-native plants. Volunteers needed: 582-3689.

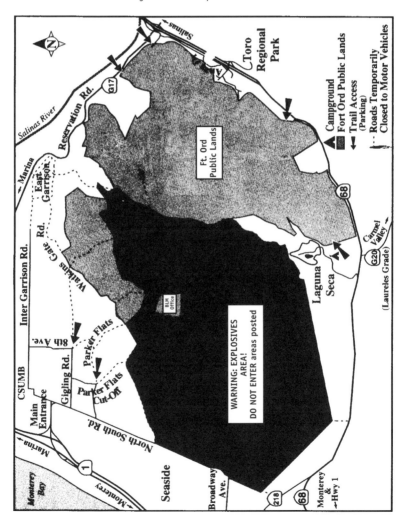

Clubs & Organizations

Meet with like-minded individuals to enrich your life and have fun. Some charge annual dues, some are free. Call for all the details.

Animals

Animal Lovers' Hour at 7:30 pm, 2nd Wednesday at Borders Bookstore, 2080 California Ave., Sand City. Monthly gathering with veterinarian JoAnn Donahoe. Bring questions about your pets. 899-6643.

Cage Bird Club, Monterey Bay. 3rd Sunday 1-3pm. For information and place, call Diane Grindol at 642-0514.

Society for the Prevention of Cruelty to Animals, SPCA, P.O. Box 3058, Monterey, CA 93942. 373-2631.

The Arts

Oriental Art Society of the Monterey Peninsula. Public welcome; refreshments. 624-7126.

Creative Edge: The Way of the Arts, 1st Saturdays with Donald Mathews at 8 Stratford Place, Monterey. 373-7809.

Friends of the Arts, Pacific Grove, meets 1st Tuesdays. This is the fundraising organization for the P.G. Arts Commission. 372-7923.

Civic & Fraternal Organizations

IOOF, the Odd Fellows and Rebekahs, 422-6418.

Jaycees, Monterey Peninsula, 644-2769. Salinas: www.salinasjaycees.org

Junior League of Monterey County, 375-5356.

Kiwanis Club of Pacific Grove, 645-4717, 655-2099.

Lions Club of the Monterey Peninsula, 646-4535.

Monterey Civic Club, 540 Calle Principal, 643-0604.

Monterey Peninsula Masonic Lodges, 375-1263. Eastern Star: Monterey, 372-4685. Carmel, 394-5273.

Optimist Club of Monterey, 883-1062 or 384-5304.

Rotary Club, meeting information, 394-0100.

Soroptimist International of Carmel Bay. Shari Hastey, 394-4279.

Collectors

Antique Glass Bottles and Glass Milk Bottles Collectors Club. Luncheon meeting every second Tuesday. 394-3257 after 7 pm.

Carmel Doll and Toy Study Group meets 3rd Mondays at The Crossroads community room at 7pm. Visitors are welcome. 373-6983.

Central Coast Chapter for Disney Enthusiasts. Call 449-9672 or 449-3408 for meeting location. Info: P.O. Box 10315, Salinas 93912-7315.

Mission Trail Historical Bottle Club, Mission Trail promotes history and collections of historical bottles. Meets 2nd Tuesday for 11:30am. Luncheon at various eateries. Call Bruce Kendall, 394-3257.

Computer

ClubMac of Monterey meets 2nd Fridays in the computer lab at PG Adult School at 1025 Lighthouse Ave., P.G. bcbelknap*redshift.com. Call 373-5717 for time.

Monterey Bay User's Group - Personal Computer Club meets 1st Fridays at 7:30pm at PG Adult Education Center, 1025 Lighthouse Ave. Novice and experienced users of IBM PCs or compatibles invited. Family membership $25; meeting open to all. 373-6245.

Conservation & Environmental

Assn. of Environmental Professionals, Monterey Chapter,408-842-3476.

Carmel River Steelhead Assn, 626-6586.

Coalition to Preserve & Protect PG Tidepools, 372-0123.

Eco-Corps, Pacific Grove, meets 2nd Wednesdays, 7:30pm, at the Pacific Grove Museum of Natural History, Central and Forest avenues, P.G. Dan Koffman, 375-2026.

Friends of the Monarchs, 375-0982.

Friends of the Sea Otter, 373-2747. Gift shop/education center, 642-9037.

Help Our Peninsula Environment, HOPE, David Dilworth, 624-6500.

Monterey Dunes Natural History Association. Meetings 1st Thursdays, 7-9pm. Call Walter Gourlay or Dave Dixon at 626-2632.

Save the Whales, 899-9957.

Ventana Wilderness Sanctuary, 624-1202.

Crafts

American Sewing Guild, Wearable Art, 372-4206, 626-4385.

Carmel Crafts Guild meets 3rd Thursdays at 10 am, Monterey Senior Center, Lighthouse and Dickman avenues, New Monterey. 646-0559.

Embroiderers' Guild of America, Monterey Peninsula Chapter, meets at 9:30am, 2nd Mondays in the Community Room in The Crossroads. 375-3878.

Monterey Peninsula Quilters Guild, 7:30 Mon, Meals on Wheels, P.G.

Dance

Greek Dancers, Sunset Center, Carmel, 375-2549.

Israeli Dancing, Marina Recreation Center, 384-8129.

Monterey Int'l Folk Dancers, Wed 7-9:45, Neighborhood Center, Lighthouse and Dickman, New Monterey. 624-6060.

Monterey Peninsula Dance Assn., 71 Soledad Drive, Monterey, has a Dance Party every Fri-Sat, fun and easy lessons. 648-8725.

Over Thirties Ballet Club meets Thursday evenings at Classical Ballet School, American Legion Hall, Carmel, and in Pebble Beach. Includes outings, lectures, free video shows. 655-5598.

SageStompers Square Dance Club meets 2nd Tuesdays at 7:30pm at Oldemeyer Center, Seaside. Refreshments, beginner and brush-up classes available. Visitors welcome. 899-0752, 375-2354.

Scottish Country Dancers of Monterey, 646-3878.

Turkish Folk Dancing, Neighborhood Center, Lighthouse and Dickman, New Monterey, 646-1916.

Ethnic

American-Scandinavians of California holds monthly or quarterly meetings concerning the culture and heritage of Scandinavians. Open to all interested persons. 659-3363 or 422-1759.

Chinese Language & Culture Club has many free events: Chinese New Year, Moon Festival, usually at MPC. Call Director C.Y. Lee, 394-2965.

Filipino American Community of Monterey Peninsula, 384-5383.

Filipino Community of Salinas Valley, 422-0830.

Korean & American Communities of Monterey County, 384-2400.

Peruvian-American Club, 443-1758, 443-8231.

Sons of Italy, Monterey Lodge No. 2003, meets 3rd Mondays at San Carlos Parish Hall, 6pm. Dinner and meeting $5. Newcomers welcome. 626-0424.

Sons of Norway, Aagaarden Lodge No.112-6. 372-3749, 424-9944.

Historical

Big Sur Historical Society, 667-0549.

Carmel Valley Historical Society, meets 1st Wednesdays. Call Jauna Gregory, 624-9611.

Central Coast Chapter of the American Historical Society of Germans from Russia. Quarterly meetings. 373-4603.

Corral of the Westerners, Monterey County, an international organization, meets 6:30pm 2nd Mondays, St. John's Chapel Parish Hall, Monterey. Potluck dinner followed by talk relating to the West and its history. Annual dues: $15 single, $25 couple. First visit free; lectures free and open to the public. Details 626-8156, 624-0435.

Daughters of the American Revolution, Commodore Sloat Chapter, invites visitors and new members. Call 624-0571.

Genealogy Society, Monterey County. Membership open to any interested person. Meets 7pm 1st Thursdays at the Family History Center, corner

Noche Buena & Plumas streets, Seaside. 759-1727. 443-8156.

Golden State Preservation Group, to preserve the State Theatre in downtown Monterey. 373-7678. www.stpg.org.

Los Amigos de la Historia y del Arte, an auxiliary of Monterey History & Art Assn., 372-2608.

Monterey County Historical Society, 333 Boronda Road, Salinas, 757-8085. www.dedot.com/mchs.

Monterey Heritage Society, Barbara Bass Evans, 372-8323.

Monterey History & Art Assn., 372-2608.

Monterey and Salinas Valley Railroad Modeling and Historical Society, Headquarters at the old Railway Express next to Amtrak. 757-6305.

Sons of the American Revolution, Monterey Bay. 625-1640, 372-5812.

Horticultural

Begonia Club meets 7:30pm, 4th Thursdays, at the Senior Center on Dickman in New Monterey. Don Englund, 373-3548.

Bonsai Club of Monterey, 649-5934.

Cactus & Succulent Society, Monterey Bay, 449-2002.

California Native Plant Society, Monterey Bay Chapter, meets at P.G. Museum of Natural History, Forest and Central, 659-2528, 659-4252.

Carmel Orchid Society meets 7:30pm, 1st Mondays at 1st Presbyterian Church, 501 El Dorado. President Sheila Bowman, 622-0292.

Fern Study Group, Monterey Bay, meets 7pm one Thursday each month at CSU Monterey Bay, Instructional Center East Building #15, Room 163, First Street and Fifth Avenue, Seaside. 659-4104.

Gardeners of America, 375-2300.

Ikebana International of Monterey Bay. Club president Carol Marchette, 373-4691.

Monterey Bay Orchid Society, meets 6:30pm, Bank of Salinas (sixth floor), Main at Alisal, Oldtown Salinas, 484-1052, 424-4972. Public welcome.

Sacred Garden Guild, headed by artist Elizabeth Murray, meets 4th Saturdays at the Thunderbird Bookshop Cafe in The Barnyard, Carmel. Visitors welcome. Free. Guest speakers. 624-1803.

Literary

Book Reading Group, Carmel Valley Library, 65 W. Carmel Valley Rd. Fridays, 2:30-4pm, adults. 659-2377.

Calligraphy Guild: The Sea Scribes meet 1st Thursday at 7 pm, The Park Place, 200 Glenwood Circle, Monterey.

Dickens Fellowship, Monterey Peninsula, meets monthly in members' homes. Call 372-7625 for details.

Gentrain Society, MPC Lecture Forum, 1:30pm, 1st and 3rd Wednesdays.

International Language and Cultural Foundation, 642-2224.

Jung Friends meet 2nd Fridays at 7pm, 284 Foam Street, New Monterey. Donation. Reservations: 649-4018.

Mystery Book Group meets 2nd Tuesdays at 6:30pm at Borders Bookstore, 2080 California Ave., San City. New members welcome. 899-6643.

Robert L. Stevenson Club, 375-0195 ext. 00.

Scrabble players meet every Wednesday from 6-9pm at the Oldemeyer Center, 986 Hilby Ave., Seaside. All levels of play welcome. No dues. 633-4649.

Thunderbird Book Club meets 10am-11:30am 2nd Tuesdays at Thunderbird Bookshop Cafe in The Barnyard, Carmel, 624-1803.

Marine

American Cetacean Society, Lecture Hall at Hopkins Marine Station, 130 Ocean View Blvd., PG. (across from American Tin Cannery). Free talks on marine mammals and fisheries. Meet 7:30pm last Thursdays of the month except Nov-Dec, meet the 1st Thurs. of Dec. Allan Baldridge, 663-9488.

Military

Fleet Reserve Association, Monterey Peninsula branch 178, meets 2nd Tuesdays at 7:30pm at Marina American Legion Post, 694 Legion Way. Membership is open to all enlisted personnel - active duty, reserve and retired - in the U.S. Navy, Marine Corps and Coast Guard, with at least one day of enlisted service. Call Shipmate Secretary Wade Willingham at 648-1058.

Ladies Auxiliary to Veterans of Foreign Wars, Post 811, offers Surf 'n Turf dinners at reasonable prices Friday evenings at the post, 3131 Crescent Ave., Marina. Public welcome. 384-6743, 384-7668.

Naval Order of the United States, open to U.S. citizens who have served as commissioned officers in the maritime services. Meets 7 Dec, 17 Feb and on call. 372-5812.

Navy League of the U.S., Monterey Peninsula Chapter, Jane Lembing, 372-5812.

Retired Enlisted Assn., 422-4964.

Retired Officers Assn., Monterey County Chapter. Call Capt. Harry Nicholson at 646-0822.

Special Forces Assn. Chapter XIV meets 2nd Thursdays at 7pm in the Marina VFW, 3131 Crescent Ave. Interested and qualified veterans are invited to attend. Call 633-4137.

Veterans of Foreign Wars Post 7895, 242 Williams Rd., Salinas, 758-5505.

Women in Military Service, 394-5686.

Mineral Societies

Carmel Valley Gem and Mineral Society, David Dimitriou, 384-8815 or 372-9215. Meets 2nd Fridays, 7:30pm, Crossroads Community Room.

Monterey Bay Mineral Society of Salinas. Meets 3rd Tuesdays, 7:30pm, Sherwood Hall, Salinas. Cindy L. Davenport, 449-6820.

Miscellaneous

Alano Club of Monterey Peninsula, 519 Hartnell, 373-0830.

Astronomical Society of the Central Coast. Meets last Tuesday, 7:30pm at MIRA, 200 Eighth St. at Second Ave., Marina. 883-1000.

Casa Abrego Club, 592 Abrego, 375-0626.

Flying Doctors, volunteer organization that treats children in Latin American countries, often presents public educational meetings. 646-8740.

Friends of Kinship invites anyone interested in attending or joining the group to call Dolores Johnson at 624-7179.

Monarca Club, 679-2787.

Monterey County Vegetarians meet 7pm, 1st Tuesdays in The Crossroads Community Room, Highway 1 at Rio Road. (Park behind Mailboxes Etc.) Bring a vegetarian dish to share without animal ingredients, a list of ingredients, a place setting, a candle for the table and a beverage. Monthly meetings include speakers and demonstrations of vegetarian food preparation. Members share recipes, pamphlets and exchange vegetarian magazines. 622-7427.

Monterey County Corral of the Westerners, 626-8156.

Monterey County Genealogical Society, 759-1727.

Pacheco Club, 602 Abrego, 373-3011.

Peace Coalition, meets at 615 Abrego. Call 372-6001.

Radio Club, meets at the Naval Postgraduate School on the 2nd Thurs of each month at 7pm. 883-0491.

Railroad Modeling and Historical, Monterey and Salinas Valley. 757-6305.

Photography

Padre Trails Camera Club meets 1st and 3rd Wednesdays, 7pm, Monterey Public Library, 625 Pacific St. Refreshments. 649-1521.

Underwater Photographers, Monterey Peninsula, meets 1st Fridays 6:30-9:30pm. Monterey Bay Aquarium Education Center, 886 Cannery Row. Guests welcome, membership open to all. Includes divers, nondivers, biologists, authors, photographers, videographers, friends and families. Educational outreach program. 455-2000.

Political

African-American Democratic Club, 394-4445.

Democrats, Monterey County. 655-3121 or 783-1980.

League of Women Voters of the Salinas Valley, 636-6759.

NAACP, Monterey Peninsula, 1104 Broadway Ave., Seaside. 394-3727.

Republican Women, Monterey County. Connie Perry, 647-9225.

Republicans, Campaign Hdqrs, 298 Pearl Street, Monterey. 646-5120.

United Nations Association, Monterey Bay Chapter, 659-3758.

World Affairs Council presentations by experts on international issues. Call 643-1855 for current programs.

Sports & Recreation

99's, Monterey Bay Chapter of the International Organization of Women Pilots. Gabrielle Adelman, 728-0692 or 722-4580; Donna Crane-Bailey, 688-9616.

Audubon Society, Monterey Peninsula. Field trips, hikes, 648-3116, Jim Booker, 624-1202.

Bridge Center of Monterey, 375-0311.

Camber Ski Club. Salinas, 633-6828. www.ski-camber.org.

Carmel Community Bridge Club, 625-4307.

Carmel Ski Club, 648-4140.

Central Coast Lighthouse Keepers, 649-7139.

Cypress MG Car Club, 373-7490.

Faultline Shootish Society, affiliate of Single Action Shooting Society. Emphasis on safety. 615-9007.

Fly Casters, Monterey Peninsula, meet 7:30pm every 3rd Wednesday, Monterey Senior Center, Lighthouse at Dickman avenues, Monterey.

Friends of Monterey County Fair, 372-5863.

Hash House Harriers, Monterey Bay: Noncompetitive 4 to 5 mile cross-country hare-and-hounds adult fun run at various locations in the Monterey Bay area every other Sunday at 1pm. Information: Tim Thomas, 728-2117 or 24-hour hot line at 267-1504.

Marina Air Flying Club, Marina Airport. Chris, 883-9680.

Monterey Chess and Dart Center, 430 Alvarado, 646-8730.

Monterey Cribbage Club, 883-0963, 422-2024.

Monterey Orienteering Club, 392-1704.

Mountain Bike Assn., Monterey, 7pm 3rd Wednesdays at Allegro Pizza, 1184 Forest Ave., P.G. 373-5656, 626-2705, 422-2380.

Pebble Beach Sports Car Club, 375-8909, 455-2268.

Sea Otters DIVE Club, Monterey Bay, meets last Wednesdays, April through October, at Marina Village Restaurant, 215 Reservation Road. No host dinner 6:30, meeting at 7pm. Guest speakers. Visitors welcome. 372-9235.

Sierra Club, meets last Thursdays. Call 624-8032 for place and time.

Ski & Social Club, Monterey. We ski in the winter and do activities year round! Meet 2nd and 4th Wednesdays. New members welcome. Call 582-9303 or gregrobi@ix.netcom.com. We participate in volunteer activities at the AT&T, Concours de Elegance and at Laguna Seca.

Social Bridge, meets Mondays at 12:30pm at Meals on Wheels, 700 Jewell Ave., P.G. $1. 657-5351.

Trail Runners of the Monterey Peninsula. All ages and levels welcome. 384-0353.

Velo Club Monterey, Monterey County Bicycle Club. Regular rides. Call Jim Gilman 649-1506. jimg@gwjcpa.com.

Seniors

AARP#97, welcomes people to its monthly meetings (call 1 week before), 2nd Fridays, 1-3pm, 1962 Mariposa, Seaside. 394-2965.

Active Seniors, Inc., 100 Harvest St., Salinas. A nonprofit organization. 424-5066.

Alliance on Aging meets every Friday at 11:30am at the P.G. Community Center, 515 Junipero Ave. Lunch 12:30. 646-4636. Salinas, call Alcida Boissonnault, information & referral specialist, 758-2811.

Singles

Primetime Singles, 644-TIME.

Parents Without Partners meets monthly, 6:30pm at the Monterey Public Library Community Room; educational-social, adult-family events. 644-2773. Salinas meets 7:30-8:30pm at John Steinbeck Library, San Luis and Lincoln, Salinas. Paul Connes 275-9057 or toll-free 888-828-6555, ext. 9602.

Single Friends, men and women 50 and older, for social outings. 659-9144.

Singles Off and Running (SOAR) discussion Wednesdays, 7:30-9pm at First Presbyterian Church, 501 El Dorado, Monterey. 373-3031.

Thunderbird Singles: A social club for men and women 55 and older. Meets Sundays at 6:30pm on the patio at the Thunderbird Bookshop Cafe, The Barnyard, Carmel, 624-7179.

What's Next Singles: outdoor, cultural, social activities, personal growth. 648-4698. Call for calendar of events.

Widowed Persons Assn. of California, Monterey chapter, 620-1927.

Toastmasters, et al

Bayview Toastmasters meets 6pm, 1st and 3rd Wednesdays, Monterey Beach Hotel, 622-9507.

Forest Toastmasters meets from 5:10-6:10pm every 1st and 3rd Tuesdays at the Pebble Beach Training Center, 2130 Sunset Ave., P.G. Open to beginners, guests and all levels of expertise. 649-6538/655-3233.

Monterey Bay Talespinners, 384-3227.

Monterey Peninsula Toastmasters 934 meets at 6:45am each Thursday at Holiday Inn Resort, 1000 Aguajito Road, Monterey, 373-4155.

Naval Postgraduate School's Toastmasters Club meets Fridays at noon, EEO Room, Herrman Hall, Naval Postgraduate School, 663-5606.

Pebble Beach Toastmasters meets at The Lodge 5pm every other Tuesday; new members welcome. 649-6538/625-8563.

Peninsula Pros Toastmasters meets last Wednesdays at 6pm at the Monterey Beach Hotel. Membership is free and open to the public. Call Steve Dellaporta at 384-5481.

Realtor's Toastmasters Club meets Fridays, noon-1pm. Visitors from all professions and walks of life welcome. For meeting place in downtown Monterey call Sandra Collingwood, 648-9673.

Salinas Sunrisers meets 6:30am Tuesdays at 1205 S. Main St. 424-0771.

Speakeasy Toastmaster Club meets noon-1pm on Wednesdays at DPIC, 2959 Monterey-Salinas Highway, Monterey, 646-1540.

Spirit of Speech Club. International training in communications; a small supportive group which teaches all forms of communication skills. Meets 1st Wednesdays at 7pm 649-8751. Call Betty Powell for place, 646-9873.

TaleSpinners, Monterey Bay, meets at 7pm on 1st Mondays at the Monterey Public Library Community Room, 625 Pacific Street, Monterey. Storytellers and would-be storytellers welcome. 384-3227.

TGIF meets every Friday in the conference room at Dennis the Menace Park, Monterey, 373-5352.

Women

Altrusa International of the Monterey Peninsula. Diane Johnson, 647-8295.

American Association of University Women, 624-6672.

American Business Women's Assn., Central Coast Charter Chapter, Connie Golden Rodriques, 883-2124, Frances Berry, 384-4568.

Business and Professional Women, Seaside, 394-3746.

Business Women's Network, Salinas Valley, 757-4311, 757-6201.

Carmel Women's Club. Clubhouse at San Carlos and Ninth, 624-2866.

Lesbian Club, 583-9602.

Panhellenic, National Alumnae, Monterey Bay Area, encourage alumnae members of national sororities who are new to the community to attend. Call Ann Marshall at 649-5449 or Lisa Hollo at 373-0542.

Professional Women's Network of the Monterey Peninsula. Meets 1st Wednesday, 6:45pm in the Community Room of the Crossroads Shopping Center, Carmel. Guests are welcome; meetings are free. For more information, call 464-0796.

Women in Military Service, 394-5686.

Women "In the Company of My Sisters," a multi-cultural women's network and support group meets 2nd Saturdays, 1-3pm at the Old Chapel, First St. Ave., PM Annex (Old Ft. Ord). For more information or copy of newsletter, call Loretta Sultzer at 394-2421.

Women in Science Association, Monterey Bay Chapter, 633-2224.

Women's Community Center meets 7-8:30pm 2nd Mondays, at the

Unitarian-Universalist Church, 490 Aguajito Road, Carmel. Enrichment, education and empowerment of women. 647-2307.

Women's League for Peace and Freedom, Monterey Branch, 372-6001.

Women's Spiritual Studies Institute, 647-1454.

Women's Works Book Club, 2nd Tuesday, 12 noon, 150 Mar Vista. Read and discuss books women have written. Free to members of YWCA of Monterey County. Call Tina Wilkensen 649-0834.

YWCA, 150 Mar Vista Drive, Monterey, 649-0834.

Youth

Boys & Girls Club of the Monterey Peninsula, 1332 La Salle Ave., Seaside. Ages 7-18, noon-8pm weekdays, 2-6 pm Sat. Teen room, computer instruction, educational assistance, weight training, sports. 394-5196.

Boys & Girls Club, Carmel Valley Branch. 24 Ford Road. Jeff Magallanes, 659-2308.

YOUTH Boys & Girls Clubs, Salinas Valley, Sherwood Unit. Activities for youth 7-17, 2:30-6:00 pm., 110 South Wood Street, Salinas, 422-2442.

Camp Fire Boys & Girls Clubs, weekly Thursday meetings of kids in Kindergarten thru 7th grades. Crafts, service projects, and other fun activities. 6:15-7:45pm. For info call Cheryl Jencks, 620-8613.

Gay Teen Alliance, Monterey, meets the 2nd and 4th Fridays at 7pm. The Salinas GTA meets every 3rd Saturday from 1-3pm. www.gtamonterey.org 393-3457, 772-8202.

YMCA, 600 El Camino Estero, Monterey, 373-4167.

YWCA, 150 Mar Vista Dr., 649-0834.

Where You Belong

iBelong helps organizations build web portals for their members. Check it out at www.ibelong.com.

Hobbyists Web Site

If you've got a hobby and have a question about it, you may want to try the Hobby Industry Association's new Web Site at http://www.chib.com/

At the site you'll find a mixture of how-to projects, tips, product samples and statistical data.   *The Monterey County Herald*

Monterey County Internet Directory

Access on the Internet

http://www.infobuy.com/freefax/ - Free fax from your e-mail account

http://www.juno.com/getjuno.html - You don't need to buy Internet access to use free Internet e-mail. Get completely free e-mail from Juno at their website, or call Juno at 800-654-JUNO [654-5866].

www.locatetravelagency.com - To locate a local travel agency; IATAN.

www.hotmail.com - get free e-mail, then configure it to check your regular e-mail account by clicking the Options link and then the External Mail link. You'll need to know the name of your POP server (for example, pop.earthlink.com), your e-mail ID (usually the first part of your e-mail address), and your e-mail password. To set up Hotmail to check up to four POP accounts, click the Options link and then the POP Mail link. (Lon Poole, *www.macworld.com*, Dec, 1998)

www.echobuzz.com and www.broadpoint.com - Free voice-mail services geared towards teens. Sign up on-line and receive an 800 number.

www.dialpad- Free telephone calls; uses a microphone.

www.homestead.com - Free personal web site

www.magicradio.com - Free personal radio web site

www.mobie.com/mobie.html - Monterey Bay Internet Enthusiasts

Access Providers

www.dra.com - DRA Business Internet

www.dedot.com - Dedot Com

www.enflow.com - Enflow Web Design & Management

www.fullsteam.com - Stoked Media

www.garlic.com - South Valley Internet

www.InternetPromotions.com - We do the scary stuff for you.

www.iprose.com - iProse Internet

www.mbay.net - Monterey Bay Internet

www.mbayweb.com - Monterey Bay Online

www.montereybay.com - Online Services

www.montereynet.net - Monterey Network Center

www.netmarc.com - Netmarc Internet Services

www.netpipe.com - NetPipe Internet Services

www.NewMediaD.com - New Media Design

www.onm.com - Online Marketing Partners

www.pacificwebcreations.com - Pacific Web Creations
www.redshift.com - Red Shift Internet Services
www.rknrobin.com - User Friedly Systems
www.ssmedia.net - Sunstar Media
www.ultimanet.com - Ultima Networks
www.universal-net.com - Universal Internet
www.visualwebcasting.com - Visual Webcasting Services
www.webgeek.com - Webgeek Communications
www.webhomepages.com - Web Home Pages

Accommodations

www.andrilcottages.com - Pacific Grove
www.asilomarcenter.com - Asilomar Conference Center, Pacific Grove
www.bigsurlodge.com - Big Sur Lodge
www.c8inns.com - Super 8 Inns, Free breakfast, newspaper, cable, calls
www.carmel-california.com - Carmel area reservations service
www.carmelliving.com - List of Carmel's dog-friendly lodging and dining
www.carmelvillageinn.com - Carmel Village Inn
www.casamunras-hotel.com - Casa Munras, Monterey
www.countrygardensinn.com - Country Gardens Inn, Carmel Valley
www.devi-inc.com/ramada - Ramada Limited - Fremont St.
www.devi-inc.com/ramadach - Ramada Limited - Carmel Hill
www.doubletreemonterey.com - DoubleTree, Monterey
www.ernestallen.com:80//tr/CA/Munraslodge
www.ernestallen.com:80//tr/CA/BestWesternParkCrest - Park Crest Motel
www.highlands-inn.com - Highlands Inn, Carmel
www.hotelpacific.com - Hotel Pacific, Monterey
www.hrs-avanti.com - Hospitality resource service
www.innaccess.com/OMI/ - Old Monterey Inn
www.innsbythesea.com - Pacific Grove
www.lhls.com - Lighthouse Lodge & Suites, Pacific Grove
www.loneoakmotel.com - Lone Oak Motel, Carmel Valley
www.loslaureles.com - Los laureles Country Inn, Carmel Valley
www.marriotthotels.com/MRYCA/ - Marriott, Monterey
www.mbay.net/embassy - Embassy Suites, Seaside

www.merritthouseinn.com - Merritt House Inn, Monterey

www.monterey.org/mcc - Monterey Conference Center, Monterey

www.monterey-reservations.com - Monterey Peninsula Reservations, no fee

www.montereybayinn.com - Monterey Bay Inn

www.montereybeachhotel.com - Monterey Beach Hotel

www.montereycoast.com - Kendall and Potter Property Management

www.montereyinns.com - Pacific Grove

www.montereyrentals.com - Vacation rentals, free lists, fax 831/655-7845

www.nepenthebigsur.com - Nepenthe, Big Sur

www.pacificgardensinn.com - Pacific Grove

www.peninsula.com - Quail Lodge Resort, Carmel Valley

www.pine-inn.com - Pine Inn, Carmel

www.postranchinn.com - Post Ranch Inn, Big Sur

www.resortdetectives.com - Resort Detectives

www.sandpiper-inn.com - Sandpiper Inn, Carmel

www.spindriftinn.com - Spindrift Inn, Pacific Grove

www.sunbaysuites.com - SunBay Suites, Seaside

www.ticklepink.com - Ticklepink Inn, Carmel

www.timetocoast.com - Lodging finder

www.travelweb.com - Hotel search

www.usa-lodging.com/motels/califn/bigsur.htm - Big Sur lodgings

www.usawines.com/hacienda - The Hacienda, Jolon

www.valleylodge.com - Carmel Valley Lodge

www.ventanainn.com - Ventana Inn, Big Sur

www.victorianinn.com - Victorian Inn, Pacific Grove

www.woodsidehotels.com - Monterey Plaza Hotel

The Arts

www.adamsgallery.com - Ansel Adams Gallery

www.amsterdamfineart.com - Amsterdam Fine Art

www.artists-equity.org - Artists Studio Tour

www.artwithasmile.com - Koffman Gallery

www.bigsurarts.org - The Big Sur Arts Initiative

www.bleich4art.com - Bleich Art

www.classicartgallery.com - Classic Art Gallery

www.creative-edge.org - The Creative Edge

www.crystalfoxgallery.com - Crystal Fox Gallery

www.danielsgallery.com - Daniel's Gallery

www.donnamoses.com - Donna Moses, Original Folk Art

www.galerieplenaire.com - Galerie PleinAire

www.hawthornegallery.com - Hawthorne Gallery

www.intag.net - Internet Auction Gallery

www.loranspeck.com - Loran Speck

www.marytitusart.com - Mary Titus

www.mastersgallery.com - Masters Gallery

www.montereyart.org - Monterey Museum of Art

www.montereyart.com - Artists co-op available August 2000

www.mbay.net/~bluedog/ - George Rodrique

www.PoupeeGallery.com - Poupee Gallery

www.richardmacdonald.com - Richard MacDonald

www.ricmasten.com - nationally known poet/artist/philosopher Ric Masten

www.stowitts.org - Hubert J. Stowitts Museum & Library

www.thomaskinkade.com - Thomas Kinkade

www.willbullasfineart.com - Will Bullas Fine & Fun Art

www.zantmangalleries.com - Zantman Galleries

Attractions & Activities

www.bigsuronline.com - Big Sur activities

www.canneryrow.com - Cannery Row

www.carmelfun.com - Carmel

www.carmelitemonastery.com - Carmelite Monastery

www.cinemacal.com - Movies

www.CometoMonterey.com - Commercial site

www.contemplation.com - Camaldoli Hermitage

www.critics-choice.com - Peninsula activities, lodging, restaurants

www.englander.com/flanders - Flanders Mansion

www.GoMonterey.com - Monterey County Travel and Tourism

www.infopoint.com/mry/index - Monterey information

www.lighthouse-pointsur-ca.org - Pt. Sur Lighthouse

www.mbayaq.org - Monterey Bay Aquarium E-Quarium site

www.mbay.net/~mshp/ - Monterey Historic Parks
www.monterey.com - Visitors and Convention Bureau
www.montereybayaquarium.com - Monterey Bay Aquarium
www.montereycountyguide.com - Visitor Guide
www.movie-tickets.com - Dream Theater, New Monterey
www.mymuseum.org - My Museum for Children
www.planetgemini.com - Comedy club, Cannery Row
www.redshift.com/~donald - Monterey County Fair
www.rent-a-roadster.com - Rent-a-Roadster, Cannery Row
www.Steinbeck.org - Steinbeck Center, Salinas
www.themorganhouse.com - Coffeehouse with entertainment
www.torhouse.org - Robinson Jeffers' Tor House, Carmel
www.toursontape.com - Audio tour tape
www.virtual-canyon.org - National Science site for Monterey Bay
www.whps.com/agtours - Agriculture tours
www.wildthingsinc.com - Vision Quest Ranch

City & County Sites

www.bestofcal - Pacific Grove and other local city information

www.bigsurcalifornia.org - Big Sur

www.carmel-by-the-sea.com - Carmel

www.carmelvalley.com - Carmel Valley

www.ci.marina.ca.us - Marina

www.ci.seaside.ca.us - City of Seaside

www.co.monterey.ca.us/sheriff - MoCo Sheriff Department

www.fora.org - Ft. Ord Reuse Authority

www.marinachamber.com - Marina Chamber of Commerce

www.mpcc.com - Monterey Chamber of Commerce

www.monterey.org - Information about the community and links to employment opportunities, the library, city parks and other departments.
www.pacificgrove.com - Pacific Grove

www.salinaschamber.com - Salinas

www.salinaspd.com - Salinas Police Department

www.sandcity.com - Sand City, available in the year 2000

www.seaside-sandcity.com - Seaside and Sand City Chamber of Commerce

Conservation/Ecology

color.mlml.calstate.edu/www/ - Moss Landing Marine Laboratories

www.bigsurlandtrust.org - Big Sur Land Trust

www.mbnmsf.org - Monterey Bay Marine Sanctuary

www.landwatch.org - Land Watch

www.oceanalliance.org - Ocean Alliance

www.rideshareweek.com - Ride Share Week to conserve energy

www.saveourshores.org - Save Our Shores

www.spcamc.org - Society for the Prevention of Cruelty to Animals

www.theoceanproject.org - The Ocean Project

www.wateroverthedam.org - Carmel River Celebration

Education

http://csumonterey.bkstore.com - CSUMB Bookstore

http://dlee.monterey.edu - CSUMB class information

www.chapman.edu - Chapman University

www.monterey.edu - California State University at Monterey Bay

www.monterey.org/lib/lib.html - Monterey Public Library

www.mpc.edu - Monterey Peninsula College

www.mpc.edu/academic/gentrain - MPC Gentrain Lecture Series - FREE

www.pgusd.org - Pacific Grove Unified School District

www.themint.org - Northwestern Mutual Life site to increase the economic and financial literacy of middle and high school students.

www.ucsc-extension.edu - University of California at Santa Cruz

Employment

www.caljobs.ca.gov - the State Employment Development Department job-search system

www.callmarshall.com - The Marshall Group Personnel Service

www.interim.com - Interim Personnel

www.manpowersj.com - Manpower Staffing Services

www.norrell.com - Norrell Staffing Services

www.universalstaffing.com - Universal Staffing Inc.

Events & Festivals

http://Montereyscotgames.com - Scottish/Irish Festival and Games

www.artichoke-festival.org - Castroville Artichoke Festival

www.attpbgolf.com - AT&T Pebble Beach

www.bachfestival.org - Carmel Bach Festival

www.bigsurjazz.org - Big Sur Jazz Festival

www.ca-airshow.com - California International Airshow

www.canneryrow.com - Cannery Row Events

www.carmelfest.org - The Carmel Performing Arts Festival

www.carodeo.com - California Rodeo Salinas

www.concorso.com - Concorso Italiano

www.cowboyjack.com - Cowboy Poetry & Music Festival

www.cvvillage.com/fiesta - Carmel Valley Village Fiesta

www.dixiejazz.com/monterey.html - Dixieland Monterey

www.firstnightmonterey.org - First Night®Monterey

www.The HolmanRanch.com - Holman Ranch, Carmel Valley

www.intlcomm.org - NPGS International Day

www.montereyblues.com - Monterey Blues Festival

www.montereyjazzfestival.org - Monterey Jazz Festival

www.montereylive.com - Monterey Live Music Festival

www.montereysquid.com - Monterey Squid Festival

www.laguna-seca.com - Laguna Seca Raceway

www.montereycountyfair.com - Monterey County Fair

www.montereyworldmusic.org - World Music Festival

www.pebble-beach-concours.com - Concours d'Elegance

www.ridepebblebeach.com - Pebble Beach Spring Horse Show

www.rocknarts.iaanet.com - Monterey Rock & Art Festival

www.seaotter.org - Sea Otter Classic at Laguna Seca

www.tomatofest.com - Tomato Fest

www.tricalifornia.com - Wildflower Triathlon Festival, Lake San Antonio

www.turkiye.net - Turkish Arts & Culture Festival

www.voyagertarot.com - Rota Psychic Fair

Free & Fun

www.freeandfun.com - free stuff galore

www.freemania.net/ - cosmetics, t-shirts and more

www.FreeShop.com - 1000+ freebies

www.rebateco.com - Products with sometimes 100% rebates

www.thefreesite.com/ - Web freebies, product samples

www.4freestuff.com/ - Product samples, magazines

Health

www.Bodysuite.com - Day Spa and Salon

www.ccvna.com - Visiting Nurse Association & Hospice

www.chomp.org - Community Hospital of the Monterey Peninsula

www.drgrant.com - J. Gary Grant, MD.

www.gestaltcenter.net - Gestalt Growth Center

www.hffcc.rog - Hospice Foundation

www.montereycpc.com - Compassion Pregnancy Center

www.natividad.com - Natividad Medical Center

www.ordwaydrug.com - Ordway Drug Store

www.ovvh.com - Ocean View Veterinary Hospital
www.spaontheplaza.com - Spa on the Plaza
www.vetdoc.com - Jo-Ann Van Arsdale, Veterinarian
www.wellnessmd.com - Abraham Kryger, MD

History

http://caviews.com - California Views Historical Photos - Pat Hathaway
www.carmelheritage.org - Carmel Heritage Society
www.dedot.com/mchs - Monterey County Historical Society Inc.
www.evansmonterey.com/MHS - Monterey Heritage Society
www.Monterey.edu/history/historicevents.html. This educational site describes the development of the Monterey area, and provides links to other local history sites.

Information

erp-web.er.usgs.gov/reports/VOL40/nc - report 98g0007.pd f- earthquake epicenters

wrgis.wr.usgs.gov/open-file/of97-30 - Monterey-Seaside geologic map

www.abooksearch.com - A Book Search Bookstore, New Monterey

www.ampmedia.org - Community Access Television

www.carmelpinecone.com - Carmel Pine Cone, newspaper

www.coastweekly.com - Coast Weekly, newspaper

www.hellashideout.com - Hella Rothwell column

www.hm-lib.org - Harrison Memorial Library, Carmel

www.internet-books.com - Thunderbird Book Store, Carmel

www.kcba.com - KCBA television station

www.keymonterey.com - Key Magazine

www.montereyairport.com - Monterey Airport

www.montereycountyguide.com - Visitor's Guide

www.monterey-herald.com - The Monterey County Herald, newspaper

www.montereypeninsulaguide.com - Your Personal Guide to Monterey

www.miis.edu - Monterey Institute of International Studies

www.newschannel46.com - KION News Channel 46

www.PanettaInstitute.org - The CSUMB Panetta Institute for Public Policy

www.pilgrimsway.com - Pilgrim's Way Bookstore, Carmel

www.salinasweekly.com - Coast Weekly

www.sunweekly.com - Sun Weekly, Carmel Valley newspaper

Music & Dancing

http://members.aol.com/kaplandisc - Ron Kaplan: jazz, swing, blues.

http://members.xoom.com/xoros/ - Greek Folk Dancing

www.abstractvision.com - Patt Spears-Casion: Original jazz.

www.beinworld.com - Amagon Mollies: original alternative rock.

www.best.com/~wulf - Visitor 42: alternative punk.

www.billboardtalentnet.com/ron_wright - Ron Wright: new age, world, pop, reggae, classical.

www.geocities.com/sunsetstrip/venue/6461/ - Moromix: alternative, electronic, rap, hip-hop, R&B, funk.

www.globalmusic.com/artists/mchrislock/mchrislock_v1.html - Melodie Chrislock: Original pop.

www.jps.net/bflat7/ - Stu Reynold Saxtet: jazz, latin, blues, funk. R&B, world beat.

www.jps.net/bflat7/outbound/ - Outbound: smooth jazz.

www.kellypro.com - Andrea Jones: Scottish/Celtic bagpiper.

www.kellypro.com - Bravo Ara: folk, classical, flamenco, international.

www.kellypro.com - Charles DeWeese: folk, rock, blues, jazz, country; world Latin, classical guitars.

www.kellypro.com - Daryl Lowery: disc jockey.

www.kellypro.com - Joe Indence: piano & keyboard: blues, jazz, Latin, big band, classical.

www.kellypro.com - Michael Culver: Pop, jazz and classical harp and vibes.

www.kellypro.com - Monterey String Quartet: jazz, classical, pop.

www.kellypro.com - Original Substitutes - 50s rock, 60s variety.

www.kellypro.com - Peter Burkhard: disc jockey

www.kellypro.com - Sound Bytes: rock, clues, jazz, country.

www.kellypro.com -Alan Berman: swing, blues, jazz, Latin, Big Band keyboard and vocals.

www.lorylynn.com - Lory Lynn: country rock, ballads.

www.maryleemusic.com - Marylee Music for children

www.mbay.net/~lascott/ferret51.htm - Ferrit 51: original rock.

www.mbay.net/~rlugo - Misshapen: Original metal.

www.messaround.com - The Broadway Band: blues.

www.nuthouse.com/contra/ - YMCA contra dancing
www.redbeans.com - Red Beans & Rice: blues
www.redshift.com/~bhpstudios/website - B H Piano Studios
www.redshift.com/~bgibson: Bill Gibson: acoustic guitar
www.redshift.com/~jlm - Jonathon Lee
www.redshift.com/~singring/ - Piper Manu band
www.rldance.com - Country Western Dancing
www.smoothjazz.com - Sandy Shore Productions 649-1223
www.sspconcerts.com - Sandy Shore Concerts
www.ultramarineblue.com - Maureen Evans-Hansen: original fusion
www.unknownjeromes.com - Unknown Jeromes: Funk, rock.

Real Estate

www.agdavi.com - AG Davi Real Estate
www.apr-carmel.com - Alain Pinell Realtors
www.apr.com (home video tours)
www.beachproperty.com - Connie Perry Realtor
www.benheinrich.com - Ben Heinrich Real Estate
www.burchellhouse.com - Burchell House Properties
www.carmel-realty.com - Carmel Realty Company
www.c21scenicbayproperties.com - Century 21
www.gregshankle.com - Greg Shankle Real Estate
www.laspalmas.com - Las Palmas Ranch New Home Communities
www.mcar.com - Monterey County Realtors
www.montereybay.com/calandra - Calandra Real Estate
www.pacificbaycorp.com - Pacific Bay Real Estate
www.pineconerentals.com - PineCone Property Management
www.redshift.com/~harborr - Harbor Realty
www.segalrealestate.com - Segal Real Estate

Restaurants

www.allegropizza.com - Allegro Gourmet Pizzeria
www.bluefin-billiards.com - Blue Fin Billiards and Cafe
www.cibo.com - Cibo Restaurant

www.critics-choice.com - Pocket guide to dining
www.eatfree.com - Free Monterey dining offers and other information
www.FiestaExpress.com - Plaza Linda Restaurant
www.gilsgourmet.com - Gil's Gourmet
www.go-dining.com - Adventures in Dining guide to the Central Coast
www.grapesofwrath.com - Grapes of Wrath, caterer
www.laboheme.com - LaBoheme, Carmel
www.lecoqdor.com - Le Coq'd Or, Carmel
www.monterey.infohut.com/laplayahotel - La Playa Hotel, Carmel
www.restauranteur.com - special offers
www.rocky-point.com - Rocky Point Restaurant, Carmel
www.sardinefactory.com - Sardine Factory, Cannery Row
www.zagat.com - Search for restaurants by city, price, decor, cuisine+

Shopping

www.ams.usda.gov/farmersmarkets - USDA Directory of Certified Farmers Mkts
www.antiqnet.com/canneryrow - Cannery Row Antique Mall
www.basquetique.com - Basket store
www.candlesandclay.com - Candle store
www.carmelcrossroads.com - Carmel Crossroads Shopping Center
www.carmelpacificgabs.com - Carmel Pacific Bags
www.carmelvalleycalifornia.com/robins.html - Robins Jewelry
www.carmoco.com - Carmel motoring company store and gallery
www.chatelco.com - Fine wristwatches and jewelry
www.chelseagca.com - women's clothing
www.citysearch.com/sfo/charmsbybay - Fine jewelry & charms
www.clairemurray.com – Hand-hooked rugs, woven throws, wearable art
www.delmontecenter.com - Del Monte Shopping Center
www.dovecote.com - Women's clothing
www.ebfarm.com - Earthbound Farm
www.ekeymall.com - Monterey shopping
www.firstnoel.com - Christmas items
www.holidayhutch.com - Gifts
www.impostors.com - Jewelry
www.ladyfingersjewelry.com - Jewelry

www.letitbead.com - Let it Bead store

www.marysboutique.com - Ladies wear

www.mole-hole.com - The Mole Hole of Carmel

www.OnLineFlowers.com - Swenson & Silacci Flowers and Gifts

www.otterlimits.com - Otters, dolphins, whales and more.

www.pacificglass.com - Pacific Etched Glass & Crystal

www.papersite-carmel.com - Paper goods

www.pearlsofpassion - Pearls of Passion Jewelry

www.phillipsmuseumshop.com - Phillips Museum Shop

www.redshift.com/~oakleaves/index.html - Oak Leaves Studio

www.romancebydesign.com - Romance by Design

www.rosamond.com - Rosamond

www.sportswiseofcarmel.com - Sportswise

www.succulentgardens.com - Succulent Gardens

www.thebackshop.com - The Backshop

www.thebarnyard.com - The Barnyard Shopping Center

www.TheDeliciousPlanet.com - Delicious Planet Cookie Co.

www.thejazzandbluescompany.com - Jazz and Blues Company

www.thewhiterabbit.com - Clothing

www.treadmill.com - Sport clothes

www.twgs.com - The Wharf General Store

www.villageprovence.com - Gift shop

www.wbucarmel.com - Wild Birds Unlimited

www.woodenickel.net - The Wooden Nickel

Sports & Recreation

http://ventana.org - Sierra Club, Ventana Chapter

www.adventuresbythesea.com - Kayaks, skate, bicycle rentals

www.athand.com - Freewheeling Cycles

www.bsim.org - Big Sur International Marathon

www.calparks.org - California Parks Foundation

www.carmelfly.com - Fly fishing

www.carmel-golf.com - Rancho Cañada Golf Club

www.carmelwalks.com - Guided tours of Carmel

www.carmelvalleycalifornia.com/cvraquet.html - CV Racquet & Health Club www.chamisal.com - Chamisal Tennis & Fitness Club

www.crusio.com/~bilswhls - Bill's Wheels

www.cruzio.com/~kayakcon - Kayak rentals

www.flymac.com - Monterey Airplane Company

www.golfinst.com - The Golf Institute

www.golf-monterey.com - Laguna Seca Golf Club

www.golfreader.com - Golf writing by Ray A. March

www.inline-retrofit.com - Skate sales and rentals

www.jrabold.net/bigsur/index.htm - Big Sur activities

www.laguna-seca.com - Laguna Seca, World Class racing

www.mbay.net/~gat - Great Adventure hikes & excursions

www.monterey-bay.net/elkhornslough - Elkhorn Slough Safari

www.montereykayaks.com - Monterey Bay Kayaks

www.montereybaywatch.com - Benji Shake cruises

www.montereybaywhalewatch.com

www.montereyexpress.com - Monterey Express Charters

www.montereykayaks.com - Kayak rentals

www.monterey.org/rec/rec.html - Monterey Dept. of Recreation

www.montereysportfishing.com - Sport fishing

www.mtadv.com/fishnet - Cameron Fly Fishing

www.nativeguides.com - Ventana Wilderness outfitters and guides

www.pacificgroverecreation.org - P.G. Recreation Department

www.randysfishingtrips.com - Fishing and whale watching

www.ridepebblebeach.com - Pebble Beach Equestrian Center

www.rideshareweek.com - Ride Share Week

www.rileygolf.com - Riley Golf

www.riogrill.com - Rio Grill Resolution Run

www.rockgym.com - Rockclimbing gym

www.sealifetours.com - Glass bottom boat tours

www.seaotter.org -Classic Cycling Festival at Laguna Seca

www.skydivemontereybay.com - Skydiving

www.soarhollister.com - Hot air ballooning

www.spaontheplaza.com - Spa on the Plaza

www.sportscenterbicycles.com - Sports Center Bicycles

www.usafishing.com/kahuna.html - Tom's Sportfishing

www.yogacentercarmel.org - Yoga Center

Travel Shops & Tours

www.baglade.com - Bag Lady
www.fdtmonterey.com - First Discount Travel
www.goodsforsale.com/dudley - Dudley Doolittle's Travel Shoppe
www.happydogtours.com - Happy Dog Tours
www.mbtours.com - Monterey Bay Scenic Tours, multilingual

Volunteer

www.blindandlowvision.org - The Blind and Visually Impaired Center
www.communitylinks.net - Community Links©
www.monterey.org/vol/vol.html - Monterey City Volunteers
www.redshift.com/~habitat - Habitat for Humanity
www.SERVEnet.org - Youth Service America
www.tmmc.org - The Marine Mammal Center
www.yesillhelp.org - Volunteer Center of Monterey County

Weather

aws.com/wx/wx.dll?crmel - Carmel Middle School weather
www.accuweather.com - Accu Weather
www.cnn.com/WEATHER - CNN weather
www.earthwatch.com - EarthWatch - Weather On Demand
www.hastingsreserve.org - Hastings Natural History Reservation
www.intellicast.com- Intellicast
www.marineweather.com - Marine Weather.Com
www.ndbc.noaa.gov - National Data Buoy Center
www.noaa.gov/ - National Oceanic Administration
www.weather.com - The Weather Channel
www.wunderground.com - The Weather Underground
www.usatoday.com/weather/wfront.htm - USA Today Weather
http://cirrus.sprl.umich.edu/wxnet - WeatherNet

Wineries

www.bernardus.com - Bernardus Winery

www.carmelvalleycalifornia.com/durney.html - Durney Vineyards

www.chalonewinegroup.com - Chalone Vineyard

www.chateaujulien.com - Chateau Julien

www.galantevineyards.com - Galante Vineyards

www.hahnestates.com - Hahn Estates, Smith & Hook

www.montereywine.com - Monterey Wine Festival

www.montereywines.org - Monterey County Vintners & Growers Assn.

www.pavona.com - Pavona Wines

www.ranchocellars.com - Rancho Cellars

www.scheidvineyards.com - Scheid Vineyards

www.secretcellars.com - Wine club

www.tastemonterey.com - Taste of Monterey, Cannery Row

www.terranovafinewines.com - Terranova Fine Wines

www.usawines.com/Cloninger - Cloninger Cellars

www.usawines.com/Jekel - Jekel Vineyards

www.usawines.com/Paraiso - Paraiso Springs Vineyards

www.ventanawines.com - Ventana Vineyards Winery

www.wineinstitute.org - Wine Institute

Weddings

www.baysidewedding.com - Wedding services

www.critics-choice.com - Complete wedding information

www.datemaker.com/Monterey

www.floresque.com - Floresque flowers

www.mbay.net/~weddings - Wedding services

www.montereyweddings.com - Wedding services

www.onlineflowers.com - Swenson & Silacci Flowers

www.romancebydesign.com

www.woodsidehotels.com - Bridal suite

www.800send.com - Salinas florist

Resources & References

A Guide to Eccentric California, P.O. Box 8744, Monterey, CA.

Adventures in Dining, 1998. Mail Mart, Carmel, CA.

Big Sur, A Complete History & Guide, Tomi Kay Lussier, 1993. Big Sur Publications

Big Sur, The Way it Was, Robert K. Blaisdell, 1995. Big Sur Country Film Co. CA.

Buying the Best, 1998. Carmel Publishing Company, Carmel, CA.

California Grassroots Tours, Eric J. Adams. 1993. Renaissance House, Frederick, CO.

California With Kids, Carey Simon and Charlene Marmer Solomon, 1989. Simon & Schuster Inc. NY.

Carmel at Work and Play, Daisy F. Bostick and Dorothea Castelhum, 1925. The Seven Arts, Carmel, CA

Carmel Pine Cone, 1998. Carmel Communications, Inc., Carmel, CA.

Central Coast Magazine, 1998. Local Videomagazine on TCI Cable Channel 2.

Coast Weekly, 1998. Milestone Communication Inc., Seaside, CA.

Complete Monterey Peninsula and Santa Cruz Guidebook, Editor B. Sangwan, 1998. Indian Chief Publishing House, Davis, CA.

Critics Choice Dining Guide, 1998. P.O. Box 221881, Carmel, CA.

Europe for Free, Brian Butler, 1987. Mustang Publishing, CT.

Ft. Ord, A Place in History, U.S. Army Corps of Engineering, Sacramento, CA.

Glorious Gardens, Priscilla Dunhill and Sue Freedman, 1993. Clarkson Potter, NY.

Guestlife Monterey Bay, 1998. Desert Publications Inc., Carmel, CA.

Guidemap to California Highway One, Map Easy, Inc., Armagansett, NY.

Key Magazine, 1998. Tri-County Publishers, Carmel, CA.

Light on Monterey, 1998. Carmel, CA.

Lover's Guide to America, Ian Keown, 1974. MacMillan Publishing Co, NY.

Monterey Bay and Beyond, Lucinda Jaconette, 1994. Chronicle Books, CA.

Monterey Bay Marine Diver's Map, E. Cooper, 1994. Pacific Grove, CA.

Monterey County Family, 1998. Salinas, CA.

Monterey County Post, 1998. Diogenes Communications, Inc., Carmel, CA.

Monterey Peninsula Exploring, Nancy M. and Neil A. Evans, 1994. Worldview Assoc. Inc., El Granada, CA.

Monterey Peninsula Guide, Somerset Publications Inc, Monterey, CA.

Peninsula Family Connection, 1998. Creative Connection, Pacific Grove, CA.

The Fairy Tale Houses of Carmel, 1974. Joanne Mathewson, Carmel, CA.

The Insiders Guide to the Monterey Peninsula, Judy Andréson and Tom Owens, 1998. Insider's Publishing, Helena, MT.

The Monterey County Herald, 1998. Knight-Ridder, Monterey, CA.

The Sun, 1998. Elizabeth Cowley, Carmel Valley, CA.

Touring California's Central Coast, 1998. Bay Publishing Company, Monterey, CA.

Trips on Tape, The Monterey Peninsula and Big Sur, 1993. The Rider's Guide, 484 Lake Park Ave., Oakland, CA.

Walk This Way Please, Irene Montagna, 1993. Afterwords, Pacific Grove, CA.

Index

W

Wagon Wheel Restaurant 64, 75
Waldenbooks Kids 115
Walking Club 181
walking tours 33, 36, 38, 97-8, 117, 137,
    145, 148, 160, 179
walks 37, 42, 55, 58-9, 66, 79, 81-2, 85, 87,
    132-3, 137, 147, 151, 160, 177-8, 180,
    190-1, 195, 207-8, 213, 220, 239
Wall of Fire 208
Wall of Flame 233
water slide 220
waterfalls 27, 66
Waterfall Spa 241
Waterfront Area Visitor's Express xiii, 165
Watsonville Slough 87
Wax Museum 147, 154
Way Station 141
Wayside Inn 61
wearable art 118, 168, 246
weather 270
Weaver Student Observatory 24
weddings 129-30, 178, 221, 271
weight room 56
Weihnachtsfest 51
Wells Fargo Game Field Walking Course 138
Welsh Cottage 37
West Wind Lodge 141
Western Hang Gliders 83
Western Stage 210
Weston Gallery 44
wetlands 82, 85
whale watching 21-2, 82, 106-7, 191, 269
whalebone sidewalk 99
whalers 84, 145, 146
Whaler's Cabin & Cove 58, 59
whales 108, 117, 160, 177, 179, 267
Whales on Wheels 13
Whaling Station & Garden 99
Whaling Station Restaurant 97, 140, 144
Wharfside 129
Whispering Pines Park 134
White Oak Grill 67, 75
White Rabbit 268
Wild Things, Animal Rentals Inc. 202
wildflowers 22, 27, 56, 85, 118, 135,
    193, 218
wildland restoration 243
wildlife 23, 24, 44, 55, 58, 82, 178
Wildlife education program 118, 125
Wilkie's Inn 182
William A. Karges Fine Art 44
Willow Creek 28
Wills Fargo 75
Wind Festival 80
Windhorst 37
windsurfing 84-5
wine 65, 118, 192, 217, 223, 271
wine tasting 49, 63-4, 67, 68, 70, 71, 109,
    118, 147, 222-8, 2700
Winfield Gallery 45
Wing Chong Market 148
Winning Wheels Bicycles 181

Winston Hotel 163
Winters Fine Art Galleries 42
Women's groups 253
wooden bridge 26
wooden pier 85
Woodhull Hall 59
Woods, Flora 148
Woodside Hotels 271
Workout trail 138
World Theater CSUMB 242
World Trail 138

Y

Yang's Happy Family 184
Yangtse Taste of Thai 211
Yellow Bird 37
Yellow Brick Road Thrift Store 62
YMCA 254
yoga 54, 69, 183, 269
Yonka Signature Day Spa 54
Young Cottage 37
Your Maitre d' Limousines xv
Youth 16, 112, 83, 127, 149, 183, 241, 254
Youth Centers 56, 68, 83, 132, 137, 183
Youth Concerts 194
Youth Hostel 148
Youth Organizations 15
Yuan, S.C. 45
yurts 69
YWCA of Monterey 194, 254
YWCA retreat 179

Z

Zantman Galleries 45, 259
Zaruk "Tak" Takali Teen Center 83
Zen Buddhist Center 69
Zeph's One Stop 202
Zimmerman Gallery 43
Zmudowski 133
Zmudowski State Beach 85